FACTORY
OUTLET
GUIDE TO THE
MID-ATLANTIC
STATES

THIRD EDITION

FACTORY OUTLET
GUIDE TO THE
MID-ATLANTIC
STATES

Delaware, Maryland, New Jersey, New York,
Pennsylvania, Virginia, and West Virginia

———

by A. Miser & A. Pennypincher

A Voyager Book

The Globe Pequot Press

Old Saybrook, Connecticut

Library of Congress Cataloging-in-Publication Data is available.
Library of Congress catalog card number 92-31142
ISBN 1-56440-079-4

Manufactured in the United States of America
Third Edition/First Printing

CONTENTS

INTRODUCTION

As you look for ways to stretch your budget, the factory store option is one we strongly recommend. When you shop at factory stores, you can take advantage of "sale" prices throughout the entire year. It is realistic to say that in the course of a year you could save 50 percent of your budgeted money if you shop at factory stores. The other side of the coin is that you can spend your budget but buy twice as much.

Do not think that factory stores have only low-quality or undesirable merchandise. Many prestigious manufacturers are involved with this marketing approach. As you browse through this book, you will see innumerable well-known brand names. Manufacturers from all levels have tried the water and decided the swimming is definitely inviting!

When we first undertook the researching of factory stores in the early 1960s, they were few and far between. Most were inside the factories themselves, often little more than an unused space converted into a makeshift sales area. Even the manufacturers weren't too sure about this aspect of their business life. Eventually, as more and more people discovered the bargains in factory stores, the sales areas were tidied up, manufacturers started to advertise their locations, and factory store shopping slowly became more respectable.

Alert manufacturers soon sensed the latent potential in this marketing approach and learned to capitalize on it. The conversion of once-busy floor space led to the congregate development we see in Reading, Pennsylvania, then to the extensive renovation of idle factory space into complexes such as CharlesTown in Utica, New York, and finally to the suburban mall with the focus on direct factory stores and distributor outlets such as Franklin Mills in Philadelphia, Pennsylvania.

Today the task of seeking relief from inflation has been greatly simplified for the shopper. There are numerous clusters of stores that offer extraordinary shopping opportunities for everyone. You can go to these complexes, finding easy parking and a diversity of top-quality stores carrying virtually everything from toys to furs at savings of 25 percent to 70 percent. You will shop in attractive surroundings and go home with twice as much for your money as a trip to your normal department store would yield.

There still remain stores in factories themselves, but they are invariably clean, attractive, and usually well stocked. They may not have luxurious fixtures, but then, you are not buying the fixtures!

Planning Your Shopping Trip

The abundance of factory store complexes has forced us to become highly organized in preplanning a shopping trip. Here are our suggestions for a productive factory store shopping expedition.

Take a loose-leaf notebook and divide it into sections. One section should be for each person for whom you buy clothing or anything else during the course of the year; jot down sizes, needs, and desires. Another section should be for your home on a room-by-room basis; keep additional pages for other categories as the need arises. With such pertinent information on hand, you can go shopping with confidence.

When you're clothes shopping for adults at a factory store you can afford to think in terms of "investment" clothing. Suits for men and women, as well as blazers and sports jackets, fall into this category. An expensive suit should be expected to last for years; for it to do so requires that you have carefully studied the styling, quality, and tailoring details. You can also afford to supplement your basic wardrobe with the less expensive items that reflect the whims of fashion. A blouse in the current "in" shades can be discarded in another season when fashion dictates a new shade; you won't feel so wasteful if that blouse only cost a few dollars at a factory outlet. But remember, a magenta ruffled blouse that will not fit in and will never be worn is not a good buy, no matter how low the price!

It is unrealistic to expect most teenagers and growing children to think in terms of "investment" clothing. They are too involved in the mainstream of current trends and fashions. However, the basic concept needs to be taught in the formative years, so try to show its value with a few strategic apparel items. Then, be glad for the low prices of factory stores that enable you to indulge your child with the fads in fashion.

Use your notebook for essential information about your home, such as window sizes, color schemes, fabric samples, furniture needs, and so on. You will find many factory stores selling a variety of items for the home; if you see a marvelous buy on one of your trips, but you aren't sure about the measurements or colors, your "find" will be of little use.

Be sure your notebook includes a list of people for whom you buy gifts. Do you have a shower, a graduation, a new baby in the offing? Put all these events in your book; you will find endless possibilities of low-cost gifts in factory stores. Your prospective Christmas gift lists definately should be included; yes, you can shop for Christmas presents all year round!

Once you have all your planning and listing completed, allow yourself some time to browse in local department stores to get a feel for prices, current styles, colors, and so on. Now you are ready to go factory store shopping. One final thought: Consider including a shopping trip in a vacation. You may find that your savings on a major shopping trip, such as before the opening of school, will help you pay for your vacation.

Using This Book

To simplify the use of this book, we have divided it into several sections:

1. In the "Profiles" section, we have described what you can expect to find at each of the outlets included in this book. Within this section you will find many direct factory outlets, such as Manhattan Factory Outlet, which are owned by the manufacturer (or affliated manufacturers). The merchandise in these outlets is offered at wholesale or close to wholesale prices. Direct factory stores also carry items produced by other manufacturers, but they may not enjoy as large a discount as the manufacturer's itmes. You will also find some off-price stores, such as Hit or Miss and Linens 'n Things, and an occasional discount store.

2. In the center (geographical) section of the books are chapters for each state, beginning with Delaware and ending with West Virginia. The towns in which factory stores and malls are found are listed in alphabetical order. A state map precedes each chapter, and the towns are numbered on the map.

3. Three specialized indexes are included at the end of the book. The first, a product index, indicates the outlets where you might shop for specific items, such as men's clothing, lamps, china, and so on. The

second index lists the towns in which all outlets can be found. The third index contains locations for the malls and large outlet complexes.

In compiling this book, we made every attempt to provide accurate information. Factory stores, however, go out of business, close for vacation, change business hours, and even move. There is no way to control or predict these changes. Do not go any great distance without first checking to see if things have changed since this book was written.

If the stores are in an area affected by tourism—as are many near amusement parks and other attractions—their hours flucutate with the tourism season. Be prepared for reduced hours in the off-season. Many stores accept credit cards; when they do not, the listing will so indicate. Take along cash or your checkbook with at least two forms of proper identification, usually a driver's license and a major credit card. Be aware that some stores do not accept personal checks; look for that information in the listing. Most outlets are fully or partially accessible to handicapped shoppers. An accessibility heading for each outlet or mall indicates the *general* conditions readers will encounter.

Factory outlet shopping is a challenge. In meeting that challenge, you and your budget become the winners. This guide provides you with the winning edge in this ongoing money-saving adventure. Go out, have fun, and save!

Finding New Manufacturers

Many manufacturers are subsidiaries or divisions of large corporations. If you become familiar with the corporate affiliations of the different manufacturers, you will learn to anticipate the brand names you can expect to find in direct factory outlets. For example, if you are planning a trip to The Branded Shoe Outlet, you can expect to find Bostonian, Clarks, and Hanover shoes there, because they all have a common parent corporation—C & I Retail, Inc. Similarly, if you go to a Vanity Fair outlet, you will find Vanity Fair as well as Lee, Bassett-Walker, Kay Windsor, Jansport, and Jantzen—all part of the Vanity Fair corporation.

Knowing the connections among apparel manufacturers will also help you to recognize the quality and value of labels that may be unfamiliar to you. For instance, perhaps you buy Evan-Picone apparel because you feel it is well made, but have you ever tried Palm Beach clothing, which is a part of the same corporation? Maybe R & K Originals clothes are a much-loved part of your wardrobe. You might be interested to know that Kollection, Misty Harbor, and Rosemarie Reid are also part of the same corporation—Jonathan Logan, Inc. Now, when you go shopping and find these labels, take a new look at them.

It is no longer feasible for us to give the exhaustive list of affliated manufacturers that we have in the past, as industries are bought and sold so frequently. But you will find much information on manufacturers' items sold in the direct factory outlets by reading through the "Profiles" section.

We encourage you to learn all you can about different manufacturers as you continue to look for the best value for your dollar.

No store owner may purchase inclusion in this book. Store inclusion is purely a personal decision on the part of the authors. In addition, some stores chose not to participate in the compilation of this book; providing pertinent information was on a purely voluntary basis. You may, however, see outlets along the roadside while you are touring the mid-Atlantic states. Refer to the "Profiles" section of this book to see if a detour is worth your while.

PROFILES

ACA Joe
Sweatshirts and casual clothes featuring Unison Sport Clothes.

Accents
Savings from 40 to 70 percent on brass, porcelain, and rattan home furnishings, including lamps.

Accessories Plus; Accessories Plus II
Save 10 to 40 percent off retail prices on women's designer jeans, sweaters, gift items, and accessories, featuring Jordache, Calvin Klein, Gloria Vanderbilt, Wrangler, and others.

Accessory Factory
Savings of 20 to 40 percent off full retail prices on Leather Shop belts, scarves, hats, gloves, and hair accessories, as well as discounts on women's belts, handbags, and jewelry.

Acme Boot Village
Specializing in western boots for men and women, featuring Acme, Dan Post, Zodiak, and Dingo.

Adidas
Save up to 60 percent on warm-up suits for the entire family, sneakers, sportswear, leisurewear, racquets, bags, and accessories.

Adolfo; Adolfo II; Adolfo Sport; Collectibles
Save 25 to 50 percent off retail prices on women's sportswear, activewear, skirt sets, pant sets, dresses, and sweaters, featuring Adolfo, Dressy Tessy, Donna Toran, Rafael, Gloria Vanderbilt, David Rose, Susan Hutton, and Hattie Carnegie.

Adrianna Papell
Save up to 70 percent off retail prices on silk dresses, blouses, and

sportswear by Adrianna Papell, Adam Douglas, Francesca of Damon, and others.

Adrienne Vittadini
Save 40 to 70 percent off suggested retail prices on sportswear, knits, dresses, and evening attire from one of America's top designers.

Aileen; Aileen Plus; Aileen Ladies Sportswear
Save at least 35 and up to 70 percent off manufacturers' suggested retail prices on sportswear and activewear in girls', petite, junior, missy, and larger women's sizes (sizes 4 to 46), on Aileen, Aileen II, Aileen Petite, and Sport I.

Airway Luggage Outlet
Save 35 to 40 percent on luggage and leather accessories, including handbags, travel items, and small gifts.

Alexander Julian
Save 30 to 70 percent off retail prices on men's suits, slacks, jackets, shirts, and more.

Alexander's Shoe Outlet
Men's and women's shoes.

Allen-Edmonds Factory Store
Save up to 30 percent on Allen-Edmonds factory seconds of dress and casual shoes, leather accessories, and selected better-name shoe brands for men and women, including sizes 6 to 16, AAA to EEE.

All-in-One Linen Outlet
Save 30 to 50 percent on designer linens for bed, bath, table, and windows, featuring Martex, Wamsutta, Springmaid, J. P. Stevens, Cannon, Burlington, and Utica.

All Sorts of Sports
Save 30 percent and more on sporting goods.

American Candle
Fifty percent savings on American candles, silk flowers, and other gift items.

American Pottery & Glass
Pottery and glassware; gifts.

American Ribbon Manufacturers Factory Outlet
Save 10 to 40 percent on ribbons for crafts and sewing projects, in small quantities or multiyard rolls.

American Tourister
Save 20 to 70 percent every day off retail prices on hard-side and soft-side luggage and business cases, featuring American Tourister, J. P. Hampton, and French West Indies.

Amity
Save 25 to 75 percent on 150 styles of men's and women's wallets. Save on luggage, handbags, clutches, briefcases, key cases, and travel gifts, featuring Amity/Rolfs, London Fog, Amelia Earhart, Stone Mountain, Jordache, Baltimore, Oleg Cassini, Saddle River, and Winn & Elizabeth.

Amy Stoudt Outlet
Twenty to 50 percent off full retail prices on large-size women's fashions, including coats, casualwear, and accessories.

Andrea Carrano
Sophisticated, elegant shoes and accessories at more than 50 percent off.

Annie Sez
Women's fashions, including sportswear, outerwear, dresses, lingerie, and accessories; some stores carry shoes and men's sportswear.

Anne Klein Outlet; Anne Klein Petites
Savings to 60 percent on designer fashions, handbags, belts, sportswear, and accessories, featuring Anne Klein and Company, Anne

Klein II, Anne Klein Knitwear, Anne Klein jeans, Anne Klein petites, Calderon bags and belts, St. Thomas leather goods, Swank jewelry, Vera scarves, Camp hosiery, Aris knitwear, Berkshire hosiery, Riviera sunglasses, and Marvella jewelry.

Ann-Michele Originals
Save up to 40 percent off retail prices on women's sportswear, dresses, and accessories, featuring Liz Claiborne, Crystal sweaters, Ricky, Mizurka, Lee jeans, Jordache, Patterns, and Esprit.

Ann Taylor
Save 20 percent and more on women's apparel and accessories by Ann Taylor.

The Answer
Twenty to 40 percent off regular retail prices on designer clothes sizes 16 and up, featuring Liz & Me, Evan-Picone, Shaker Sports, and Chaus Woman. Accessories available.

Argenti
Save 33 to 75 percent off retail prices on women's apparel, including silk dresses in petite and plus sizes.

Argo Factory Store
Save 40 to 70 percent on activewear and casualwear for the entire family, featuring Coyote, Tulip Tops, Runner Up, Head Sport, Spalding, New Connections, and other brands.

Arrow
Save up to 40 percent on Arrow shirts.

Art and Frame Outlet
Savings of 25 to 75 percent on oil paintings, prints, lithographs, sculptures, and ready-made and custom-made frames.

Artist's Outlet
Save up to 50 percent on art supplies.

Astor Swimwear

Save 30 to 50 percent on swimwear, cover-ups, skirts, and hats in junior, missy, and women's sizes.

Athlete's Den Outlet

Clothing and supplies for almost every sport.

Athlete's Foot

Sneakers, socks, T-shirts, and shorts at 20 to 60 percent savings.

Athlete's Outlet

Featuring Nike, Timberland, Reebok, New Balance, OP, and most other major brands for men, women, and children.

Athletic Outlet

Save up to 60 percent on sneakers and active apparel, featuring Nike, Timberland, Reebok, New Balance, OP, Avia, Tretorn, Etonic, and most other major brands for men, women, and children.

Aunt Mary's Yarns

Save 20 to 75 percent off retail prices on books, needles, accessories, craft kits, art supplies, silk and dried flowers, needlepoint, and yarns—more than 500 basic and fashion yarn colors available—featuring Caron, Unger, Reynolds, and others.

B & J Children's Outlet

Savings of up to 70 percent on infant accessories, apparel, bottles, gift items, linens, supplies, and toys.

Baby's Outlet

Savings of up to 70 percent on infant clothing, supplies, apparel, furniture, and toys.

Bag & Baggage Luggage and Handbag Outlet

Twenty to 50 percent off suggested retail prices on luggage, business cases, handbags, and more, featuring Atlas, Elizabeth, Griffon, Monarch, Pegasus, Samsonite, Earhart, London Fog, Ricardo, Skyway,

Ventura, Contessa, Borelli, Empress, Great American Leather, Judith Lynn, Palizzio, Stone Mountain, Saddle River, and other brands.

Bag & Baggage of Virginia
Thirty to 50 percent off Samsonite and American Tourister luggage; 20 to 40 percent off small leather goods; and 20 to 50 percent off handbags.

Bag City
Save 20 to 70 percent on luggage, handbags, and business cases.

Bagmakers Factory Outlet
Up to 60 percent discount on handbags, casual luggage, business cases, backpacks, and wallets, featuring Stone Mountain, Etienne Aigner, Palana, John Romain, Borelli, and Sarne.

The Bag Outlet
Save 20 to 60 percent off retail prices on handbags, backpacks, and accessories.

Bagtime
Save 20 to 50 percent on handbags, women's accessories, and small leather goods.

Bally Shoe Outlet Store
Save 25 to 60 percent off suggested retail prices on men's and women's shoes, attachés, men's leather jackets, hosiery, portfolios, briefcases, belts, silk ties, wallets, and women's handbags.

Banister Shoe; Freeman; Banister/Capezio
Save up to 50 percent on Adidas, Amalfi, Arpeggios, Avia, Bandolino, Bandouno, British Walker, California Cobblers, Capezio, Cobbies, Etonic, Evan Picone, Famolare, Freeman, French Shriner, Garolini, Georgetown, Joyce, Liz Claiborne, Manistee, Mushrooms, Pappagallo, Puma, Reebok, Rockport, Selby, Soft Spots, Sperry, Sportivo, Sociality, and Streetcars shoes.

Barb Bee's Factory Outlet
Save 20 to 60 percent on women's sportswear up to size XXL.

barbara's outlet
First-quality, up-to-the-minute sportswear and smart career looks in coats, pants, skirts, blouses, dresses, and sweaters.

Barbizon Lingerie
Thirty to 60 percent savings on pajamas, gowns, panties, fleece robes, Cuddleskin and Feathaire sleepwear, Dearfoam slippers, and lingerie by Barbizon, Hanes, Carole, and Youthcraft.

Bare Necessities
Save 20 to 60 percent on bras, panties, robes, and gowns, featuring nationally known brands.

Bargain Sneakers
Save 25 to 60 percent on Reebok, Nike, Adidas, Converse, Puma, Russell Athletic, L.A. Gear, Tretorn, Etonic, New Balance, and other athletic footwear for infants, children, women, and men to size 16. Athletic clothing also available.

Bass Shoes; G. H. Bass
Save 25 percent and more on Weejuns, Bucs, Sunjuns sandals, and other classic footwear and on accessories.

Bauer Shoes
Savings of up to 65 percent on men's and women's shoes in dress, casual, and athletic styles, featuring hard-to-fit sizes.

Bay Carpets
Save 30 to 50 percent on wall-to-wall carpet, wood floors, no-wax vinyl flooring, ceramic and other kinds of tile, wall coverings, custom draperies, and vertical blinds. Professional installation and free in-home estimates within service area.

Bear Mountain Books
Save 10 percent and more on current and back-listed books and magazines.

Beauty Barn
Save 20 percent and more on cosmetics and fragrances.

Beauty Scenter
Up to 70 percent off suggested retail prices on leading department store brands of toiletries and such gift items as potpourri and candles.

Bed, Bath & Beyond
Save 20 percent and more on bathroom, kitchen, bedroom, and other household linens and notions.

Bed 'n Bath
First-quality and designer sheets, towels, bath accessories, bedspreads, comforters, pillows, and tablecloths.

Beer Arena
Cut-rate prices on beer and other beverages.

Benetton Outlet
Save up to 50 percent on a large selection of summer and winter clothing, available all year, at the United Colors of Benetton.

Bentley Books
Best of current family reading; best-selling hardcover and softcover books, magazines, and more at special prices.

Bentwood Company
Savings of about 20 percent on gifts, collectibles, and Pennsylvania handcrafted furniture.

Benzel's Pretzel Factory Outlet
Benzel's pretzels, as well as other brands of cookies, candies, potato chips, corn chips, cheese dips, mustards, pickles, and hot bologna.

Best Jewelry
Twenty-five percent off jewelry and accessories, featuring Seiko, Gruen, Mikimoto, and others.

Best of Times
Extensive line of costume jewelry, including watches, earrings, rings, necklaces, and bracelets. Informal leisurewear for today's active woman.

Best Things
World-famous prestige cosmetics and designer fashions at 30 to 50 percent off retail prices.

Biederlack of America (Biederlack Blanket Company)
Blankets, down comforters, pillows, cuddle wraps, and material.

Big & Tall
Save 15 percent and more on big and tall–size men's clothing.

Big Ben Jewelers
Save 40 to 60 percent off suggested retail prices on sterling silver, fourteen-karat gold, and diamond jewelry, including rings, pendants, chains, earrings, bracelets, charms, wedding bands, pearls, and colored stones, as well as Seiko, Belair, Pulsar, and Lorus watches. Jewelry and watch repairs.

Bijou Catrin
Complete line of European fashion accessories catering mainly to young girls and women. Some items for men are available.

Binghamton Knitting Company
Save 50 percent on sweaters for the entire family, featuring Escort and Brimwick; also sportswear and knitting yarns.

Black & Decker
Hardware, power tools, lawn-care equipment, and accessories.

Black & Decker Reconditioned Outlet
Large selection of reconditioned and blemished products, including power tools and small household appliances, at substantial savings. Hard-to-find replacement parts and accessories available. Fully warranted products. Shipping service.

The Black Sheep featuring Woolrich
Sweaters, skirts, and pants for men and women.

Blair New Process Company
Up to 80 percent savings on seconds men's and women's clothing—including men's ties, belts, hats, shirts, and slacks and women's blouses, sweaters, pantsuits, dresses, and separates—featuring Botany 500, McGregor, and the company's private brands, John Blair and Lady Blair; shoes and housewares available too.

Blenko Glass Company, Inc.
Seconds, sale items, and discontinued handblown glassware. Crafters at work daily from 8:00 A.M. to 12:00 noon and from 12:30 to 3:15 P.M.

Bleyle
Save 35 to 70 percent off regular retail prices, with personal service, on Bleyle, Mayon, and Sisignora womenswear.

Bloomingdale's Outlet
Save up to 50 percent on end-of-season and surplus merchandise from Bloomingdale's department stores.

Bollman Direct Hat Factory Outlet (George W. Bollman & Co., Inc.)
Save up to 60 percent on first-quality and select irregulars on men's dress felt hats; Dynafelt western hats for men, women, and children; women's millinery; knit and sport headwear in seasonal styles; neckties and belts; and caps, cloth hats, and straw hats.

Bon Worth
Save 35 to 50 percent on first-quality misses' sportswear, featuring Bon Worth, Lee, and other names.

Book Cellar
Hardback and paperback books discounted.

Book Hutch
Save up to 80 percent on a wide variety of hardback and paperback books. Special orders welcome.

Books-a-Million
Save up to 75 percent on books and other publications.

Booksellers Warehouse
Save up to 80 percent off publishers' retail prices on hardback and paperback books.

Book Stall
Save up to 70 percent on discontinued books and greeting cards. Magazines, newspapers, and current videos (for rent and sale) also available. *New York Times* best-seller books discounted.

Book Warehouse
Save 50 percent to 90 percent off publishers' retail prices on overrun books and related items from all major publishers. About 4,000 titles per store.

Bostonian Factory Outlet; Branded Shoe Outlet
Savings of 10 to 60 percent off retail prices on men's and women's shoes, including Hanover, Bostonian, Clarks, Maine Woods, Converse, Reebok, Nike, Rockport, Naturalizer, and other brands.

Boston Traders and Boston Trader Kids
Savings of 30 to 70 percent off suggested retail prices on fine sportswear for men, women, and children; also carries men's big and tall sizes.

Branded Shoe Outlet
See Bostonian Factory Outlet.

Brands Factory Outlet
Savings of 30 to 70 percent off retail prices on fashions by Bill Blass, Michii Moon, Perry Ellis, Chaps by Ralph Lauren, Nancy Heller, Leon Levin, Sanyo, MIGHTY-MAC, Echo, Lord Jeff, and Lakeland.

Brass Factory
Savings of 50 to 70 percent off retail prices on 2,000 different brassware items.

Brass Works
Specializing in fine lacquered brassware by Hampton Brass, including door knockers, Christmas decorations, and more than 200 styles of picture frames, at 40 to 60 percent savings.

The Braun Company
Sterling, pewter, giftware, and tableware, including water pitchers, Thomas Jefferson stainless flatware, Tidewater desk accessories, apple and pear salt-and-pepper shakers, and Williamsburg tankards, coffee sets, and tulip fluted champagnes, from America's oldest silversmiths. Commissionable pieces; engraving service. Call (301) 338–6000 for guided tour.

Briefcase Unlimited
Display and sale of briefcases, portfolios, backpacks, wallets, and leather goods. Monogramming on premises.

Brooks Outlet
See T. Edwards.

Bruce Alan Bags
Save 35 percent off regular retail prices on first-quality, brand-name leather handbags, wallets, hard-side and soft-side luggage, attachés, belts, and briefcases, as well as on backpacks, umbrellas, costume jewelry, and travel accessories.

Bubbles and Scents
Savings of up to 70 percent off suggested retail prices on leading department store brands of toiletries including home fragrances, bath luxuries, and children's character toiletries featuring Barbie, Care Bear, Muppets, Looney Tunes, G.I. Joe, Teenage Mutant Ninja Turtles, and Real Ghostbusters.

Buffalo's Added Touch Boutique
Savings of 25 to 60 percent below retail prices on lingerie, casual-wear, loungewear, and swimwear. Also sells famous brand colognes, jewelry, and gifts at discount prices.

Bugle Boy Outlet
Save 20 to 60 percent off retail prices on family apparel and athletic clothing for children, juniors, and preps and on young men's and women's contemporary sportswear featuring Nesi, Bugle Boy, and Vincente.

Burlington Brands
Thirty to 50 percent savings on men's and women's brand-name sportswear.

Burlington Coat, Dress and Linen Factory Outlet; Burlington Clothing Factory
Savings of 25 percent on nationally advertised brands of coats, dresses, and sportswear in sizes from 5 to 24½. Seasonal sales offer additional savings.

Burlington Coat Factory
Save 40 to 60 percent on coats, year-round rainwear, and other apparel, featuring Misty Harbor, Perry Ellis, Calvin Klein, Bill Blass, Anne Klein, Charles Klein, London Fog, Evan-Picone, J. G. Hook, Jill Jr., Bert Newman, Ashley Scott, and Forecaster.

Buttons and Things Factory Outlet
Sensational selection of hard-to-find buttons at wholesale prices, including novelty buttons, holiday buttons, bell and heart buttons, craft buttons, and buttons by the pound. Also carries books, button findings, sewing accessories, crafts, collectors' thimbles, Christmas collectibles, Fun 'n Learn toys, and unique gift items.

By the Yard
Savings of 40 to 60 percent on decorative fabrics for the home, directly from the manufacturer.

Cabin Creek Furniture
Savings of 10 percent and more on dining-room, bedroom, and occasional furniture, entertainment centers, and custom furniture.

Calvin Klein
Savings to 70 percent on designer sportswear for women; casual sportswear for men and women.

Calvin Klein Jeans Outlet
Savings of 40 to 70 percent on Calvin Klein jeans, skirts, sweaters, and shirts.

Cambridge Dry Goods Outlet Store
(New England Trading Company)
Save 35 to 50 percent on first-quality sportswear and careerwear for women, featuring Cambridge Dry Goods, Cambridge Sport, and Cambridge Sports Club.

Camera Shop
Save up to 30 percent on photographic supplies.

Cami'z
Save 25 to 50 percent off retail prices on men's, women's, and children's sportswear and accessories.

Campus Factory Outlet
Save 40 to 50 percent off suggested retail prices on first-quality men's and boy's apparel in regular, big and tall, and boy's sizes 4 to 20, featuring Campus, Letigre, and J. J. Cochran.

Canadian's Outlet
Savings of 25 percent and more on Canadian-made products.

Candle Factory
Reduced prices on candles and supplies.

Candle Towne U.S.A.
Large supply of candles and candle-making products at reduced rates.

Candy Barrel Outlet
Sweets at sweet prices.

Candy Kitchen
Reduced prices on candies and other treats.

Canterbury of New Zealand
Men's, women's, and children's rugbywear and assorted sports activewear, including tall and large men's sizes.

Cape Craft
Discounts of up to 40 percent on country home furnishings and accessories, including brass-framed pictures, baskets, and products sold as seconds.

Cape Isle Knitters
Savings of up to 60 percent on similar branded or private-label knitwear for men and women, featuring current, best-selling styles and colors in all sizes. A "no questions asked" return policy.

Capezio
Shoes, featuring Evan-Picone, Nina, Bandolino, Jazz, Bellini, Capezio, A.K. Sport, and other names.

C. A. Reed
Savings of up to 70 percent on a complete line of paper products for all occasions (weddings, birthdays, showers, graduations, anniversaries, etc.). Items include napkins, hot cups, tablecovers, skirting, champagne glasses, centerpieces, candles, nut cups, cake decorations, decorated streamers, bells, cake knives, folds, plume pens, curling ribbon, thank-you notes, and more.

Cargo Factory Outlet
Solid-wood casual furniture and decorative accessories.

Carlos Falchi
Save from 30 to 60 percent off retail prices on handbags and leather accessories by i santi, Michael Rome, and Carlos Falchi.

Carole Hockman Lingerie
Save 40 to 70 percent on petticoats, camisoles, teddies, bridal sets,

lingerie, daywear, bras, robes, hosiery, and loungewear, featuring Carole Hockman, Bordeaux, Mollie Parnis, Christian Dior, Sara Beth; also Lily of France lingerie, sleepwear, and bras.

Carole Little
Save 35 to 70 percent off retail prices on casual and career sportswear.

Carolina Furniture of Williamsburg
Save 25 to 50 percent on more than 600 of America's finest furniture lines, featuring Henkel Harris, Council Craftsman, Southwood, Henredon, Thomasville, Craftique, Thayer Coggin, Karastan, Greeff, Leathercraft, Link Taylor, Dixie, Stiffel, Hitchcock, and Century.

Caroline's Treasure Hut
Costume and fine jewelry at a discount.

Caron Yarn
Savings of 20 to 70 percent off retail prices on yarns, plus books, needles, and accessories relating to yarns and crafts.

Carpet Factory Outlet
Full rolls, mill ends, remnants, Orientals, and area rugs from Masland carpets and Mannington vinyls.

Carpet and Rug Outlet
Savings of up to 60 percent on Orientals, dhurries, handmade and machine-made carpets, and rugs. Shipping service.

Carroll Reed
Savings of 20 to 70 percent on sportswear, dresses, accessories, and handbags by J. G. Hook, John Meyer, Izod, Carroll Reed, Eagle's Eye, Scrader Sport, Lombardi, and others.

Carter's Childrenswear
Save 30 to 60 percent on clothing for boys and girls to size 14 and on a complete line of layette merchandise.

Carter's Little Gallery
Twenty to 60 percent discount on layette merchandise and on infant and toddler clothing, sizes 4–14, by Carter.

Carvel Hall
Fifty percent off retail prices on Carvel Hall cutlery; brass, crystal, pewter, and silver-plated giftware; candles; housewares, including pots, pans, and teakettles; and pewter- and nautical-themed jewelry. The Crisfield outlet is part of the Carvel Hall factory, a division of Towle Silversmiths, and in summer carries local Maryland souvenirs.

Champion Activewear Outlet
Save 30 to 50 percent on athletic apparel—T-shirts, jerseys, sweat-suits, sweaters, nylon jackets, crewneck sweatshirts, mesh half-jerseys, tube and other styles of socks, gym shorts, coaches' shorts, golf shirts, and knitwear; also custom printing.

Champion Hanes Activewear
Fleece and cotton warm-ups, shirts, skirts, pants, and jackets in the latest fashion colors for men, women, and children at discount prices. Also a wide variety of accessories.

Charles Chips Outlet Store
Featuring nationally advertised Charles Chips and Charles Pretzels, along with a wide variety of fresh cookies, candies, and other snacks.

Charles P. Rogers Factory Showroom
Save 25 to 60 percent (occasional sales) on brass beds.

Chaus
Savings of 25 percent off retail prices on Chaus, Ms. Chaus, Josephine, Chaus Sport, Chaus Petite, Chaus Women, and Josephine Chaus clothing for women.

Chesapeake Pottery
Large outlet store featuring Anchor Hocking, Bahlsen of Germany, Bucilla, Burlington, Cannon, Capel Rugs, Chicago Cutlery, Corelle, Corning, Farberware, Fitz & Floyd, Gerber Cutlery, J. G. Durand,

Libbey, Lindt Chocolates, Martex, Miracle-Gro, Noritake, Oneida, Ortho, Pfaltzgraff, Pyrex, RevereWare, Royal Worcester, Rubbermaid, Salisbury Pewter, Springmaid, Stotter, Toscany, Villeroy & Boch, Wedgwood, Yankee Candle, and more. Pennsylvania Dutch farmer's market open Thursday through Saturday.

Chico's Outlet
Retailer of men's and women's southwestern-style apparel manufactured exclusively for Chico's. Accessories also available.

Children's Mill Factory Outlet Inc.
Save up to 75 percent on closeouts, overruns, and special promotions for infants', toddlers', and children's clothing from birth to size 18, including outerwear, slacks, tops, sweaters, sleepwear, hosiery, underwear, baby bedding, jogging suits, and dresses.

The Children's Outlet
Save 20 to 40 percent on fashion clothing and accessories for children, newborn to size 14, featuring OshKosh, Health-Tex, Levi, Lee, Pattles, On-Track, Images, and others.

China Plus
Dinnerware, crystal, cranberry glass, gifts, and decorative accessories.

Christian Benard
Savings of 25 to 70 percent on a full line of fine jewelry. Jeweler on premises Saturday and Sunday.

Christmas Goose
Candles and Christmas gifts, decorations, and collectibles at low prices.

Christmas Mouse
A wonderland of ornaments, decorations, gifts, and other Christmas needs.

Christmas Tree Hill
Constantly changing mix of gifts, home accessories, and collectibles for the Christmas season at discount prices.

Church's English Shoes
Savings of 35 to 65 percent off retail prices on shoes, belts, wallets, ties, and more.

Claire's Factory Store
Save 40 to 80 percent off suggested retail prices on women's apparel in petite, misses, and half sizes, featuring Studio 36, Lorlyn, I. Appel, and Joan's of New York, as well as Appel robes, Smart Time dusters, Formfit bras, and Myonne panties.

Claire's Outlet Boutique
Fun accessories at fabulous prices.

Classic Caramel Company
Manufacturer of the famous York old-fashioned caramels, toffee, taffy, nougat, and soft butter-and-cream caramel, as well as hard candy, chocolates, snack food, and "munch" more. Bargains on seconds, plus monthly "superspecials."

Clifford Michael
Luxury shearlings, leathers, and wools, as well as sportswear, rainwear, and coats, for ladies and men; specializes in petites.

Clifford & Wills
Savings of 30 to 50 percent on traditional women's apparel from their catalog, with a career and sportswear emphasis.

Clock Center
Save 20 to 50 percent on fine collectibles, including items by Lladro, Swaroski, and M. J. Hummel, plus nutcrackers and more. Carries more than 700 clocks, including grandfather, mantel, and cuckoo clocks; also offers more than 600 Seiko watches at 40 percent off retail prices.

The Clothes Out Closet
Popular, first-quality misses' fashions in current styles for work and play, all at discount prices.

The Clothes Outlet

Twenty-five to 40 percent off classic, traditional brands of men's and women's clothing, including Robert Scott, Tallyho, Duckhead, and many private labels.

Club House

Save 50 to 75 percent off retail prices on better blouses and separates in petite and plus sizes by La Chine Classics and Galinda Wang.

Cluett Apparel Factory Stores; Cluett Peabody

Forty percent savings on first-quality family apparel, featuring Arrow, Lady Arrow, Gold Toe socks, Burberry's, R.P.M.; Jon Marc slacks; Saturdays, Sundays Sportswear; Alexander Julian sportswear; Arrow boyswear; and Dobie childrenswear. Slight irregulars and sales representatives' samples sold at even greater savings.

The Coach Store

Save 30 percent on slightly irregular Coach products, including gloves, belts, and handbags.

Coat Factory

Primarily coats and swimwear at a discount.

Coat World, a Division of Flemington Fur Co.

A huge collection of cloth coats, leathers, suedes, imported woolens, cashmeres, all-weather coats, suits, jackets, fur hats, "fabulous fakes," fun furs, and fur-lined garments for men and women.

Cobbler's Factory Outlet

Savings to 70 percent on women's shoes and boots, sizes 4 to 12 AAAA to WW.

Cocoon Silk

Save 50 to 70 percent off retail prices on women's silk apparel.

Cole-Haan

Savings of up to 50 percent on fine Cole-Haan apparel, accessories, and leather footwear for men, women, and children.

Colonial Wood Benders, Inc. Outlet
Early American and colonial replicas of wooden items, such as butter churns, wooden buckets, forks, and racks, as well as toys and gifts. Many items are factory seconds at discounts of up to 50 percent. Wholesalers welcome. UPS shipping.

Colors by Alexander Julian
Savings on fashions by Colors.

Columbia Garment Co.
From slight discount to below-wholesale prices on laces, sewing needs, material, trims, patterns; some garments and robes carried.

Compare Menswear by Ted Louis Shop, Inc.
Thirty-five to 50 percent off men's suits and clothing, including Botany 500 suits and garments by Arrow, Izod, Halston, Enro, Van Julian, Damon, Robert Bruce, and others.

Contemporary Man
Brand-name sportswear and suits for men and young men, all at a discount.

Converse Factory Outlet
Save an average of 50 percent off retail prices on Converse athletic shoes and activewear.

Corner House
Fashion apparel for women.

Corning Factory Store (Corning/Revere Factory Store)
Great savings on Corning Ware, Pyrex, Corelle, Visions range-top cookware, Thermique thermal servers, hurricane globes, glass and plastic covers, drinkware, parts, coordinated accessories, microwave products, and RevereWare. Some stores carry only Corning or Revere, but most stores carry both.

Country Casuals
Savings on first-quality casualwear for the entire family by OP, Liz Claiborne, Newport Blue, Woolrich, David Brooks, and others.

Country Cheese 'N Jam Gift Outlet
Wholesale and retail prices on gourmet selection of imported cheeses, mouth-watering fruit jams, crackers, mustards, coffees, teas, and gift items. Affordable cheese gift baskets made with the personal touch. Shipping.

Country Road Australia
Savings of 30 to 40 percent off retail prices on men's and women's suits, topcoats, dresses, skirts, shorts, sweats, shoes, and accessories by Country Road Australia.

Crazy Franks Accessory Outlet
Savings of up to 70 percent off retail prices on his-and-her fashion sportswear and accessories, from bathing suits to jogging suits.

Crazy Horse
Savings of 40 to 60 percent off retail prices on natural-fiber sportswear, sweaters, and career separates for women in sizes 4 to 14. Also features Russ Togs for sizes 8 to 18 and a selection of men's better knits.

Crib
Baby- and infantwear.

Crystal Sportswear by Kobe
All merchandise is 50 percent off manufacturer's suggested retail price on sweaters, sweatshirts, T-shirts, and skirts in missy and large sizes.

Crystal Works Factory Outlet
Save 20 to 60 percent off retail prices on first-quality, full-lead crystal, stemware, bowls, vases, decanters, candlesticks, barware, table lamps, chandeliers, and more, featuring Nachtmann.

Custom Sportswear
Save up to 50 percent or more on women's, misses', and juniors' brand-name dresses, sportswear, blouses, skirts, sweaters, and slacks.

Daffy's Clothing Bargains for Millionaires
Family apparel, handbags, and lingerie.

Dali B
Save 50 percent off retail prices on women's apparel and sportswear by Semplice.

Dalzell Viking
See Viking Glass Company

Damon Shirts
Forty to 60 percent off regular retail prices on men's better sweaters; knit, sport, and dress shirts; and ties, slacks, belts, underwear, and outerwear—featuring Damon, Bill Blass, Enro, Courcheval, and other brands. Big and tall men's department.

Dan River
Sheets, pillowcases, comforters, shams, dust ruffles, priscillas, bedspreads, country curtains, bed pillows, decorative pillows, mattress pads, towels, kitchen and bath accessories, blankets, table linens, Dan River fabrics, and Sunbeam electric blankets. Direct mail-order service.

Dansk Factory Outlet
Save up to 60 percent on dinnerware, teakwood serving pieces, flatware, glassware, cookware, gifts, seconds, discontinued patterns, and limited editions of Dansk's classic tabletop designs. Ship UPS.

Danskin Outlet
Save 50 percent off suggested retail prices on Danskin women's and girls' bodywear, leotards, swimwear, aerobicwear, legwear, tights, unitards, foundations, accessories, belts, cosmetics, luggage, pantyhose, daywear, and nightwear. Phone orders and mailing service.

Danson Jewelers
Save 20 to 60 percent off manufacturers' suggested list prices for jewelry, including loose stones and diamonds. Repairs, remountings, special orders, and custom work available.

Danville Factory Outlet
Fifty percent and more off retail prices on women's clothing, includ-

ing sportswear, nurses' uniforms, coats, underwear, and robes—featuring Christian Dior sleepwear, Members Only, Farah Pablo Collection, Miss Liz, David Brett, and Haegar, as well as White Swan and Crest uniforms.

Dazzles
Accessories at a discount.

Deb Fashion Outlet
Direct savings on fashions from this popular juniors' clothing store (sizes 3–13).

Delta Hosiery Outlet
Savings from 25 to 70 percent on leotards, tights, socks, panties, pantyhose, stockings, bras, and slips, from Burlington, Round the Clock, Hanes, Liz Claiborne, Evan-Picone, Humpty Dumpty, Givenchy, Charles Jourdan, Calvin Klein, and Blossoms—for the entire family.

Designer Luggage Depot
Savings of up to 75 percent on Samsonite, Pierre Cardin, Oscar de la Renta, Gloria Vanderbilt, Lucas, and John Weitz luggage.

Designer Jewelry
The finest designer fashion jewelry at affordable prices.

Designer Wholesale Outlet
Popular and brand-name designer creations in junior, missy, and large sizes, at a savings of 30 to 50 percent.

Designer Yarns
Savings of 10 percent and more on yarns and on knitting and craft supplies.

Dexter Shoe Factory Outlet
Save up to 50 percent on a variety of men's and women's quality leather footwear.

Diamonds Unlimited
Save up to 50 percent or more off regular department store prices on costume jewelry, handbags, accessories, and watches.

Diane Freis
Diane Freis/Designer Collection features limited-edition day and evening dresses. One-size-fits-all styles.

Diane Gilman
The "Washable Silk Capital" of Secaucus, with dresses, blouses, slacks, lingerie, and more, all in 100 percent washable silk. Also Kriss Kross sportswear. Misses, petites, and large sizes.

Diesse Shoes
Discounts on women's shoes and men's sneakers.

Doe-Spun Factory Store
Save 40 to 70 percent on clothing for infants, toddlers, and girls to size 14 and for boys to size 7, featuring Doe-Spun, Billy the Kid, Wrangler, Sasson, Buster Brown, Rothchild, and other brands.

Dollar Bills
Accessories, knickknacks, and other stuff at $1.00.

Dollar Save Outlet
Household gadgets and other items at $1.00 or more.

Donna Karan
Save 10 percent and more on designer apparel and accessories from Donna Karan and DKNY.

Donnkenny
Save 20 to 60 percent off retail prices on women's apparel by Donnkenny, DK Gold, Kenny Classics, Flirts by Donnkenny, and others.

Dooney & Bourke
Save 20 to 60 percent off retail prices on leather wallets, belts, purses, briefcases, and more.

Door Store
Contemporary home and office furniture, with a wide selection of chairs, desks, and dining, bedroom, and storage units. New, first-quality goods in stock and special clearance area for as-is merchandise.

Down East Factory Outlet
Save 30 to 70 percent on skiwear, sportswear, sweatsuits, and apparel for cycling and hiking, as well as on books, sneakers, and sports aids and medical supplies—featuring Gerry, Raven, Zero, Avia, Timberland, and others.

Draperies Etc.
Linens, domestics, draperies, curtains, and bedspreads.

Dress Barn
Save up to 50 percent off department store prices on dresses and suits, career to casual, for misses and juniors, including Lizwear, Larry Levine, Calvin Klein, Sasson, Act III, Villager, harvé benard, Casper, Cherokee, John Meyer, and Gloria Vanderbilt.

Dress Barn Woman
Save 20 to 50 percent on women's fashions in sizes 14 to 24.

Dunham Footwear
Save 25 to 50 percent off retail prices on footwear, featuring first-quality boots by Dunham, Quoddy, and L.A. Gear.

Eagle's Eye
Savings of 30 to 50 percent off regular retail prices on overproduced colors, styles, and irregular women's classic and novelty sweaters made from the finest natural materials, as well as a full line of sportswear coordinates for women and children.

Eastern Shore Uniform Company
Hotel, motel, and hospital uniforms, aprons, and shoes. Variable discount, according to purchaser and quantity, from 5 percent for hospital and nursing home employees, to 10 percent for students, to negotiation for large corporations.

East Prospect Factory Outlet
One mile from the factory, the East Prospect outlet handles Curtain Call costumes, including dance shoes, fabric, and trims, as well as Alpha Factor gymnastic clothing and Gantner swimwear. Halloween costumes, doll clothing, and a potpourri of other unexpected items are a specialty.

Eddie Bauer
Save 30 to 60 percent off retail and mail-order prices on men's and women's apparel by Eddie Bauer and others.

E. K. Bags
Manufacturer of handbags and luggage at a discount.

The Electronics Outlet
Savings on home, car, and office stereo and electronic equipment, televisions, radios, CBs, and accessories.

Elegant Boutique
Savings of 20 to 40 percent below suggested retail prices on dresses, skirts, suits, pants, blouses, and more—featuring Liz Claiborne, Leslie Fay, Laura Osbourne, Giorgio, and Susan Hutton.

Elkay Factory Outlet
Sweatclothes, corduroys for children, and other merchandise direct from the factory.

Ellen Tracy
Savings from 35 to 50 percent on designer sportswear, dresses, blouses, skirts, jackets, sweaters, and coats in misses and petite sizes for women.

Emerson Radio
Factory-authorized outlet store offering a selection of consumer electronic products, tapes, and accessories.

Endicott Johnson
Save 20 to 35 percent off retail prices on shoes, footwear, and acces-

sories, featuring Nike, Puma, Carolina, Endicott Johnson, Wolverine, and other brands.

Enterprise Golf Outlet
Men's clothing, including casual pants, warm-up suits, sweaters, jackets, and topcoats, featuring Jordache, Calvin Klein, Gabrielle, and Bugle Boy. Specializing in golf clubs, golf accessories, club fitting, club making and repair, and computer swing analysis.

Eric Allan Factory Store
Save 30 to 50 percent on brand-name men's clothing, including silk sportcoats and Dacron/wool-blend suits, featuring Christian Aujard, J. G. Hook, and Egon von Furstenberg.

Escada
Savings of up to 65 percent off retail prices on women's apparel and accessories, featuring Escada, Laurl, and Crisca.

Esprit
Savings of 30 to 70 percent off retail prices on women's and children's ready-to-wear and women's careerwear, sportswear, sweaters, and shoes, as well as all sheets, all by Esprit.

Etienne Aigner
Savings of 30 percent and more off retail prices on women's apparel, handbags, and footwear and on small leather goods for men and women, featuring Etienne Aigner.

Euro Collections
Save 30 to 70 percent off department store prices on clothing, featuring Oleg Cassini. Visit the private collections room for a large selection of eveningwear, black-tie, and mother-of-the-bride merchandise.

European Designer Outlet
Savings of 30 to 70 percent off retail prices on women's dresses, blouses, pants, suits, sweaters, and coats; men's suits, pants, sportswear, and shirts; and more.

Evan-Picone Factory Store; Evan-Picone/Gant
Save 35 to 70 percent off suggested retail prices on Evan-Picone, Gant, Austin Hill, Palm Beach, John Weitz, Seinsheimer, Eagle, Hunter Haig, Haspel, and other apparel and accessories labels for men and women.

Everything's a $1.00
Thousands of items, from housewares to toys, each costing $1.00.

Executive Neckware
Save 30 to 70 percent on a variety of neckwear, wallets, accessories, gift items, and much more for men and women—featuring Pierre Cardin, Buxton, Prince Gardener, John Henry, Swank, Johnny Carson, Halston, and Alexander Julian. Small leather goods at 50 percent savings.

Fabric Factory Outlet
Carrying a large selection of fabrics from the top designers' studios in New York City, including linens, woolens, and cottons. Notions and patterns also carried.

Factory Linens
Save from 30 to 40 percent off regular retail prices on bed linens, bath towels, tablecloths, place mats, kitchen linens, and much more in current product lines—plus substantial savings on overstocks and discontinued items—from Ritz, Saturday Knight, Spring Maid, Northern Feather, Tobin, and Cannon.

Famous Brands Housewares
Savings on everything for the kitchen and the house, from cookbooks to closet hooks.

Famous Brands Outlet
Clothing for men and boys, featuring Cherokee Style, Original Product, Balboa, and Robert Bruce.

Famous Brand Yarns
Save 25 to 60 percent on yarns, needlepoint, crewel, canvases, craft kits, and needlework of all kinds.

Famous Footwear
Save 10 to 50 percent on shoes and accessories for the family, featuring Adidas, Candies, Mushrooms, Nike, Nunn Bush, Reebok, Tiger, and U.S. Keds.

Famous Galleries of Williamsburg
Twenty to 50 percent off regular prices on original oils, limited- and open-edition prints, framing, and gifts; specializing in colonial and wildlife art.

Fan Fever
Everything for the sports fan, particularly those who follow Pennsylvania, New Jersey, and New York teams.

Fanny Farmer
Save 25 to 50 percent on Fanny Farmer Almost Perfect™ chocolates, first-quality bulk chocolates, nonchocolate candy, nuts, fudge, holiday candy, and ice cream.

Farah Menswear; Farah Factory Clearance Store
Save 30 to 35 percent on men's clothing, featuring all Farah brands, Farah, W.F.F., Savanne, E'Joven, N.P.W., and Generra.

Fashion Bug
Twenty-five percent savings on major brand-name and private-label women's apparel and accessories, featuring Stefano, Maggie Lawrence, American Line, Gitano, Levi, and Jordache.

Fashion Bug Plus
Updated line of sportswear; casualwear, careerwear, and formalwear; coats; lingerie; and accessories for women in larger sizes.

Fashion Express
Casual sporty attire for men, women, and juniors, featuring Lee, Levi, and Jordache.

Fashion Factory
Carrying a complete line of casual, comfortable, and unique brand-name sportswear, with savings of 30 to 70 percent on all the season's

hottest looks and colors for men and women; junior sizes carried for school, work, and play apparel.

Fashion Finds
Women's clothing, with everything for $10.

Fashion Flair
Savings starting at 40 percent on Izod, LaCoste, Ship 'n Shore, and Monet sports and casualwear for men, women, and children.

Fashion Jewelry Exchange
Save up to 50 percent or more off regular department store prices on fine and costume jewelry, accessories, and watches.

Fashion Shoe Outlet
Save 25 to 50 percent on brand-name women's and teens' shoes, featuring Candies.

Fenton Art Glass Company
Fifty percent discount on individually blown or pressed glass, with first-line items, as well as seconds and some discontinued items.

Fieldcrest Cannon
Save 40 to 60 percent on irregular and discontinued merchandise for the bedroom, bathroom, and kitchen. Bathrobes also.

Filene's Basement
Save up to 50 percent on end-of-season and surplus merchandise from Filene's department stores.

Finder's Keepers
Savings of 20 to 70 percent on jewelry, shells, gems, and crystals.

Fine Jewelry by Solange
Savings of up to 50 percent off wholesale prices on diamonds and precious gemstones with fourteen-karat gold, ten-karat baby jewelry, Mexican sterling silver, men's accessories, and genuine and simulated cultured pearls.

First Choice
Save 60 to 80 percent off retail prices on women's apparel, accessories, and sportswear, with selections from previous collections by Escada, Laurel, and Crisca.

Flemington's Coat World
Savings of 25 to 35 percent on first-quality famous maker and designer cloth and leather coats and all outerwear for the whole family.

Flemington Fashion Outlet; Flemington Plus; Flemington Petites
Designer and famous-name labels in women's sportswear, separates, suits, sweaters, blouses, skirts, pants, blazers, and coordinates, in regular, plus, and petite sizes.

Flower and Plant Cove
Savings on everything for the green thumb.

Foggy Bottom
Discontinued and overstock selection of imported gifts from Holland, Scotland, England, and France, including pewter and Delft, kitchenware, and bakeware.

The Footfactory
Save 10 percent or more on brand-name shoes.

Forever Accessory
Discounts on jewelry, watches, and hats for women.

Formal Celebration
Savings of 20 percent and more on bridal gowns and tuxedo rentals

Formfit Outlet
Save a minimum of 40 percent off retail prices on first-quality items, closeouts, and overruns on sleepwear, robes, activewear, and intimate apparel, featuring Formfit, Myonne, I. Appel, and others.

Fostoria Glass Factory Outlet
Fostoria glassware, Nelson McCoy pottery, candles, and giftware 100 percent packaged.

Fowler's Chocolate Factory
Specializing in quality chocolates, fudges, and nuts, direct from the manufacturer.

Fragrance Cove
Save 15 percent and more on cosmetics, fragrances, and accessories.

Fragrance World
Savings of 10 percent and more on fragrances, cosmetics, and accessories.

Freddy's Discount Drugs
Save 50 percent and more on personal-care items, health-care products, cosmetics, and fragrances.

Frederick Clothiers
Thirty to 50 percent savings on men's clothing, specializing in formalwear and men's big and tall sizes, with dress shirts to size 20 and sports shirts to size 4XL, in standard and athletic cuts. Accessories and some women's suits also carried.

Freeman Shoes
Save up to 50 percent on shoes from Adidas, Amalfi, Arpeggios, Avia, Bandolino, Bandouno, British Walker, California Cobblers, Capezio, Cobbies, Etonic, Evan Picone, Famolare, Freeman, French Shriner, Garolini, Georgetown, Joyce, Liz Claiborne, Manistee, Mushrooms, Pappagallo, Puma, Reebok, Rockport, Selby, Soft Spots, Sperry, Sportivo, Sociality, and Streetcars.

Frisco Blues
Save 40 percent and more off regular retail prices on closeouts and irregulars, featuring Levi Strauss for men, women, and children.

From Me to You
Cards, Precious Moments, newspapers, magazines, candy, stuffed animals, and collectibles.

Frugal Franks
Savings of up to 50 percent or more on top-quality, brand-name shoes for men, women, and children, featuring Del Cino, Sibelli, 9 West, Puma, Nike, and other names.

Fuller Brush
Shop here when the Fuller Brush man (woman) doesn't stop by your house. Savings of at least 10 percent on the complete line of Fuller Brush products and other items.

Full Size Fashions
Savings of 25 to 40 percent on brand-name items, specializing in women's sizes 16 and up.

Fur Vault
Save 20 to 50 percent or more off prices in traditional fur stores on furs and leathers, including blue fox, mink jackets with fox trim, natural or dyed mink coats, and natural or dyed female mink coats.

Gabrielle
Savings of up to 60 percent off suggested retail prices on men's collegiate licensed products: jackets, coats, sweaters, pants, shirts, jeans, and sneakers.

Galt Sand
Savings of 30 to 70 percent on activewear, including sweatshirts, sweatpants, hoods, T-shirts, and shorts.

Gant
Save 25 to 50 percent on men's shirts, sportswear, and sweaters, including cashmere, Shetland, and lamb's wool, and on women's blouses, skirts, sweaters, and slacks.

Gap
Men's, women's, and children's apparel at discount prices.

Garage
Discounts on brand-name teenwear and sports gear.

Gem Vault; Baskin & Sons Inc.
From the cutters to you. Huge savings on fourteen- and eighteen-karat gold jewelry with fine colored gems and custom handmade mountings.

General Shoe Factory to You; Factory to You
Save 35 to 50 percent off regular retail prices on men's and women's shoes, featuring J & M, Jarmon, Charm Step, Mademoiselle, Air Step, and Laredo boots.

Generra
Savings of 30 to 70 percent off retail prices on Generra fashion sportswear for the entire family.

Genesco
Savings of 35 to 50 percent off regular retail prices for men's and women's shoes and boots.

Gentile Glass Company, Inc.
Twenty percent discount on first-line items, specializing in handmade paperweights and hand-cut crystal tableware and featuring Fenton, Pilgrim, Indiana, Crystal Clear, and other lines. Some seconds.

Gentlemen's Wearhouse
Save 30 to 50 percent on first-quality men's suits, sport coats, slacks, and accessories. Women's tailored clothes and weekend fashions at substantial savings.

Geoffrey Beene
Savings of 20 to 50 percent off retail prices on men's apparel by Geoffrey Beene.

Georgetown Leather Designs Outlet
Selection of leather goods for men and women from the Georgetown Leather Designs stores.

George W. Bollman & Co.
See Bollman Direct Hat Factory Outlet.

Georgiou

Savings of 40 to 75 percent on women's natural-fabric apparel by Georgiou, Balkan, and Kolanki.

G.H.Bass

See Bass Shoes.

Gilligan & O'Malley

Save 35 to 60 percent off retail prices on sleepwear and robes by Gilligan & O'Malley in sizes X-small to XXX-large.

Gitano

Save up to 50 percent on all girls', juniors', misses', plus, maternity, and men's casualwear, activewear, and sportswear, direct from the manufacturer. Selection includes a full line of Gitano accessories—footwear, outerwear, underwear, watches, socks, camp shirts, tank tops, girls' denim skirts, girls' pocket T-shirts, crepe de chine shells, and more. Frequent-shopper bonus of $25 toward a purchase after $250 worth of purchases.

Gitano Kids Factory Stores

Save one-third off retail prices on children's casual and active sportswear and accessories, featuring Gitano and E. J. Gitano labels.

Gitano Warehouse Clearance Center

Save 50 percent off retail prices on women's, men's, and children's casual and active sportswear and accessories, featuring Gitano.

Glass Resort

A minipottery, with savings of 20 to 70 percent on china, glassware, wicker, and dishes.

Glen-Gery Brick Factory Outlet

The best selection of Glen-Gery face brick, paving brick, and masonry products, offered at factory outlet prices.

Gloray Knitting Mills

Savings of up to 70 percent on 100 percent cotton sweaters, golf shirts, jogging suits, and knit dress sets, all of which Gloray makes for fourteen prestigious brands found in better stores coast to coast.

Golden Chain Gang
Costume and fine jewelry.

Golden Talents
Handmade quilts, pillows, afghans, toys, and a host of desirable gifts made by Hunterdon's senior citizens.

Gold Exchange
Display and sale of fourteen- and eighteen-karat gold jewelry. Large and diverse collection of gold, diamond, and precious-gem jewelry, with four jewelers on the premises making and repairing jewelry.

Gold-N-Silver
Special savings on all first-quality Speidel watches, plus fourteen-karat gold and silver jewelry.

Gold 'n Things Jewelry
Forty percent savings off regular prices every day on fourteen-karat gold and sterling silver from both Italian and U.S. manufacturers. Chains, charms, and earrings, plus fashionable costume jewelry.

Gorham
Gorham silver flatware, hollowware, silver pieces, stainless steel, and silver-plated flatware; china dinnerware; full lead and fine crystal; and dolls, teddy bears, hand-painted sculptures, musical figurines, Norman Rockwell collectibles, and Christmas ornaments.

Great Outdoor Clothing Co.
Savings of 30 to 70 percent off retail prices on brand-name outdoor clothing.

Green Onion Kitchen Shoppe
Kitchenware, Fenton glass, Christmas room, snow village, heritage villages, German nutcrackers, and gourmet coffees and teas.

Gucci

Savings of 40 to 50 percent off retail prices on men's and women's fashions, shoes, leather goods, gifts, luggage, and accessories.

Guess? Factory Store

Savings of 50 percent off retail prices on men's, women's, and children's apparel and accessories.

H. L. Miller Tops & Tees

Adult and youth knit sportswear, including T-shirts, shirts, sweatshirts, and pants; also custom decals and letters for individuals, schools, and businesses. Irregulars available at even greater savings.

Hagerstown Shoe Factory Outlet

Save 10 to 60 percent and more on first-quality, selected irregulars, samples, overruns, and closeouts of nationally advertised brands of men's and women's shoes and athletic footwear.

Hahn's Shoes Outlet

Save as much as 50 percent on shoes from Bass, Capezio, Bandolino, Socialites, Cobbies, Joyce, 9 West, Selby, Pappagallo, Reebok, Jazz, Liz Claiborne, Cobbie Cuddlers, Rockport, Esprit, Nunn Bush, Florsheim, Hush Puppies, French Shriner, Clarks, and Wm. Hahn—with a large selection of hard-to-find sizes.

Hamilton Luggage & Handbags

A variety of famous-brand luggage, handbags, business cases, and leather accessories at a discount, featuring Hartman, Atlas, Lark, Skyway, Bosca, Ventura, Princess Gardner, and many others.

Hamilton Watch & Clock Shoppe

Savings on Hamilton watches and clocks—designer samples, factory overruns, and discontinued models.

Hamrick's

Apparel for the entire family.

Handbag Company Outlet
Leather handbags and accessories, casual and work gloves, and wallets for men and women, all at a discount.

Handmade Quilts, Etc.
Handmade quilts, wallhangings, pillows, tablerunners, and hot pads made in Amish Country. Handcrafted wooden toys, quilt-it-yourself printed panels, quilt books, and delicious Pennsylvania Dutch breads.

Hanes Activewear
Closeouts on Hanes casual activewear, mix-and-match sweatsuits, and other styles, plus additional savings on slightly imperfects.

Hanover Shoe Store
Up to 50 percent or more savings on factory-damaged shoes by Hanover and Bostonian for men, plus a few cancellation styles for women.

Happy Hatter
Fashion jewelry, sunglasses, hair accessories, scarves, belts, gloves, and hats, for the whole family, featuring Stetson, Betmar, and Barbisio.

Hartstrings Childrenswear Outlet
Save 30 to 50 percent off retail prices on updated traditional sportswear, dresses, and accessories for children, all in fine fabrics and beautiful colors. Sizes from 12 to 24 months, girls' Hartstrings sizes 2T to 14, and boys' Kitestrings sizes 2T to 10.

Hartz & Company Factory Outlet
Men's clothing, suits, sport coats, trousers, and overcoats.

harvé benard
Savings of 40 to 60 percent on the full line of men's and women's designer fashions, jewelry, accessories, and handbags.

Harvey Electronics
Top-name audio and video products from such manufacturers as

Sony, Bang and Olufsen, Adcom, Bose, Boston Acoustics, Carver, Infinity, KEF, Klipsch, McIntosh, Monster Cable, NAD, Nakamichi, Polk, Proton, Yamaha, Mitsubishi, and Denon, at greatly reduced prices. Manufacturers' overruns, one-of-a-kinds, and demonstration models.

Hathaway
Savings of 40 percent and more on merchandise for men, including Hathaway dress and sport shirts, Christian Dior sportswear and elegant dress shirts, and Chaps and Ralph Lauren sportswear. Men's ties and women's White Stag sportswear, as well as Olga and Warners intimate apparel for women.

Heacock's Deerskin Factory Store
Leather handbags and accessories, casual and work gloves, wallets for men and women, and soft deerskin moccasins and slippers.

Head over Heels
Save 20 to 70 percent off retail prices on women's fashion footwear, hosiery, and accessories, featuring Nickels, Jazz, Via Spiga, Studio Paolo, Glacee, and Paloma.

Heirloom Lace Country
Battenburg Lace and other handmade laces in the form of bedding, fine table linen, and curtains. Huge selection of lace trim by the yard.

Heirlooms
Savings of up to 80 percent off retail prices on Philadelphia's newest manufacturer of better women's sportswear.

Helen's Handbags
Twenty to 50 percent off retail prices on briefcases, totes, small leather goods, and, of course, handbags—from casual shoulder bags to designer evening purses.

Heritage Shop
Visit the furniture factory and see craftsmen build quality furniture. Browse in showrooms of wood furniture and eye-catching upholstery and decorative accessories.

He-Ro Group Outlet
Savings of up to 70 percent on ladies blouses, sportswear, dresses, leathers, and evening-wear fashions by Bob Mackie, Oleg Cassini, Blassport, Fabrice, d'ore, pia rucci, and Palmer & Palmer.

Hilda of Iceland Outlet
Save 30 to 70 percent on men's, women's, and children's Iceland woolen knit sweaters, jackets, coats, and accessories.

Hi-Tec Outlet
Liquidations and closeouts on brand-name stereos, videos, car stereos, and phones. Also installation of car stereos and cellular phones and repair of stereos and VCRs.

Hit or Miss
Twenty to 50 percent off retail prices on national-brand misses' and career fashions.

Home Again
Savings of up to 75 percent on home gifts items, knickknacks, picture frames, brass items, and more.

The Housewares Store
Save up to 60 percent or more on Krups, Melitta, Bormioli glassware, appliances, bakeware, coffee makers, cookware, cutlery, dinnerware, flatware, kitchen gadgets, gourmet foods, salt/pepper mills, espresso/cappuccino makers, travel accessories, spices, and other quality items. Shipping service available.

I.B. Diffusion
Save 30 to 60 percent off full retail prices on women's apparel and accessories, featuring I.B. Diffusion, I.B. Sport, and Rediffusion.

IKEA
Scandinavian furniture and home furnishings, most unassembled in boxes.

Imp Pedlar

Thirty to 65 percent off retail prices on men's and women's apparel, featuring Anne Klein, Levi, Jantzen, Liz Claiborne, and many others.

Instant Decor

Ready-to-assemble, take-home furniture, featuring living-room pieces, dinettes, wall units, utility carts, desks, lamps, mailboxes, mats, and more.

International Boutique, Inc.

Unique shop specializing in Indian, European, and American fashions, with a selection of women's clothing, jewelry, and handicrafts from India and other countries. Savings of 20 to 50 percent on brand names.

International Clothing Company

Savings to 60 percent on men's and young men's clothing and sportswear. Men's and young men's outlet for suits, tank tops, shorts, sweatpants, bike shorts, and capri tights, featuring Champion Reverse Weave sweats.

International Diamond Cutters Exchange

Diamonds, gold, watches, and other jewelry.

International Footwear Co. Outlet Store

Save 30 to 70 percent on men's and women's current-fashion, brand-name dress and casual shoes, featuring Bostonian, Westies, Mia, Keds, Grasshopper, Bellini, Maine Woods, Florsheim, and other brands.

International Lingerie, Cosmetics, & Children's Wear

Savings of 20 to 70 percent on luxurious feminine apparel, cosmetics, health and beauty aids, children's apparel, and more.

Intimate Eve

Save 40 to 70 percent on all-cotton panties, camisoles, nightshirts, pajamas, lingerie, swimwear, funwear, and daywear, all in fashion colors and novelty prints and featuring St. Eve—for women, men, juniors, and children.

In-Wear Matinique
European styling in clothing for men and women.

Island Gear
Swim- and sportswear for men, women, and children.

Iva's
Antique collectibles, including the *Gone with the Wind* series.

Izod/LaCoste; Izod/Evan Picone; Izod/Gant
High-quality sportswear by Izod/LaCoste, Ship 'n Shore, and Monet for men, women, and children. Savings of 40 to 60 percent off manufacturers' suggested retail prices.

Jaeger Outlet
Save 50 to 70 percent off retail prices on European woolens, cashmere, and silks, all in career looks, as well as on matching accessories, footwear, handbags, and leather goods.

J. C. Clinton's
Ray-Ban and other brands of sunglasses, plus other accessories.

J. C. Penney Outlet
General merchandise, including small electronics.

J. Crew
Men's and women's casual clothing and accessories.

Jeans 'n Things
Basic, stretch, and fashion jeans by Chic, Lee, Levi, Wrangler, Jordache, and Gitano. Sizes for juniors, misses, women, and men. Tops and jewelry as well.

Jessica McClintock
Save as much as 50 to 75 percent off suggested retail prices on Jessica McClintock and Gunne Sax women's fashions.

Jewel Master
Savings on costume and fine jewelry, including fourteen-karat gold and sterling silver.

Jewelry Connection
Fourteen-karat gold and sterling silver, in addition to the latest in costume jewelry.

Jewelry Outlet
Popular lines of contemporary fashion jewelry, famous-name watches and clocks, fourteen-karat gold jewelry, sterling silver, jewelry boxes, sunglasses, and belts.

Jewelry Vault
Forty percent savings off regular prices every day on fourteen-karat gold and sterling silver. Chains, charms, and earrings, plus fashionable costume jewelry.

J. G. Hook Co. Store
Save one-third and more off retail value on dresses, jackets, skirts, pants, blouses, and sweaters in misses and petite sizes.

JH Collectibles
Misses and petite sizes for women.

Jindo Furs
Save 20 to 50 percent or more off prices in traditional fur stores on furs and leathers, including blue fox, mink jackets with fox trim, natural or dyed mink coats, and natural or dyed female mink coats.

Joan & David
Savings to 50 percent on women's first-quality designer shoes and leather accessories.

John Henry; John Henry & Friends
Savings of 30 to 60 percent off men's and women's sportswear, shirts, and blouses, by Manhattan, Perry Ellis, John Henry, and Anne Klein.

John Wright Warehouse

A restored warehouse overlooking the Susquehanna River, featuring a factory outlet and country store with more than 2,000 items for home and garden. Among the items are cookware, collectibles, cast-iron accessories, muffin pans, cookie molds, candy pans, kettles, steamers, trivets, doorstops, fire marks, decorative eagles, foot scrapers, cast-iron toys, wheel toys, mechanical banks, still banks, shutter hinges, hooks, and shelf brackets. The Country Store features home decorative items and furnishings, including baskets, lamps, furniture, china, tinware, aprons, potpourri, and crafts. The Stove Shop has John Wright stove accessories, Vermont Castings products, and other manufacturers' products.

Johnston & Murphy Factory Outlet

Save 40 to 60 percent on men's shoes, featuring Johnston & Murphy, Sebago, British Walker, Keith Highlander, Bass, and Durango.

Jonathan Logan Outlet

Save 40 to 70 percent on activewear, dresses, blouses, outerwear, and coordinates from major manufacturers, including the Jonathan Logan line, in sizes for petites, juniors, misses, and women. Featured are Misty Harbor, Chaus, Counterparts, Private Club, Calvin Klein, Maggy Boutique, Diane Von Furstenburg, Josephine Ace & Company, Alpeslick, Breckenridge, Anne Klein, Alice Stuart, Domino, Judy's Place, Villager, Villager Petites, Bill Blass Action Scene, R & K Originals, Kollections, Amy Adams, Rose Marie Reid and Bill Blass swimwear, and Etienne Aigner accessories.

Jones New York; Jones New York Women; Jones New York Sport, Misses, and Petites

Save 30 to 50 percent off suggested retail prices on women's apparel, featuring Jones New York, Jones Sport, Christian Dior suits and separates, and Saville suits.

Jordache

Savings of 25 to 60 percent off retail prices on Jordache apparel and accessories.

Judy Bond Blouses
Save 40 to 60 percent off retail prices on Judy Bond–label women's apparel.

Just'a Sweet Shoppe
Savings of up to 40 percent on candy, dried nuts, and crackers.

Just Coats 'n Swimwear
Save 40 percent off full retail prices on women's pantcoats, coats, suits, down coats and jackets, and leathers, and on men's overcoats and down- and polyester-filled jackets, featuring London Fog. Some stores carry resort and swimwear for women and rainwear and outerwear for men.

Just Kids Outlet Store
Save 25 to 60 percent off retail prices on children's apparel, featuring Her Majesty and other major brands.

Just My Size
Intimate apparel, including hosiery, bras, lingerie, slips, and panties, made exclusively for full-figured women and featuring slightly imperfects, discontinued items, and overstocks. Expert bra-fitting service available.

Kandy Korner
Hard and soft candy at a discount.

Kay Bee Toys
At least a 10 percent discount on brand-name toys.

Kenar-Nicole Matthews
Catering to the contemporary woman's lifestyle with sportswear, dresses, and leisurewear featuring Kenar Studio, Kenar Dresses, Kenar Sportswear, and Kenar Leathers at discount prices.

Kid City
Children's clothing at a discount.

KIDrageous
Save 30 to 70 percent off regular retail prices on children's clothing and accessories—for infants, toddlers, girls' sizes 4 to 6X and 7 to 14, and boys' sizes 4 to 7 and 8 to 20.

Kid's Barn
Savings of 30 to 50 percent on children's clothing and accessories, from newborn through girls' size 14 and boys' size 18.

Kids Creations
High-quality European children's clothing, infants through preteen, featuring items of 100 percent cotton.

Kids, ETC.
Save 30 to 60 percent on better-quality childrenswear, including shirts, pants, sweaters, sleepwear, outerwear, hosiery, and underwear, from newborn to size 16 and featuring Buster Brown, Kleinerts, Shirt Tales, and Cradle Togs.

Kidsfeet
Savings on all children's footwear, for activities ranging from school to sports.

Kids Port USA
Savings of 20 to 40 percent on Health-Tex clothing for infants, toddlers, girls through size 14, and boys through size 8.

Kidstuff
Apparel and accessories for children, from infants to boys and girls.

Kidswear
Twenty to 60 percent savings on brand-name children's apparel, including OshKosh B'Gosh, Izod, OP, Polly Flinders, and London Fog.

Kids Wearhouse
Savings of 40 to 60 percent off name-brand children's apparel including OshKosh B'Gosh, Izod, OP, Polly Flinders, and London Fog.

Kimberton Outlet
Fifty percent savings on women's and men's golf shirts, tops, skirts, and sweaters.

Kinder Bin
Fashion for infants and children, featuring OshKosh B'Gosh, Hartstrings, Esprit, Sara Kent, and more. Also educational toys, gifts, and jewelry.

Kindermart
Savings of about 20 percent off clothing for babies, infants, boys up to size 16, and girls up to size 14.

Kitchen Collection
Save 20 to 70 percent on first-quality and factory seconds of Wear-Ever cookware, ProctorSilex appliances, and Bissell and Anchor Hocking products.

Kitchen Linens Etc.
See Factory Linens

Kitchen Place
Utensils, dinnerware, flatware, and accessories, featuring Durand, Rubbermaid, Wear-Ever, Libby, Anchor Hocking, and more.

The Knittery
At least 40 to 70 percent discounts on first-quality, current lines from Susan Bristol and on Keneth Too sweaters and coordinating merchandise; Robby Len swimwear and cover-ups at savings of up to 40 percent.

Kuppenheimer Men's Clothier
Men's suits, sport coats, and slacks from Kuppenheimer, as well as accessories, outerwear, and jackets. Alterations available.

Lace Factory Outlet
All forms and designs of lace.

La Chine Classics
Save 50 to 75 percent off retail prices on better blouses and separates, sarong and split skirts, silk separates, and sportswear in petite and plus sizes, by La Chine Classics by Galinda Wang.

Ladies Factory Outlet
Women's clothing in sizes from petite to large, specializing in SK & Company, SK Wear, and Laura & Jayne.

Lady Footlocker Outlet
Brand-name athletic sneakers, sports apparel, and accessories for women and children.

Lady Leslie
Save 20 to 50 percent on such fashion labels as Cricketeer, Evan-Picone, Ann Randolph, J. G. Hook, Shrader, Ultra Suede, Chaus, Pendleton, and Leslie Fay. Alterations and special orders.

Lady Leslie Woman's World
Classic sportswear, dresses, suits, and leisurewear in sizes 14½–24½, 30–38, 36–46, and 12–20 and featuring Cricketeer, Evan-Picone, Leslie Fay, Castleberry, Shrader, Ultra Suede, Chaus, French Vanilla, Pendleton, Alley Cat, and Shaker Sport. Accessories carried too.

Lamp Factory Outlet
Twenty to 50 percent savings on lamps, accessories, chandeliers, Tiffany lamps, desk lamps, floor and table models, shades, lamp parts, mirrors, bulbs, and more—featuring Stiffel, Robert Abbey, Keystone, and other brands.

Lancaster Lingerie Outlet; Fifth Avenue Design
Famous-name lingerie and sportswear at 25 to 75 percent off manufacturers' suggested prices.

Lancaster Pottery & Glass Outlet
Save 20 to 50 percent on a complete selection of first-quality and current Corning Ware products; decorative and tabletop glassware; country crafts, wagons, and giftware; American-made pottery and gadgets; handblown Pilgrim glass vases; and candles and rugs. Shipping service available.

Land & Seas
Cotton sweaters and clothing for the entire crew, nautical gifts, and Niagara Falls T-shirts and sweatshirts.

Laura Ashley Outlet
English designs in natural-fiber fashions for women and children.

Leather and Fur
Savings of up to 50 percent on leather and fur coats and related items.

Leather Gallery
Save 40 to 60 percent on a variety of small leather and eelskin goods, wallets, belts, briefcases, attachés, handbags, and novelty items.

Leatherland
The area's largest selection of men's and women's leather garments, all at 30 to 60 percent savings.

Leather Loft
Forty to 60 percent savings on leather items, including luggage, brief-cases, handbags, wallets, belts, gloves, executive gifts, and domestic and Italian desk accessories. Designer items feature Edward Harvey, Carlo Amboldi, Exeter Ltd., Lisa Loren, Cary's of California, London Fog, Oleg Cassini, High Sierra, Renwick of Canada, and Tumi.

Leather Plus
Savings of up to 50 percent (sometimes more) off department store prices on leather and suede clothing and accessories for men and women, including outerwear, sportswear, gloves, wallets, belts, and handbags, as well as scarves, sweaters, hats, novelty T-shirts, and sweat-shirts.

Leather Warehouse
Discounts on the company's own label, featuring apparel, coats, and bags.

Lechters Inc.
Discounts on kitchen and household gadgets.

L'eggs/Hanes/Bali Factory Outlet

Twenty to 50 percent and more off suggested retail prices on slightly imperfects, closeouts, and overstocks of L'eggs, Hanes, Bali, Bill Blass, and Gem Dandy hosiery, lingerie, socks, sweatsuits, and underwear for men, women, and children. Hosiery-club membership earns six free pairs of slightly imperfect pantyhose after purchase of seventy-two pairs of same; request membership card.

Lenox Crystal & China Clearance Center; Lenox Factory Store

Save 40 to 60 percent off retail prices on select seconds of Lenox dinnerware, china, crystal, stemware, handblown items, candles, pewter, and other tabletop accessories and gifts, as well as discontinued Hartmann luggage.

LF (Leslie Fay) Factory Outlet

Savings of 30 to 90 percent on nationally advertised separates, coordinates, better dresses, blazers, sweaters, blouses, shorts, and slacks in misses, petites, and women's sizes, featuring Leslie Fay.

Lightfoot Manor

Twenty to 35 percent savings on Council Craftsmen reproduction furniture, Jefferson cups, tobacco jars, humidors, Distinction Leather Furniture, Kirk Stieff, Tudor, Baldwin Brass, and Virginia Metalcrafters Brass.

Lighthouse Factory Outlet

Savings of 10 to 50 percent off suggested retail prices on table, floor, and desk lamps; replacement lamp parts; and shades. More than fifty manufacturers featured, including Westwood, Cycle 2, and Robert Abbey.

Lillian Vernon

Save 25 percent off regular catalog prices.

Limited Editions for Her

Savings of up to 50 percent on exceptional American designer fashion coordinates in quality fabrics.

Linens 'n Things
Linens, bathroom and bedroom accessories, gift wrap, quilts, comforters, and more, featuring Martex, Fieldcrest, Cannon, Stevens, Wamsutta, Dan River, and others.

Linen Warehouse
Twenty to 30 percent off suggested retail prices on towels, sheets, comforters, shower curtains, and table linens by J. P. Stevens, Fieldcrest, Martex, and Springmaid.

Lingerie Shop
First-quality, current lingerie and sleepwear in petite through extra-extralarge sizes, at discount prices. National brands. Shipping service.

Little Red Shoe House
Save 20 to 50 percent on footwear for business, play, or dress—sneakers, sandals, work shoes, boots, and casual styles for men, women, and children. Senior citizen discount.

Liz Claiborne
Save up to 75 percent off retail prices on discontinued, first-quality Liz Claiborne merchandise for men and women, including dresses, leather goods, sportswear, Claiborne menswear, handbags, and fashion accessories.

L. J. Fashions
Discounts on women's fashions.

L. L. Bean
Selections from the company's catalog.

LMC Factory Store
Watch the garments being made while you shop at the factory store. Savings on women's sleepwear/loungewear, selected women's sportswear, and children's items.

London Fog Factory Outlet Store; Londontowne Factory Outlet Store
Fifty percent off regular retail prices for first-quality rainwear, jackets, outerwear, toppers, pantcoats, leathers, slacks, sport shirts, sweaters,

hats, and scarves—for children, men, and women and in all lengths and sizes. Special seasonal sales.

Lots of Linens
Lowest prices year-round on famous-maker towels, bath sheets, cotton blankets, fingertip towels, beach towels, water-bed sheets, mattress pads, pillows, comforters, tablecloths, place mats, rugs, doilies, napkins, and kitchen accessories. Featured are Abouchar, Bess, Bibb, Brentwood, Barth & Dreyfus, China Art, Wamsutta, Quallofil, Quallofirm, Corscill, Crown Craft, Foreston Trends, Fieldcrest, Ginsey, Springs, Spirella, Sunweave, Stevens, Tobin, and Vohann.

Lucia . . . That's Me!
Thirty-five to 40 percent off suggested retail prices on coordinated missy and junior sportswear featuring Lucia . . . That's Me.

Luggage World
Discounts of up to 60 percent on luggage, briefcases, totes, carry-ons, duffles, backpacks, trunks, pullmans, garment bags, and travel accessories, featuring Lark, Samsonite, American Tourister, Members Only, Jordache, and Amelia Earhart. Repair service.

Macy's Specialty Stores
Savings of 50 to 75 percent on designer names and labels that have made Macy's famous—offering women's, men's, and children's fashions, plus designer shoes.

Madd Maxx
Ten to 20 percent off retail prices on appliances and electronics, featuring General Electric, Hitachi, RCA, Sony, and others.

Madran Tools
Discounts on small tools.

Maidenform Outlet Store
Save up to 50 percent off retail prices on Maidenform first-quality, discontinued, and closeout merchandise, including bras, panties, camisoles, half and full slips, garter belts, and other lingerie.

Maison Emanuelle

Save as much as 60 to 70 percent on perfume, cologne, and cosmetics—featuring Joy, Shalimar, Halston, Chanel, Estée Lauder, Nina Ricci, and Pierre Cardin—and on specials of sweaters, tops, and skirts by Krazy Kat, Body Focus, and St. Michel.

Male Ego

Men's and young men's clothing, from underwear to outerwear, in sizes from student to big and tall (XXXXXL). Clothes for all occasions, including swimwear and skiwear.

Manhattan

Save up to 60 percent off retail prices on men's and women's fashions from Manhattan, Perry Ellis, John Henry, Anne Klein for New Aspects, Peters Ashley, Henry Grethel, Lady Manhattan, Manhattan shirts, Yves Saint Laurent, and Vera accessories. Also carries women's sportswear in plus sizes and big and tall shirts at 25 to 60 percent off suggested retail prices. Frequent-buyer club.

Man's Town

Savings of 30 to 80 percent on men's clothing.

Manufacturer's Surplus Outlet (MSO)

Discount savings on furniture from bedroom to dining room, with lots of lamps and decorator pieces and a great variety of curio cabinets, featuring such brands as Bassett, Hooker, Schweiger, Koster, Beechbrook, and Howard Miller.

Manufacturer's Shoe Outlet

See Banister.

Marburn Curtain Warehouse

Save up to 70 percent (sometimes more) on curtains, linens, rugs, miniblinds, shades, sheets, and towels—at "almost wholesale prices."

Mark Cross

Beautifully selected merchandise for women and men, substantially below the regular prices found in Mark Cross stores, including such items as handbags, small leather goods, luggage, gift items, scarves, ties, briefcases, attachés, portfolios, desk sets, and executive items.

Marketplace Sneakers
Savings of 20 percent and more on major brands of sneakers.

Marty's Shoes
Save 30 to 70 percent off prices in department stores and specialty shoe stores on famous-label and designer footwear for the entire family, featuring Andrew Geller, 9 West, Kenneth Cole, Nickles, Air Step, Westies, Caressa, Bally, Florsheim, Bostonian, Bass, and others. Also offered are handbags, hosiery, and accessories.

Maternity Wearhouse
Fifteen percent off maternity fashions for the mother-to-be, sizes 4 to 44, including dresses, tops, pants, coats, and lingerie, and featuring Ma Mere, Puccini, Great Times, Jeanette, Sasson, M. H. Fine, Japanese Weekend, Oliver Peace, Belle France, and others.

Maternity with Love
Save 60 percent on maternity and nursing apparel in sizes to XXL and on unique outfits for children, from preemie to 24 months. Baby gifts, christening outfits, and crib sets carried too.

Maxine's Books
Savings on hardback and paperback books and magazines.

Melton Clothing Factory
Save 40 to 70 percent off family apparel, including shirts, jeans, sweaters, jackets, boots, underwear, socks, and wool pants. Sizes include big and tall. Featured are Deerskin, Melton, Melton Wintermaster, Lee, Trebark, Wigwam, London Fog, Fruit of the Loom, Screen Stars, Dee Cee, Outdoor Products, Healthknit, Career Club, Polarfleece, Ideal, Hollofil 808, Dingo, Kool Dri rainwear, Coleman, Duxbak, Thinsulate, Terramar, Dr. Denton, Chic, White Stag, Gore-Tex, Garanimals, Golden Fleece, Northlake, Boss, Dickies, Fieldline, Dexter, Johnson Garment, Sorels, RefrigiWear, Kenilworth, Health-Tex, 10X, Red Ball, Wrangler, Weather Tamer, Zena, SafTBak, Texas-

brand boots, Wilson, Hanes, Columbia, OshKosh B'Gosh, Penfield, Keneth Too, BVD, Walls, Wells Lamont, Converse, Carhartt, Key, and Redhead.

Members Only Outlet Store
Twenty to 80 percent off retail prices on clothing for the entire family.

Menagerie Discount Outlet
Savings of 10 to 40 percent on paperback books, greeting cards, and plush animals.

Men's Market
Discounts on men's clothing.

Mercantile
Offering customized, handmade leather belts and other items at prices well below retail.

Merit Outlet
Gifts for under $2.00.

Merry Go Round Outlet
Casual to dressy clothing and accessories for men and women, all at discounted prices.

MFO; Murray's Menswear
Suits, sport coats, slacks, and furnishings for men, including portlies, portly shorts, extralongs, regulars, and longs to size 54 and featuring Stuart Davis, Eagle Clothes, and Botany 500. Alterations available.

Micki
Fifty percent off comparable retail prices on in-season women's suit separates, dresses, and accessories.

Mid-Atlantic Glass Company
First-quality items at wholesale prices in small to medium lot sizes, such as four large decanters or six dozen glasses. Guided and self-guided tours can be arranged when the factory is open.

Middishade Factory Stockroom
Men's apparel, with such specials as two suits for $199 or two pair of slacks for $25.

Mikasa Factory Store
Savings of up to 80 percent on dinnerware, stemware, cookware, table linens, flatware, housewares, crystal servingware, ceramic gifts, holiday and other gift items, and bone china giftware.

Mill Outlets
Save an average of 20 percent off retail prices on linens, domestics, and towels, featuring Fieldcrest, Springmaid, Cannon, Martex, and J. P. Stevens.

Moda Fashion Apparel
Savings of 30 to 50 percent off retail prices on men's and women's fashion apparel by Valentino, Ungaro, Joseph Abboud, Emmanuel, Giorgio Armani, and Mani.

Mondi
Save up to 75 percent on European sportswear for women, sizes 4-14.

Morey's Jewelers
Fine jewelry, plus watches by Longines, Wittnauer, Bulova, and Pulsar, all at discount prices. Swarovski crystal and Lladro figurines also available.

mothercare
Affordable fashions for moms-to-be and babies too, including maternity dresses, sportswear, lingerie, layette needs, and children's clothing through size 4T.

Munsingwear
Save 50 to 75 percent off retail prices on men's underwear and sportswear, sizes 28 to 60, and on women's lingerie and intimate apparel, sizes S to 3X, featuring primarily Munsingwear and Vassarette. Socks for all sizes and babywear by LeRoi.

Murray's Menswear
See MFO/Murray's Menswear

Mushroom Factory Store
Air-cushioned Mushrooms, Cobbies, and Selby shoes in functional and fashionable styles for women.

Music Den
Compact discs, tapes, and records, carrying current hits, easy sounds, classics, oldies, and country, big band, soul, and kiddies' music.

Names for Dames (featuring Adolfo)
Thirty-three to 60 percent discounts on fashion blouses, sweaters, knit skirt and pant sets, and activewear, featuring Donna Toran, Dressy Tessy, and Adolfo Sport.

Nanny's Shoppe
Handcrafted gifts, calico specialties, folk art, primitives, slates, "apple people" dolls, and more.

Napier Co.
Savings up to 40 percent off retail prices on Napier first-quality costume jewelry.

National Locker Room
Licensed sportswear, including shirts, jackets, and sporting plaques available with team, college, and league designs.

Nautica
Save a minimum of 30 percent off retail prices on men's and women's Nautica sportswear, activewear, and outerwear.

NBO Warehouse Store
Forty to 60 percent off retail prices on national brands of men's apparel.

NCS Shoe Outlet
Savings of 50 to 75 percent off retail prices on the latest styles from Nickles, Jazz, Via Spiga, Paloma, Studio Paolo, and Glacee shoes.

Neiss Collectibles

Save 20 to 50 percent off regular retail prices on a broad line of giftware, dolls, plush animals, pewter, music boxes, figurines, bears, nutcrackers, smokers, bells, china cups and saucers, collectibles, and more.

Nettle Creek

Save 35 to 50 percent off retail prices on a complete selection of Nettle Creek bed covers, accessories, decorative pillows, upholstered furniture, window treatments, and fabric by the yard. Custom orders handled with decorator assistance, plus a shop-at-home service for window treatments.

Newberry Knitting Company, Inc.

Knitted clothing, including sweaters, mittens, gloves, and socks for the entire family.

Newport Sportswear

Men's current-season activewear, sweaters, sport shirts, dress shirts, neckties, and outerwear.

New York Electronics

Electronics, video software, watches, calculators, televisions, and more, by AIWA, Sanyo, Sony, Sharp, Texas Instruments, and others.

Nickels

Savings of 25 to 70 percent off retail prices on fashion shoes by Jazz, Nickels, Glacee, Via Spiga, and others.

Nike Factory Outlet

Save 30 to 50 percent off full retail prices on selected closeouts and irregulars of Nike footwear, apparel, and accessories for the entire family.

Nilani Outlet

Twenty to 60 percent savings on dresses, blouses, sweaters, shirts, pants, and sportswear in sizes for misses, juniors, and women, featuring Nilani and Billy Jack.

$9.99 Stockroom
Featuring the latest sportswear, in junior, missy, petite, and plus sizes, for $9.99 or less.

9 West & Co.
Savings of 30 percent and more on hundreds of 9 West & Co. dress shoes, casual shoes, and boots.

Noel's Hosiery Outlet
Save 20 to 50 percent on pantyhose, knee-highs, and men's and women's socks and underwear.

No Nonsense
Save 30 to 70 percent off comparative retail prices on women's brand-name sportswear, lingerie, and hosiery.

Nordstrom Rack
Savings of 30 to 70 percent off the original prices on top-name apparel, accessories, and footwear for men, women, and children. Special-purchase values as well.

The North Face
Save up to 40 percent off retail prices on men's and women's sportswear, down and synthetic outerwear, skiwear, Gore-Tex, and Versa-Tech activewear, featuring North Face and Windy Path brands.

Norty's Factory Outlet; Norty's Clearance
First-quality Norton McNaughton sportswear for women, including pants, skirts, tops, shorts, and blazers; sizes include petite, missy, and Maggie (plus).

Not Just Barrettes
Savings on barrettes and other accessories.

Not Just Jeans
Sweaters and jeans for both sexes.

N.T. Tahari
See Tahari Outlet.

NWS Electronics Outlet
Savings on stereo and electronic equipment, televisions, radios, and accessories.

Ocean Avenue
Savings of 20 to 70 percent on women's clothing, including styles by Donnkenny, Russ, Woolrich, and others.

Ocello Sportswear
Women's and children's fashion thermals, knit tops, daywear, and lingerie.

Office Furniture Outlet
Save up to 60 percent on new and used filing cabinets, desks, chairs, bookcases, tables, computer tables, and room dividers. Cash-and-carry policy.

O'Furniture
Save 30 to 70 percent on brand-name furniture.

The Old Candle Barn Outlet
Save 50 percent on No. 2 candles; wholesale and retail sales.

Old Mill; Old Mill Ladies Sportswear Outlet
Save 25 to 70 percent on women's sportswear, coordinates, related separates, dresses, and tailored suits, from career to casual styles and in junior and missy sizes 4 to 18 and petite sizes 4 to 16. Featured are Country Suburban, Handmacher, Suburban Petites, and Weathervane Petites.

Olga/Warner's
Savings of 30 to 50 percent off department store prices on a large selection of first-quality lingerie, from basic bras and panties, to fashion daywear and slimwear coordinates, to these manufacturers' exclusive designer sleepwear.

Oneida Factory Store; Oneida Silversmiths
Save 20 to 70 percent on tableware, seconds, closeouts, and discon-

tinued items from Oneida, including stainless or silver-plated flatware, hollowware, cutlery, crystal, dinnerware, and items for children and babies.

Oriental Rug Outlet
Savings of 30 to 80 percent on 100 percent pure wool, hand-knotted Oriental rugs and dhurries.

Oriental Weavers
Savings on Oriental rugs.

Original I. Goldberg
Savings on camping gear, sportswear, apparel, and outdoor equipment.

OshKosh B'Gosh Outlet
Save up to 50 percent on OshKosh B'Gosh sportswear and workwear for men, women, and children.

Outer Banks
Savings of 25 to 30 percent on knit shirts and casual clothing from Outer Banks.

Outlet Store
Featuring some of the world's finest clothing, at prices from 50 to 80 percent off suggested retail prices. The original outlet store in Secaucus!

Oxford Brands, Ltd.
Men's, women's, and children's sport- and casualwear, featuring Merona, McGregor, Trotters Club, Holbrook, and Polo.

Pacific Party Co.
Savings of 50 percent on party goods and decorations, gift wrap and accessories, home and office paper supplies, and books.

Palace Music Outlet
Compact discs, tapes, and records, carrying current hits, easy sounds, classics, oldies, and country, big band, soul, and kiddies' music.

paldies
Fifty percent off retail prices on menswear, including shorts, shirts, and pants, featuring paldies sweater collection.

Palm Beach Company Stores; Palm Beach; Palm Beach Factory Stores
See Evan-Picone Factory Store.

Pandora Factory Outlet
Save 50 percent off nationally advertised prices on sweaters and coordinated sportswear for men and women in juniors' and misses' sizes, featuring Pandora, Waterville, Thackery, and Excello.

The Paper Factory
Fifty percent savings on party goods and decorations, gift wrap and accessories, home and office paper supplies, books, games, and puzzles.

The Paper Outlet
Gift wrap, some of it unusual, and party and other paper supplies.

Parade of Shoes
Footwear for women, including all-leather shoes, boots, and sneakers.

Paris in Secaucus Perfumes
Savings of 30 to 80 percent on perfumes, including Christian Dior scents, and cosmetics, including Lancôme and Chanel items.

Party II
Decorations for all occasions, Mylar and latex balloons, helium-tank rental, piñatas, Wilton baking- and candy-making supplies, and more.

Passport Foods
Savings of 25 to 75 percent on first-quality international delicacies; special weekly features.

Paul Revere Shoppe
Revere cookware; stainless-steel, copper-clad, and aluminum cookware; discontinued bakeware; and teakettles. Seconds at 50 to 70 per-

cent savings. Shipping service. Sometimes combined with Corning Factory Store.

Payless ShoeSource; Payless Shoes
The latest shoe styles cost less at Payless ShoeSource, America's number-one family shoe store.

The Peddler's Wagon
Gift, scent, and basket outlet, featuring Crabtree & Evelyn, Scarborough soaps, potpourri, gourmet foods, salt-glaze pottery, crocks, handcrafted quilts, tole-painted wood, dolls, pillows, dried flowers and herbs, glass, brass, Remington sculptures, porcelain musicals, Precious Moments figurines, and antiques.

Pennsylvania House Furniture Factory Outlet
Savings of 50 percent and more on seconds of Pennsylvania House Furniture–brand items, including some upholstered items and some case goods or wooden pieces. Merchandise is sold on an as-is basis, with no guarantee and no returns, and you must take the item(s) with you on the day of purchase. Special sales reduce prices even more drastically.

Perfumania
Twenty to 60 percent savings on American and European perfumes and cosmetics.

Perrella Factory Outlet (B & G Leathers)
Men's and women's golf gloves, cape and deerskin lined and unlined dress gloves, leather handbags, knits, woolens, and scarves.

Perry Ellis
Save 30 to 60 percent off retail prices on Perry Ellis men's and women's sportswear and fashion accessories.

Peruvian Connection
Savings of 30 to 60 percent off catalog prices on designer alpaca and Peruvian Pima sweaters.

Petal Pushers
Great savings on everything in silk flowers, stems, wreaths, arrangements, bouquets, and floral supplies.

Petals Factory Outlet
Save 40 to 70 percent on silk flowers, dried flowers, plants, trees, containers, gifts, and home-decorating items. Commercial "plantscaping" and bridal designing; custom and holiday floral decorations.

Petite Shop Outlet
A discount store specializing in career-geared dresses, sportswear, and accessories for the woman who is five-foot-four or shorter.

Petticoat Corner
Save from 25 to 75 percent on bras in sizes 32A to 48E and on gowns, slips, and camisoles in sizes small to 4X. Featured are Playtex, Exquisite Form, Loom, Slyray, and Baby Dolls.

Pewtarex Factory Outlet Stores
First- and second-quality Pewtarex merchandise at 25 to 70 percent savings. Also available at discount prices are Disharoon Valley (American country) furniture; baskets, candles, and candies, original flower arrangements and potpourri; decoys and Richard Morgan–painted birds; and more.

Pfaltzgraff Factory Stores
Savings of 30 to 70 percent on a wide selection of stoneware, bakeware, and decorative accessories, from place settings to place mats, with irregulars priced at 50 percent savings and more. First-quality Pfaltzgraff products, which carry a one-year warranty, are available at full price. Replacement parts available. Also carried are MaLeck decorative woodenware, Oneida stainless flatware, Fallani & Cohn table linens, and general housewares. Shipping available via UPS. Free Pfaltzgraff factory tours in York, Pennsylvania.

Phar-Mor
Save up to 50 percent on health and beauty aids, pharmacy items, cleaning supplies, greeting cards, books, and much more.

Phil's Shoes
Discounts on brand-name shoes for men and women.

Philly Fever
Everything for the sports fan, particularly those who follow Pennsylvania, New Jersey, and New York teams.

Piece Goods Shop
Discounts on fabrics, notions, and sewing items.

Pier 1
Home furnishings, unusual handmade items from more than forty countries, porcelain collectibles, earthenware, linens, brass, stemware, candles, baskets, and furniture.

Pierre Cardin
Savings of 40 to 60 percent off retail prices on designer knit coordinate sportswear.

Pilgrim Glass Corporation
Specialties are cobalt, crystal, and cranberry glass, with first-line items at a 25 percent discount and seconds at wholesale prices. Glass-enclosed gallery allows shoppers to view stages of production.

Pinehurst Lingerie
Savings of 40 to 60 percent off retail prices on Pinehurst lingerie.

Plumm's Outlet
Save 20 to 50 percent off retail prices on women's apparel, lingerie, and accessories in misses and junior sizes—for work, day-into-night dressing, and weekend occasions.

Pocono Candle Shop
Savings of 50 to 60 percent on a large selection of candles, hand-carved ribbon candles, Precious Moments, Norman Rockwells, Pocono Mountains souvenirs, brass, pewter, and Fenton glassware.

Pocono Kitchen & Curtains
Kitchen gadgets, curtains, draperies, hardware, and linens, plus shower curtains.

Pocono Linen Outlet
Linens, towels, kitchen goods, tablecloths, comforters, and bedspreads, as well as a complete line of water-bed linens. Factory closeouts, first-quality items, and some slight irregulars at discount prices.

Pocono Odd-Lot Outlet
Savings of up to 50 percent on a huge selection of Pocono souvenirs, T-shirts, sweats, hair accessories, adult gifts, novelties, and general merchandise, including toys, housewares, and hardware.

Pocono Toy Outlet
Brand-name toy closeouts, including Sesame Street, Mickey Mouse, and cartoon friends at discount prices. Large selection of miniature furniture, Rock'n Horses, wagons, doll strollers, personalized items, and more. New doll section and baseball-card center.

Polly Flinders Factory Stores
Save 40 to 60 percent off retail prices on Polly Flinders children's apparel.

Pol-o-Craft
Patented home-decorator plaques and three-dimensional floral arrangements (including the alphabet in script) created by a local artist.

Polo/Ralph Lauren Factory Store
Savings from 25 to 75 percent off suggested retail prices on men's, women's, and boys' apparel; leather goods and footwear; fragrances; accessories featuring Polo and Ralph Lauren; and Ralph Lauren home furnishings.

Popular Greetings
Savings of 20 to 70 percent on greeting cards, wrapping paper, party goods, and other paper supplies.

Portraits Plus
Savings on family portraits.

Ports of the Orient
Exotic gifts from the Far East.

Ports of the World
Clothing, accessories, and sportswear, for women, children, and juniors.

Potpourri
Crabtree & Evelyn toiletries, collectible porcelain dolls, pewter figurines, Austrian crystal, and Victorian gifts.

Pottery Factory Outlet
Thirty percent off retail prices on housewares and gifts by Mikasa, Anchor Hocking, Libby, and others.

Potting Shed
Largest selection of silk flowers and foliage in the area. Free arranging with silk purchase. Silk wedding bouquets, corsages, and centerpieces. Extensive collection of dried flowers. Specializing in houseplants and related items.

Prancing Pony
Musical carousels, painted ponies, craft supplies, folk-art gifts, and accessories.

Prato's Menswear
Savings of 50 percent off market prices on men's clothing, including Calvin Klein apparel, Oscar de la Renta suits, and Jordache jeans.

Prestige Fragrance & Cosmetics
Save 25 to 70 percent on prestigious brands of men's and women's fragrances, toiletries, and cosmetics, featuring Yves St. Laurent, Calvin Klein, and other brands.

Price Jewelers
Diamonds, gold, watches, and other jewelry.

Princess Gardner
Discounts on Princess Gardner leather goods.

Pro Image
Major-league and college sportwear.

Puma Outlet; Puma USA
Save up to 70 percent off retail prices on athletic and sports apparel, accessories, and shoes.

Quality Discount Apparel
Savings of 40 to 50 percent off suggested retail prices on men's suits, sport coats, slacks, shirts, and ties.

Quoddy Crafted Shoes Factory Direct Stores; Dunham Footwear Factory Outlets
Save 20 to 40 percent on first-quality, current-style crafted footwear for the entire family—for work, dress, and play. Hand-sewn boat shoes, camp and beaded moccasins, penny loafers, tassel loafers, walkers, slippers, sandals, boots, pumps, and flats.

QVC Network
First-run merchandise from the home-shopper television network, featuring items in quantities too small to present on the air. All merchandise has a "no questions asked," thirty-day money-back guarantee.

Rack Room Shoe Outlet
Men's, women's, and children's brand-name footwear and accessories, discounted every day and direct from the manufacturer. Savings up to 60 percent.

Radio Shack
Thirty percent off everything in boxes, plus other sales, all on current merchandise.

Rawlings Sporting Goods

Savings of 25 percent on men's apparel for baseball and football, sweatsuits, and some sporting goods.

Reading Bag Company

Handbags, purses, wallets, and other leather products.

Reading China & Glass Outlet

Twenty-five to 70 percent discounts on china, glass, crystal, cutlery, housewares, cookware, bakeware, plush animals, silk flowers, linens and domestics, and gourmet foods, featuring Reading, Calphalon, Noritake, Lenox, Royal Doulton, Libby, Anchor Hocking, and Corning.

Reading Christmas Outlet

Savings of 25 to 60 percent off most any Christmas decoration, including trees from 6 inches to 10 feet, lights, ornaments, electrified candles, animated figures, silk flowers, ribbon, Santa collectibles, novelties, wreaths, garlands, musicals, gift wrap, and cards.

Record World

Savings on compact discs, tapes, and records, carrying current hits, easy sounds, classics, oldies, and country, big band, soul, and kiddies' music.

Reebok

Save 20 to 50 percent off suggested retail prices on all Reebok and Avia athletic footwear, apparel, and accessories for men, women, and children.

Reed & Barton

Save up to 50 percent on flatware, serving pieces, and decorative pieces of sterling, silver plate, stainless steel, pewter, brass, and more.

Regal Outlet Store; Regal Ware Factory Outlet

Save 30 to 70 percent on seconds and closeouts of cookware, small electric appliances for the kitchen, stainless-steel and aluminum cookware, frying pans, food processors, coffee makers, and microwave cookware, and more, featuring Regal and La Machine.

Remembrance Shoppe
Hallmark cards, gifts, and souvenirs for those special events and holidays.

Remington Factory Outlet
Savings of 20 to 50 percent off retail prices on personal-care products, accessories, clocks, knives, and shavers from Remington.

RevereWare Factory Store
See Corning Factory Store.

The Ribbon Outlet Inc.
Save up to 50 percent off retail prices on more than 2,500 varieties of ribbons and trims—cut your own, buy by the yard, or choose precut lengths or entire spools. Also carried are handcrafted gift items, craft supplies, and novelty, bridal, and seasonal items. Personnel are knowledgeable about home sewing and craftswork.

Richard Roberts Jewelers
Large selection of diamonds, precious and semiprecious gemstones, sterling silver, Citizen and Pulsar watches, and gold bracelets, chains, charms, and earrings, all at incredibly reduced prices.

Rings 'n Things
Specializing in rings, fashion sterling silver, and turquoise. Also gold- and silver-plated chains and charms.

Rite-Aid
Health and beauty aids, sundries, and more.

Ritz Camera & Video Outlet Center
Photography and video supplies.

Robert Scott & David Brooks
Savings of 35 percent off retail prices on women's classic apparel, including shirts, separates, and blouses by Andrew Harvey, Robert Scott, and David Brooks.

RockBottom Jeans
Specializing in jeans, featuring Lee, Levi, Jordache, and Calvin Klein, and in accessories such as shirts, casual pants by Bugle Boy, and sweaters by various top-quality manufacturers.

Rodier Paris
From France, the outstanding fashion statement of impeccable designs for women.

Rolane Factory Outlet
Save 30 to 60 percent off comparable prices for factory overruns, discontinued and slightly imperfect styles, and other products—featuring BVD, Burlington, No Nonsense, Dockers, and Oscar de la Renta. The outlet uses a "price-point ending" policy, with 0 meaning that merchandise is slightly imperfect; 5, that merchandise is first quality; and 8, that merchandise is at sale or clearance prices.

Ronlee Fur Warehouse
Mink, fox, beaver, raccoon, coyote, and leather coats.

Rosenbaum Jewelry
Save 20 to 50 percent on fourteen-karat gold, diamonds, pearls, fashion rings, watches, and other jewelry, sterling silver, crystal, brass, ceramics, pewter, glassware, and famous-name gifts, featuring Lladro, Hummel, Towle, Lenox, Waterford, and Cross.

Ross Dress for Less
Substantial savings on dresses, suits, skirts, blouses, slacks, outerwear, sport jackets, slacks, ties, sport and dress shirts, sweaters, sportswear, lingerie, sleepwear, at-home attire, shoes, handbags, and belts—for men, women, teens, children, and toddlers. Also carried are luggage, towels, sheets, pillows, comforters, bedspreads, and kitchen linens. Prices are 20 to 60 percent below those of department stores and specialty shops.

Rowe Showplace Gallery
Discounts on furniture, particularly sofas and chairs.

Royal Book Outlet

Called the biggest and best bookstore in Westchester County, with current best-seller hardbacks at 35 percent off list prices, best-seller paperbacks at 25 percent off list, all other hardcovers at 15 percent off list, and closeouts at 70 percent off list.

Royal Doulton

Save 20 to 60 percent on Royal Doulton dinnerware, giftware, and crystal; greater savings on select overstocks, discontinued merchandise, and special imports. Featured are firsts, seconds, and closeouts of Royal Albert, knickknacks, character and Toby jugs, figurines, Bunnykins, Beatrix Potter, and more. Shipping service and telephone orders.

Royal Grouse; Royal Grouse II

Quality candles at less than factory prices, finer giftware, Baldwin brass, cranberry glass, Woodbury pewter, and plush animals.

Royal Jewelers

Savings of 5 to 60 percent off retail prices on fourteen-karat gold, sterling silver, and other metal jewelry.

Royal Robbins

Save 35 percent off retail prices on men's and women's classic outdoor clothing of natural fibers, including shirts, skirts, shorts, pants, and sweaters.

Royce Hosiery

Save 30 to 60 percent on Royce cashmere, silk, and woolen socks, made in the Martinsburg factory.

Rubin Gloves Factory Store

Quality leather and knit gloves, imported Scottish scarves, and other cold-weather knit items.

Ruff Hewn

Savings of 35 to 50 percent on casual men's and women's sportswear, featuring Ruff and Pretty Ruff lines.

Rug Outlet

Wool dhurries, braided rugs, Turkish hand-knotted rugs, wool hand-knotted accent rugs from China and India, Oriental-design rugs, wool flokatis from Greece, hand-hooked rugs, and Karastan rugs. Shipping service.

Rugs, Etc.

A Chapel Mill outlet for braided rugs, including hand-knotted Orientals, exotic Indian dhurries, and colorful Turkish kilims, with savings of 20 to 50 percent off retail prices. Oriental accent furniture also available.

Run of the Mill

Junior, misses, and women's brand-name sportswear, including blouses, plus novelty transfer shirts and custom printing.

Russell Jerzees Outlet

Savings of 30 to 50 percent off retail prices on family sports apparel, leisurewear, and knitwear.

Russ Togs

Factory outlet specializing in first-quality casual and career dressing in misses and petite sizes (4–18), as well as a selection of girlswear and young junior sizes (6–14).

St. Thomas Inc.

Forty-five percent discount on St. Thomas and Anne Klein leather accessories for men and women.

Saks Fifth Avenue Clearinghouse

Savings of 30 to 70 percent off the original prices on top-name apparel, accessories, and footwear for men, women, and children. Special-purchase values too.

Salisbury Pewter

Pewter mugs, trays, and giftware.

Salt Glaze Pottery

The famed process that made Williamsburg Pottery so popular.

Sam Goody
Savings on compact discs, tapes, and records, carrying current hits, easy sounds, classics, oldies, and country, big band, soul, and kiddies' music.

Sam's Tailoring
Discounted men's clothing.

Sassafras (Perryville, Maryland)
This Perryville, Maryland, store is the only East Coast Sassafras outlet for Sassafras stoneware planters, bowls, terra-cotta chip-and-dip dishes, kitchen items, beach balls, tubes, educational blocks, backpacks, soft luggage in pastel and primary colors, deep-dish pizza dishes, and more at savings of 30 to 40 percent off department store prices.

Sassafras (Woodbridge, Virginia)
This Woodbridge, Virginia, store has savings of 40 to 52 percent off comparable department store prices on dresses, related separates, pants, blazers, jeans, blouses, sweaters, and more. The store features primarily women's career apparel, with some casual attire as well.

Sassco Fashions
Savings of 20 to 50 percent below retail prices on women's suits and dresses, featuring Nolan Miller, Albert Nipon, Kasper for A.S.L. Nights, Kasper for A.S.L. Petites, Kasper II (plus sizes), and LeSuit.

Satchels
Savings of up to 60 percent off suggested retail prices on handbags and accessories, featuring Carlos Falchi, Stone Mountain, Saddle River, Empress, and other brand names.

Scotfoam Corporation
Heavy-duty foam and vinyl for homes, campers, boats, cushions, mattresses, and pillows—cut while you wait—as well as paper products in case lots, carpeting, and padding.

Sears Outlet
Overstocks from Sears stores—family apparel, housewares, tools, and general merchandise.

Secaucus Handbag Outlet

Women's handbags, hosiery, small purse accessories, gloves, hats, belts, rainwear, and related items.

Sergio Valente

Latest designer sportswear for men and women. Savings of up to 70 percent.

Shades of America

Fashionable designer sunglasses and accessories sold at discount prices. T-shirts and tank tops also available.

Shady Lamp Shop

Thousands of lampshades, plus lamps, handmade chandeliers, furniture, and rugs.

Shap's

First-quality women's clothing and shoes, featuring Lifestride, Westie, Reebok, and Tretorn at discount prices.

The Sheet & Towel Outlet

Sheets, towels, tablecloths, place mats, shower curtains, bedspreads, comforters, and more.

Sheri's Moccasin Outlet

Southwest and Indian art, crafts, collectibles, sterling silver Indian jewelry, and Minnetonka moccasins.

Ship 'n Shore

See Fashion Flair

Shoe-Town Outlet; Shoe Town

Save 20 to 50 percent on famous-brand and designer footwear and handbags for women.

Shoe Works

Women's dress, casual, and athletic shoes from many nationally famous brands.

Silk Garden
Savings of 20 to 70 percent on silk flowers, plants, and arrangements.

Silver Sky Jewelers
Outlet prices on boutique and sterling silver jewelry.

S & K Brand Menswear
Brand-name suits, sport coats, slacks, sportswear, and accessories, at 30 to 50 percent off regular retail prices.

Sleepy's Mattress Outlet
Savings of 30 to 80 percent on Sealy, Simmons Beautyrest, and Serta mattresses.

Small Delights
Gifts from $2.00 to $3.00 and gorgeous silk floral arrangements for weddings.

Small Talk
Savings of 50 percent off retail prices on children's apparel, featuring Small Talk.

Snack Factory
One of the largest selections of candy, nuts, dried fruit, and many other specialty snack items, all at discounted prices.

Sneakee Feet
Save 10 to 25 percent on athletic and leisure footwear, sports apparel, and accessories for the entire family.

Socks Galore & More
Twenty-five to 85 percent off retail prices on dress socks, sport socks, tubes, and knee-highs—for men, women, teens, and children and featuring Anne Klein, Burlington, Classic Toe, Dri-Sox, Christian Dior, E. J. Plum, Humpty Dumpty, Giggles, Trimfit, Camp, World's Softest Sock, and others. Toll-free telephone ordering service at (800) 626–SOCK (7625).

Socks Plus

Save up to 50 percent on Jard-brand socks for men, women, boys, and girls; also featured are Converse, Wilson, Weekend, Botany 500, Calvin Klein, Burlington, and "The Super Sock."

Soho Mill Outlet

Save 25 to 30 percent on sheets, towels, and comforters by Cannon, J. P. Stevens, and others.

Solid Brass Inc.

Save 20 to 70 percent on Bowon picture frames, lamps, home accessories, switch plates, door knockers, candlesticks, planters, bugles, and giftware.

Spain's Hallmark

Hallmark cards, gifts, and souvenirs for those special events and holidays.

Special Seasons

Big savings on unique, affordable gifts for all seasons: glassware, candles, and accessories. Christmas items.

Specials, Exclusively Levi Strauss & Co.

Save up to 50 percent off the ticketed prices on family apparel by Levi Strauss & Co.

Spiegel Outlet

Savings of 30 to 70 percent off the original prices on catalog overruns and other merchandise.

Splash Creations

Individual designs on T-shirts and sweatshirts, created with a cotton-candy-type dying machine.

Sports & Sorts

Savings to 50 percent on authentic major-league baseball products, featuring Felco jackets, Mizuno gloves, Franklin batting gloves, Majestic batting jerseys, Spaulding gloves, Easton bats, baseball plaques,

Sportcraft summer games, and items from Speedo, Rhodegear, Spenco, Academy Broadway, and Russell Athletic.

Sports Fans
Savings of 20 to 70 percent on sneakers, sports clothing, team apparel, and more for the whole family.

Sportshoe Center
Always $5.00 to $20.00 off list prices on first-quality athletic footwear and apparel from Nike, Reebok, Rockport, Asics, Hi-tec, Saucony, New Balance, Foot Joy, Adidas, Keds, Tretorn, and L.A. Gear.

Sports Wearhouse
Save 40 to 60 percent off suggested retail prices on outerwear for infants through adults, featuring Reebok, O'Neills, OP, Dunlop, Rose Marie Reid, and Fresh Squeeze, and on sportswear decorated with NFL, NBA, MLB, NHL, and college-team names. Also carried are Disney and Snoopy character items.

Springmaid Wamsutta
Savings of 20 to 60 percent off retail prices on sheets, comforters, bedspreads, and accessories by Springmaid, Wamsutta, Performance, Pacific, Andre Richard, and Graber.

Square Circle
Savings on compact discs, tapes, and records, carrying current hits, easy sounds, classics, oldies, and country, big band, soul, and kiddies' music.

S. Schwab Company
Twenty to 70 percent discounts on infants' and children's clothing, accessories, and more.

Stationery Outlet
Closeouts from 20 to 50 percent off regular prices on supplies for office, school, and home. Greeting cards at half price. Art supplies, games, a large inventory of children's books, videos, and educational materials as well.

Stauffer's Nut, Candy, Cookies

Specialties include more than 50 varieties of cookies, fresh from the bakery; 250 kinds of candies; more than 50 types of nuts and dried fruits; more than 50 snack-related food products; candy-making supplies; and beautiful gift canisters. A large variety of Christmas cookies is available during the season.

Sterling Super Optical

Savings on eyeglasses, contact lenses, and accessories.

Stockroom/Evan-Picone

See Evan-Picone Factory Store.

Stone Mountain Handbags

Save 20 to 50 percent off retail prices on handbags, leather goods, jewelry, and accessories, featuring Stone Mountain, Saddle River, and 9 West handbags and Ande evening bags.

Stormcrow Leather

Hand-tooled leather goods, including belts, wallets, and accessories; also shoe repair.

Stroud Handbag Outlet

Largest selection of handbags in the Poconos, from more than 50 manufacturers, including Stone Mountain, Capezio, Davey's, and Le Sport Sac. Also carried are men's and women's wallets, attachés, and soft-side luggage.

Summerdale Mills Fabric Outlet

Fabrics for dresses, suiting, woolens, curtains, leather, notions, patterns, fur, vinyl, foam, and trimmings; custom-made draperies and slipcovers.

Sunday Best

Specializing in designer sunglasses and accessories sold at a discount.

Sunglasses Outlet

Save on famous-maker sunglasses by Ray-Ban, Serengeti, Vuarnet, Gargoyles, and many others.

Sunglass World
Featuring Ray-Ban, Serengeti, and all famous brands.

Sunshades
Save 20 percent and more on sunglasses by Bausch & Lomb (Ray-Ban), Serengeti Drivers, Porsche, Vuarnet, Revo, Oleg Cassini, Carrera, Pucci, Ted Lapidos, and others.

Supply Outlet for Lovable Pets
Almost everything for your pet: foods, toys, accessories, and more.

Susan Greene
Savings of 20 percent and more on fine pocketbooks and jewelry.

Susquehanna Glass; Susquehanna Glass Outlet and Clearance Center
Save 10 to 50 percent on lead crystal, barware, dinnerware, and related tabletop and gift accessories. A glass cutter demonstrates the art of hand-cutting glassware and custom-monograms barware, stemware, serving accessories, and gift items. Clearance center in Columbia, Pennsylvania, store.

Swank Factory Outlet
Men's leather goods, ties, belts, wallets, briefcases, travel accessories, cuff links, and key rings, featuring Swank, Pierre Cardin, Alexander Julian, Anne Klein, Royal Copenhagen, and Richard Scott. Women's jewelry too.

Sweater Mill
Save 30 to 70 percent on sweaters for women, girls, and men, including full sizes and big and tall men's sizes, and on sportswear and activewear.

Sweaters, Ski & Sports
Wool, cotton, and hand-knit sweaters for men and women; skiwear for the entire family; and jackets, pants, gloves, turtlenecks, hats, sporting goods, swimwear, and tennis clothing—at savings of up to 60 percent.

Sweatshirt Company
Mix-and-match styles, in colors and sizes for the entire family, including big and tall sizes for men and plus sizes for women.

Sweets Street
Save on desserts, gourmet cakes, and lunches.

Syms
Brand-name men's, women's, and children's apparel and accessories.

Syracuse China Factory Outlet
Fifteen to 50 percent off retail prices on dishware, flatware, cookware, and glassware, featuring Syracuse, Anchor Hocking, and Chicago Cutlery.

Table de France
Savings of 40 to 70 percent off retail prices on tabletop items imported from Europe, including Limoges porcelain, Guy Degrenne silverware, flatware and cookware, Sabatier cutlery, and handblown crystal stemware and giftware.

Tahari Outlet; N. T. Tahari
Save 30 to 75 percent off suggested retail prices on the Tahari Collection line of women's sportswear, dresses, suits, blouses, trousers, and knits.

Talbots Surplus Store
Leftovers from Talbot clothing stores, at drastic reductions.

Tanner Dress Shop
Save 25 to 75 percent on dresses and sportswear, featuring Tanner, Tanner Sport, Tanner Country, Doncaster, and other famous lines.

Tapemeasure
Savings of 30 to 70 percent on first-quality, contemporary sportswear for women, children, and plus sizes.

Taylor Made Products
Travel and recreational bags, in colorful nylons and bench ends; flags; storage covers; and more.

TC Sports
Men's and women's clothes for sports and physical fitness, including college and pro logo items.

Techline Furniture
Savings of 30 to 80 percent on quality modular furniture, including wall units, home offices, workstations, and bedroom sets.

T. Edwards/Brooks Outlet
Women's sportswear, tops, shorts, skirts, and some dresses at 20 to 60 percent off retail prices.

Tempo Luggage
Savings on luggage and small leather goods, including such brands as Andiamo, London Fog, and Lark.

T. H. Mandy
Offering a line of discounted apparel for career-oriented women. Accessories and designerwear available.

Thos. David Factory Store
Save 20 percent and more on men's and women's pure wool and blend suits, slacks, skirts, sport coats, shirts, blouses, and furnishings.

TieLand
Designer ties, bow ties, suspenders, leather and canvas belts, cummerbund sets, tie and scarf sets, extralong ties, blazer buttons, pocket scarfs, and more.

Ties & More
Ties, belts, and other accessories at a saving.

Timberland Factory Outlet
Save 35 to 50 percent off full retail prices on Timberland boots, handsewn casuals, and leather accessories.

Time World (Hamilton Watch & Clock Shoppe)
Official factory outlet for Hamilton, Swatch, Tissot, and Rado, with savings of up to 50 percent.

T. J. Maxx
A deep discounter of overruns and discontinued fashions and accessories for the entire family. Shipments vary in styles and prices on a weekly basis.

Top of the Line Cosmetics
Savings of 30 to 60 percent off retail prices on makeup, fragrances, and accessories for women and men. Featured are more than fifty nationally advertised brands. Free make-overs and color analyses.

totes Direct Factory Outlet; totes Warehouse Store
The complete line of totes and associated brands of rainwear, hats, caps, umbrellas, accessories, cooler bags, travel items, and luggage—for men and women and at savings of 30 to 70 percent. Some overstocks, irregulars, closeouts, and discontinued styles and colors are available.

Touch of Class
Many nationally known brands of wood and glass gifts, decorative accessories, and jewelry and boutique items, as well as a variety of Lancaster County handcrafted items and souvenirs at discounted prices.

Touch of Gold Jewelry
Discounts of up to 70 percent on diamonds, gemstones, fourteen-karat gold, sterling silver, and fashion jewelry.

Towle Factory Outlet; Towle/1690 House
Discounts of 50 to 70 percent on housewares, giftware, and crystal; cutlery at retail prices. Featured are Towle Silversmiths, F. B. Rogers, National Silver, Carvel Hall, Javit Crystal, Supreme Cutlery, Gailstyn Sutton, Shelton-Ware, and others.

Town & Country Menswear
Save 25 to 75 percent on first-quality, name-brand tailored clothing and sportswear, including Botany 500, Members Only, and Pierre Cardin.

Toy Liquidators
Savings of up to 75 percent on toys from Hasbro, Tonka, Universal Matchbox, Milton Bradley, Playskool, Mattel, Fisher-Price, and more.

Toys Unlimited
Closeout toys, featuring Mattel, Fisher-Price, Milton Bradley, and others.

Toy Works
Save 20 to 80 percent off retail prices on toys from Mattel, Fisher-Price, Kenner, Ideal, Tonka, Playskool, Tomy, Matchbox, Coleco, Milton Bradley, Tyco, Hasbro, and others.

Trader Kids (Boston Traders)
Savings of up to 40 percent on Trader Kids' label clothing in boys sizes 4 to 7 and 8 to 20 and in girls' sizes 4 to 6X and 7 to 14. Also infant and toddler sizes.

Tuesday Morning, Inc.
Save 50 to 80 percent off retail prices on overstocks, closeouts, and discontinued items, including artificial flowers, ceramics, giftware, glass, metalware, plastics, wood products, toys, luggage, linens, and domestics. Featured are Hauer, Members Only, Mikasa, Orrefors, Spiegel, Studio Nova, Johnson Bros., Wedgwood, Oneida, Battenburg, Playskool, Anne Klein, Couristan, Kosta, and others. Stores are open four times a year (winter, spring, summer, and Christmas) for six to eight weeks.

Tultex Mill Outlets
Save 20 to 70 percent off retail prices on family apparel and lingerie, featuring Tultex Fleece, Alfred Dunner, Harot, Katz, BVD, and other brands.

Uddermost
Savings of 40 to 50 percent on decorative houseware gifts.

Uniform Factory Outlet
Save 20 to 60 percent on brand-name uniforms, including lab coats, pants, and skirts; dresses; and leather shoes. Featured are Barco, Whiteswan, Meta, Crest, Nursemates, and more.

Union Bay
Savings of 25 to 70 percent off retail prices on juniors', young men's, and children's apparel, including items from Union Bay, Reunion, and Sync.

Unisa
Savings of 30 to 50 percent off retail prices on footwear and handbags by Unisa.

United Shoe Outlet; United Outlet
Women's and men's dress and casual shoes, plus athletic shoes for men, women, and children.

Unlimited Design Fine Jewelry
Save 30 to 60 percent off major stores' regular advertised prices on a large selection of fine jewelry, diamonds, and watches. Resetting, special orders, custom design, and remounting services available.

Urban Clothing Company
Career dressing for women and young ladies.

U.S.A. Classic Outlet Store
Savings of 30 to 35 percent off retail prices on children's and young men's sportswear and activewear by Everlast, Nautica Youthwear, and B.U.M. Equipment Youthwear.

Vakko
Substantial savings on designer leather and suede clothing for women.

Valley Fair
American and European designer scents, famous-name cosmetics, health and beauty aids, 30 percent off greeting cards, 30 percent off party goods, and up to 60 percent off luggage.

Val Mode Lingerie Factory Stores
Save 40 to 60 percent on Val Mode lingerie by Jessica Lynn and on lingerie carrying other private labels. Also offered are a selection of brand-name intimate apparel, slippers, and accessories.

Van Heusen Factory Store; Van Heusen/Bass
Save up to 50 percent on current, in-season fashion merchandise for men and women, featuring Van Heusen, Lady Van Heusen, 417, Allyn St. George, Buxton, Cacharel, Corum, Etienne Aigner, Gear, Geoffrey Beene, Hennessey, McGregor, PGA, Windbreaker, and others. A "no questions asked" return policy.

Vertucci Gloves
Men's and women's leather dress gloves and mittens.

VF (Vanity Fair) Clearance
Men's, women's, and children's clothing by Vanity Fair, Lee, Bassett-Walker, Heron Cove, Kay Windsor, and Jantzen.

VF (Vanity Fair) Factory Outlet
Save 50 percent off ticketed prices on activewear, jeans, knit and woven shirts, outerwear, pants, shorts, socks, sweaters, sweatwear, swimwear, nightgowns, pajamas, robes, scuffs, slips, hosiery, loungewear, and underwear. Featured are such brand names as Vanity Fair, Lee, Bassett-Walker, Kay Windsor, Heron Cove, Jansport, and Jantzen. Merchandise for men, women, girls, and boys, including children's, petites', juniors', and extralarge sizes.

Viking Glass Company; Dalzell Viking Glass Company
First-line products, as well as seconds and discontinued items, at 40, 50, and 60 percent discounts.

Village Jewelry
Savings of 40 to 60 percent on fourteen-karat gold, silver, and costume jewelry, as well as on pearls.

Villeroy & Boch
Save 30 to 70 percent on fine-china seconds and discontinued items and on bakeware, featuring Villeroy & Boch and Wilkens. Phone orders and UPS shipping.

VIP Mill Store
Men's and women's Gloray cotton sweaters; No Nonsense and

Burlington hosiery; Bostonian, Hanover, and Rockport shoes; and handbags.

Virginia Apparel Outlet
Savings of at least 25 percent off suggested retail prices on quality, brand-name clothing, including apparel by Alfred Dunner, Vanity Fair, Patterns, and Stanley Knits for women; items by Osh Kosh B'Gosh for children; and clothing by Botany 500, Santan, and Chapel Hill for men.

Waccamaw Pottery
Pottery, dinnerware, glassware, Christmas decorations, woodenware, pewter, candles, cutlery, lamps, pictures, paper products, toys, flatware, brass, housewares, wicker, dried and silk flowers, flower arrangements, giftware, and much more—discounted as much as 80 percent off regular department store prices. Featured are Anchor Hocking, Black & Decker, Cannon, Corning, Hoan, Libby, Mikasa, Rubbermaid, Wedgwood, and other lines.

Waldenbooks
A complete bookstore, featuring new releases, best-sellers, and audio/video items.

Wallach's Outlet
Offering a line of brand-name apparel and related ready-to-wear accessories for men and women.

The Wallet Works
Save 25 to 75 percent on 150 styles of men's and women's wallets. Save on luggage, handbags, clutches, briefcases, key cases, and travel gifts, featuring Amity/Rolfs, London Fog, Amelia Earhart, Stone Mountain, Jordache, Baltimore, Oleg Cassini, Saddle River, and Winn & Elizabeth.

Wallpaper Outlet
Discounts on favorite wall coverings and supplies.

Warehouse
Savings on leather goods, particularly luggage and purses.

Warnaco Outlet Stores
Save 40 to 70 percent off suggested retail prices on men's and women's apparel, including that by Thane, Puritan, White Stag, Hathaway, Christian Dior, Geoffrey Beene, Rosanna, Spalding, Speedo, Hirsch, Weis, Warner's, Olga, Pringle of Scotland, Jack Nicklaus, Albert Nipon, and Chaps by Ralph Lauren.

Watch Outlet
Seiko, Timex, Casio, and Lorus watches, plus a unique variety of fashion watches and jewelry, all at factory-direct savings.

Waterford/Wedgwood
Featuring Wedgwood, Adams, Queensware, Midwinter, Johnson Brothers, Franciscan, and Coalport, with a large selection of discontinued merchandise. Savings of up to 90 percent off suggested retail prices on bone china, earthenware, and ironstone dinnerware and on giftware and crystal.

Wathne
An Icelandic company featuring clothing, luggage, and other accoutrements for those who ride horseback, go on safaris, take fishing trips, or engage in similar kinds of activities.

Waxie Maxie's Warehouse Store
Savings on compact discs, tapes, and records, carrying current hits, easy sounds, classics, oldies, and country, big band, soul, and kiddies' music.

Webster Warehouse
Overstocks of men's clothing from the chain of Webster Men's Wear.

Welcome Home
Cape Craft products at 30 to 50 percent off suggested retail prices and including wooden decorative items, giftware, kitchen textiles, rugs, candles, porcelain dolls, and wicker.

Weldon Factory Salesroom
Savings on clothing for infants to adults, including sizes XXXX and tall in men's apparel.

Wemco

A fantastic selection of men's brand-name neckwear and classic sportswear at incredible prices.

Westchester Apparel

Women's apparel, both brands that the company manufactures and closeouts from other sources, with each item priced at $10.

WestPoint Pepperell Mill Store

Fifty percent off retail prices on accessories for bed and bath, table napery, linens, draperies, and assorted home furnishings, featuring Martex, Lady Pepperell, and Attelier.

Westport Ltd. Outlet

Fashions from the factory to you; top-quality labels for women, including Westport Ltd., Princeton Club, Atrium, and Milano. Sizes 4–14.

Westport Woman; Westport/Dress Barn

Savings of 20 percent and more on top-quality labels in larger sizes.

West Virginia Fine Glass

Featuring Fenton, Blenko, Beaumont, West Virginia Glass, Pilgrim, Gibson, Gentile, L. G. Wright, Hamon, Red Mill, Boyd, Mosser, and Greenbriar.

Whims

Savings of 10 to 70 percent off retail prices on jewelry and accessories from Sarah Coventry, 1928, and others.

Wholesaler's Shoe Outlet

Savings of 25 percent or more off current retail prices on footwear for men and women. First-quality, nationally advertised brand names, in this season's styles and in dress, casual, sport, and athletic shoes.

Wholesale Stores Incorporated

Save 30 to 70 percent on men's and women's tailored suits, jackets, and skirts.

Wibbies
Colorful cotton clothes for children, with prices at or below wholesale.

Wicker Basket Outlet
Savings of 30 percent on flowers, greenery, baskets, furniture, and other things in between.

Wicker Outlet
Wicker furniture, accessories, home decorations, and baskets galore, as well as cards, wrapping paper, Crabtree & Evelyn and Scarborough products, candles, clay pottery, home fragrances, jewelry, gourmet foods, coffee and confections, and personal and gourmet gift baskets.

Wicker Unlimited
A wicker-and-silk-flower store, offering baskets and furniture and 20 percent savings on silk flowers, plants, and arrangements.

Widman Deep Discount
Save up to 50 percent on fragrances and cosmetics and other discount amounts on designer luggage and paper and party goods.

Wilbur Chocolate Factory Outlet
A wide and unusual selection of candy, at economical outlet prices, by the company that makes chocolate for other companies—Pepperidge Farm, Godiva, and dozens more. Chocolate museum, room for watching hand dipping of candies, and a large collection of chocolate pots on display.

Wild Birds Unlimited
Savings of 20 to 70 percent on bird food, feeders, and other supplies.

Wildlife Treasures
Savings of about $30 to $40 on wildlife items, hand-carved decoys, prints, and related objects.

The Williamsburg Shirt Company
T-shirts and patented William & Mary designs for the whole family.

Williamsburg Soap & Candle Factory Outlet

Firsts and seconds of soaps and candles, as well as needlework and imports. A country store, candy shop, restaurant, and Christmas shop.

Wilton Armetale Factory Outlet

Save up to 60 percent off suggested retail prices on seconds and closeouts of Wilton Armetale–brand dinnerware, serving pieces, and giftware, plus products by Bruce Fox, Countryware, and Color Accents. Shipping service.

Windsor Shirt Company

Savings to 50 percent off everyday prices on men's and women's dress and casual shirts, ties, belts, underwear, socks, sweaters, and rugby shirts.

Woodward & Lothrop Outlet Center

Overstocks of men's and women's clothing and shoes from the chain of Woodward & Lothrop department stores.

World Fare Trading

Primarily men's sportswear manufactured for the store, at a discount.

World of Values

Gifts, dinnerware, glassware, and silk flowers.

Young World

Savings on children's clothing, from newborns to children age fourteen.

Your Toy Center

A complete line of toys and games, featuring Fisher-Price, Mattel, Coleco, Playskool, Milton Bradley, Matchbox, and other names.

DELAWARE

Delaware has no sales tax.

1. Elsmere
2. Rehoboth Beach

3. Smyrna
4. Wilmington

DELAWARE

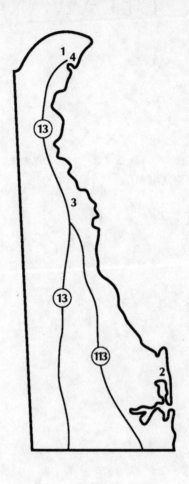

ELSMERE

All-in-One-Linen Company
2101 Kirkwood Highway
Route 21

Directions: Take I-95 to Newport 141 exit, to Elsmere exit. Follow ramp and store is on the right.
Phone: (302) 999-8100
Hours: 10:00 A.M.-9:00 P.M.; Monday-Saturday; 10:00 A.M.-5:00 P.M., Sunday
Credit Cards: American Express, MasterCard, Visa
Personal Checks: Yes, with address imprinted on check, social security card, and Choice card
Handicapped Accessible: Yes
Bus Tours: No

REHOBOTH BEACH

Ocean Outlets Factory Center
Route 1

Directions: Highway 1, 1 mile north of Rehoboth Beach city line, southbound side
Phone: (302) 227-6860
Hours: May 23-September 13: 10:00 A.M.-9:00 P.M., Monday-Saturday; 10:00 A.M.-6:00 P.M., Sunday. September 14-May 22: 10:00 A.M.-6:00 P.M., Sunday-Thursday; 10:00 A.M.-9:00 P.M., Friday and Saturday
Credit Cards: MasterCard, Visa
Personal Checks: Yes
Handicapped Accessible: Yes
Bus Tours: Yes
Food: Available
Notes or Attractions: Beach resort community; children's playground

Outlets:
Aileen Factory
American Tourister
Banister Shoes
Bass Shoe
Bermuda's
Bon Worth
Book Warehouse
Candy Kitchen
Capezio
Carter's Childrenswear
Champion Hanes
Corning/Revere
Creative Impressions Art
Eagle's Eye
Finders Keepers
Formfit
Glass Resort
Izod/Gant
Kitchen Collection
Leather Loft
L'eggs/Hanes/Bali
London Fog
Lots of Linens
Ocean Avenue
Oneida
Pfaltzgraff
Prestige Fragrance and Cosmetics, Inc.
Rehoboth Golf Outlet
Ribbon Outlet
Socks Galore & More
Sports Fans
Sweater, Ski & Sport
totes
Toy Liquidators
Van Heusen
Wallet Works
Welcome Home
Westport Ltd.
Westport Woman
Wicker

Ocean Outlets Seaside
Route 1

Directions: Highway 1, 1 mile north of Rehoboth Beach city line, northbound side
Phone: (302) 227–5800
Hours: May 23–September 13: 10:00 A.M.–9:00 P.M., Monday–Saturday; 10:00 A.M.–6:00 P.M., Sunday. September 14–May 22: 10:00 A.M.–6:00 P.M., Sunday–Thursday; 10:00 A.M.–9:00 P.M., Friday and Saturday
Credit Cards: Most major credit cards accepted at most stores
Personal Checks: Yes, with identification
Handicapped Accessible: Yes
Bus Tours: Yes
Outlets:
Bugle Boy
Cape Isle Knitters

Christmas Tree Hill
Eddie Bauer
Etienne Aigner
Famous Brands Housewares
Generra
Geoffrey Beene
Gitano
Housewares Store
Lise J. Fashion Outlet
Lucia
9 West
Popular Greetings
Prestige Fragrance & Cosmetics
Reebok
Ruff Hewn
Satchels
Sergio Valente
Silk Garden
Silver Sky Jewelry
T. H. Mandy Career Image Company Store
Union Bay
Welcome Home
Wild Birds Unlimited
Windsor Shirts

SMYRNA

Manhattan
6 Village Square
Route 13

Directions: Route 13, 2 miles south of Smyrna city line, on right
Phone: (302) 653–5037
Hours: 9:30 A.M.–5:30 P.M., Monday–Saturday; noon–5:00 P.M., Sunday

Credit Cards: American Express, Discover, MasterCard, Visa
Personal Checks: Yes, with two forms of identification and a driver's license
Handicapped Accessible: Yes
Bus Tours: Yes

WILMINGTON

Delta Hosiery
721 Market Street

Directions: Take I–95 North to Delaware Avenue exit; bear right, proceeding down to Market Street Mall; turn right on the mall; proceed down 2 blocks. Store is on the right.
Phone: (302) 655–0614
Hours: 10:00 A.M.–5:00 P.M., Monday–Saturday; closed Sunday
Credit Cards: No
Personal Checks: Yes, with driver's license
Handicapped Accessible: Yes
Bus Tours: Yes

MFO/Murray's
101 Greenbank Road

Directions: Take I–95 North to Route 141 North exit; proceed to Boxwood Road exit. Approximately 1 mile to store.
Phone: (302) 998–5656
Hours: 10:00 A.M.–9:00 P.M., Monday–Friday; 10:00 A.M.–5:00 P.M., Saturday; 11:00 A.M.–4:00 P.M., Sunday
Credit Cards: American Express, Discover, MasterCard, Visa
Personal Checks: Yes
Handicapped Accessible: Yes
Bus Tours: No

MARYLAND

1. Annapolis
2. Chester
3. Cockeysville
4. Crisfield
5. Cumberland
6. Ellicott City
7. Forrestville
8. Frederick
9. Gaithersburg
10. Glen Burnie
11. Greenbelt
12. Hagerstown
13. Hancock
14. Hunt Valley
15. Laurel
16. La Vale
17. Ocean City
18. Perryville
19. Princess Anne
20. Queenstown
21. Randallstown
22. Reisterstown
23. Rockville
24. Salisbury
25. Silver Spring
26. Thurmont
27. Towson
28. Wheaton

MARYLAND

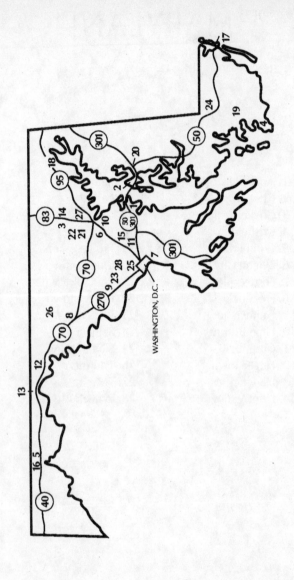

ANNAPOLIS

Bay Bridge Market Place
595 Route 50

Directions: One mile west of the Chesapeake Bay Bridge
Phone: (302) 227–4800 (management company)
Hours: 10:00 A.M.–8:00 P.M., Monday–Friday; 10:00 A.M.–6:00 P.M., Saturday; noon–5:00 P.M., Sunday
Credit Cards: MasterCard, Visa
Personal Checks: Most stores accept checks with proper identification.
Handicapped Accessible: Yes
Bus Tours: Yes
Food: Available
Outlets:

Adolfo Sport
Aileen Factory
Bargain Sneakers
Bass Shoes
Cape Craft
Cape Isle Knitters
harvé benard
International Footwear
Lady Leslie
Lady Leslie's Woman's World
Linen Warehouse
Micki Designer Separates
Mikasa
Old Mill
Pandora Factory
Paper Factory
Perfumania
Ribbon Outlet
Royal Doulton
Rugs, Etc.
Van Heusen
Wallet Works
Welcome Home

Tuesday Morning
Bay Ridge Plaza
123 Hillsmere Drive

Directions: Take U.S. 50 to Riva Road; turn left onto Forest Drive; turn right and proceed for 4 miles; then turn right on Hillsmere. Store is in the complex on the left.
Phone: (410) 280–2015
Hours: 9:30 A.M.–6:00 P.M., Monday–Wednesday, Friday, and Satur-

day; 9:30 A.M.–9:00 P.M., Thursday; noon–6:00 P.M., Sunday
Personal Checks: Yes
Credit Cards: Discover, MasterCard, Visa
Handicapped Accessible: Yes
Bus Tours: Yes

CHESTER

Kent Narrows Factory Stores
U.S. 50, exit 41 at Piney Narrows Road

Directions: Three and one-half miles east of Bay Bridge, just before Kent Narrows Bridge
Phone: (410) 643–5231
Hours: 10:00 A.M.–6:00 P.M., Sunday–Thursday; 10:00 A.M.–8:00 P.M., Friday–Saturday
Credit Cards: MasterCard, Visa
Personal Checks: Yes
Handicapped Accessible: Yes
Bus Tours: Yes; promotional package and discount coupons offered.
Food: Available
Outlets:

American Tourister Factory
Banister Shoes
Bugle Boy
Carter's Childrenswear
Champion-Hanes Activewear
Corning/Revere
Izod/Gant
Jantzen & Lee Casuals
Jonathan Logan

Kitchen Collection
Leather Loft
L'eggs/Hanes/Bali
Pfaltzgraff
Sports Wearhouse
Toy Liquidators
Van Heusen
Vanity Fair
Westport Ltd.

COCKEYSVILLE

Clothes Outlet
22-A Church Lane

Directions: Take I–83 North to exit 17, Padonia Road; bear right to third traffic light. Turn left onto York Road until just past the first traffic light. Turn left into Signet Bank driveway; store is in shopping complex behind the bank.
Phone: (410) 628–1020
Hours: 10:00 A.M.–9:00 P.M., Monday–Friday; 10:00 A.M.–6:00 P.M., Saturday; noon–5:00 P.M., Sunday
Credit Cards: American Express, Discover, MasterCard, Visa
Personal Checks: Yes
Handicapped Accessible: Yes; some dressing rooms specifically set up for handicapped customers.
Bus Tours: Yes

CRISFIELD

Carvel Hall
Route 413

Directions: Take U.S. 13 south to Route 413, just before entering the town of Crisfield. Outlet is on the left.
Phone: (410) 968–0500
Hours: 10:00 A.M.–6:00 P.M., Monday–Sunday; closed Thanksgiving, Christmas, and New Year's Day
Credit Cards: American Express, Discover, MasterCard, Visa
Personal Checks: Yes, with bank approval
Handicapped Accessible: Yes
Bus Tours: Yes

CUMBERLAND

Biederlack Blanket Company
Route 220 North, Bedford Road

Directions: Take I–68 to Route 220 North, to the traffic light. Turn right; the store is about 100 yards down, on the left.
Phone: (301) 759–3633
Hours: 9:00 A.M.–5:00 P.M., Monday–Friday; special holiday hours
Credit Cards: MasterCard, Visa
Personal Checks: Yes, with driver's license
Handicapped Accessible: Yes
Bus Tours: Yes, if notified in advance

ELLICOTT CITY

Tuesday Morning
Normandy Business Center
8492 Baltimore National Pike
Suite 107

Directions: Take I–695 to Ellicott City (Route 40) exit, proceeding for about 4½ miles to Center Drive, and turn right. Turn left at the traffic light into the Normandy Business Center. Store is on the lower level.
Phone: (410) 465–5503
Hours: 9:30 A.M.–6:00 P.M., Monday–Wednesday, Friday, and Saturday; 9:30 A.M.–9:00 P.M., Thursday; noon–6:00 P.M., Sunday
Credit Cards: Discover, MasterCard, Visa
Personal Checks: Yes
Handicapped Accessible: Yes; wheelchair ramp at end of center
Bus Tours: Yes

FORRESTVILLE

Burlington Coat Factory Warehouse
3420 Donnell Drive

Directions: Take I–495 to exit 11B. Proceed through two traffic lights, turning right onto Donnell Drive; turn right to warehouse.
Phone: (301) 736–6685
Hours: 10:00 A.M.–9:00 P.M., Monday–Saturday; 11:00 A.M.–6:00 P.M., Sunday
Credit Cards: American Express, Discover, MasterCard, Visa
Personal Checks: Yes
Handicapped Accessible: Yes
Bus Tours: Yes

FREDERICK

Frederick Clothiers
420 East Patrick Street

Directions: Take I–70 to the first Frederick exit, taking East Patrick Street for 1 mile. Store is on the left.
Phone: (301) 663–1355
Hours: 10:00 A.M.–8:00 P.M., Monday–Friday; 10:00 A.M.–5:45 P.M., Saturday; noon–5:00 P.M., Sunday
Credit Cards: MasterCard, Visa
Personal Checks: Yes
Handicapped Accessible: No
Bus Tours: Yes

Hartz & Company
1341 Hughes Ford Road

Directions: Take Route 270 to Market Street. Follow signs to Frederick Airport. Store and factory are next to airport.

Phone: (301) 695–5877
Hours: 10:00 A.M.–5:30 P.M., Monday–Friday; 9:00 A.M.–5:30 P.M., Saturday
Credit Cards: MasterCard, Visa
Personal Checks: Yes
Handicapped Accessible: Yes
Bus Tours: Yes

GAITHERSBURG

Tuesday Morning
311 Muddy Branch Road (at Festival shopping center)

Directions: I–270 to Route 370 exit. Take Route 370 (Sam Eigt Highway) to second light. Go right on Diamondback to second light. Go right on Muddy Branch to second light.
Phone: (301) 921–9542
Hours: 9:30 A.M.–6:00 P.M., Monday–Wednesday, Friday, and Saturday; 9:30 A.M.–9:00 P.M., Thursday; noon–6:00 P.M., Sunday
Credit Cards: Discover, MasterCard, Visa
Personal Checks: Yes
Handicapped Accessible: Yes
Bus Tours: Yes

GLEN BURNIE

Tuesday Morning
Southgate Market Place
337 Hospital Drive

Directions: Take Route 3 to Route 100 East to Oakwood Road; then turn right immediately and take another immediate right onto Hospital Drive. Shopping complex is 1/2 mile on the left.
Phone: (410) 760–9034
Hours: 9:30 A.M.–6:00 P.M., Monday–Wednesday, Friday, and Satur-

day; 9:30 A.M.–9:00 P.M., Thursday; noon–6:00 P.M., Sunday
Credit Cards: Discover, MasterCard, Visa
Personal Checks: Yes
Handicapped Accessible: Yes
Bus Tours: Yes

GREENBELT

Burlington Coat Factory
6158 Greenbelt Road

Directions: Take I–495 to Greenbelt Road South exit; take Greenbelt Road West to the first traffic light. Turn right.
Phone: (301) 982–2386
Hours: 10:00 A.M.–9:30 P.M., Monday–Saturday; 11:00 A.M.–6:00 P.M., Sunday
Credit Cards: American Express, Discover, MasterCard, Visa
Personal Checks: Yes, with driver's license
Handicapped Accessible: Yes; elevator in rear of store
Bus Tours: Yes

Greenway Center
7565 Greenbelt Road

Directions: Take Baltimore-Washington Parkway to Greenbelt Road East, into the shopping center.
Phone: (202) 293–4500
Hours: 10:00 A.M.–9:00 P.M., Monday–Friday; 10:00 A.M.–6:00 P.M., Saturday; noon–5:00 P.M., Sunday
Credit Cards: Most individual stores accept major credit cards.
Personal Checks: Yes
Handicapped Accessible: Yes
Bus Tours: Yes
Food: Available

Outlets:
The Answer
Dress Barn
Linens 'n Things
Maternity Wearhouse
Ross Dress for Less
Shoe Town

HAGERSTOWN

Izod Factory Store
Route 40 East
1845 Dual Highway

Directions: From I–70 take the Route 40 East exit. Proceed approximately 1 mile; store is on the westbound side.
Phone: (301) 797–7920
Hours: 9:00 A.M.–6:00 P.M., Monday–Thursday; 9:00 A.M.–9:00 P.M., Friday; 9:00 A.M.–8:00 P.M., Saturday; noon–5:00 P.M., Sunday
Credit Cards: American Express, Discover, MasterCard, Visa
Personal Checks: Yes, with driver's license
Handicapped Accessible: Yes
Bus Tours: Yes

Hagerstown Shoe
Route 40 East
1835 Dual Highway

Directions: From I–70, take the Route 40 East exit. Proceed approximately 1 mile; store is on the westbound side
Phone: (301) 797–7244
Hours: 9:00 A.M.–9:00 P.M., Monday–Saturday; 11:00 A.M.–5:00 P.M., Sunday
Credit Cards: American Express, Choice, MasterCard, Visa
Personal Checks: Yes
Handicapped Accessible: Yes
Bus Tours: Yes

Radio Shack
Washington County Business Park
100 Tandy Drive

Directions: Take I–81 to the Route 40 East exit (Hagerstown), to the traffic light at Nottingham Road. Turn right, proceeding to the stop sign at Washington Street. Turn right; 1/4 mile on the left is Washington County Business Park. Turn left into the park and the store is on the left.
Phone: (301) 739–1312
Hours: 9:30 A.M.–6:00 P.M., Monday–Friday; 9:30 A.M.–5:00 P.M., Saturday
Credit Cards: American Express, Discover, MasterCard, Visa
Personal Checks: Yes
Handicapped Accessible: Yes
Bus Tours: Yes
Notes or Attractions: New deliveries every Thursday evening; call then or Friday morning if you're looking for something specific

HANCOCK

London Fog
285 W. Main Street

Directions: Take I–70 to Route 522 South; turn right onto West Main Street, proceeding about 1/4 mile
Phone: (301) 678–5601
Hours: 9:00 A.M.–6:00 P.M., Monday–Thursday and Saturday; 9:00 A.M.–8:00 P.M., Friday; 10:00 A.M.–5:00 P.M., Sunday
Credit Cards: MasterCard, Visa
Personal Checks: Yes, with driver's license
Handicapped Accessible: Yes; store aisles are, however, narrow
Bus Tours: Yes

HUNT VALLEY

Tuesday Morning
11021 York Road

Directions: Take I–83 to Schwann Road past Hunt Valley Mall. At the traffic light turn right onto York Road. Store is 1½ blocks on the left.
Phone: (410) 527–0051
Hours: 9:30 A.M.–6:00 P.M., Monday–Wednesday, Friday, and Saturday; 9:30 A.M.–9:00 P.M., Thursday; noon–6:00 P.M., Sunday
Credit Cards: Discover, MasterCard, Visa
Personal Checks: Yes
Handicapped Accessible: Yes
Bus Tours: Yes

LAUREL

China Plus
8740–14 Cherry Lane

Directions: Take U.S. 1 North to Cherry Lane. Turn right; then turn left into a brick warehouse complex, past Pace. Store is in the back.
Phone: (301) 470–1110
Hours: 10:00 A.M.–6:00 P.M., Monday–Saturday; noon–4:00 P.M., Sunday
Credit Cards: MasterCard, Visa
Personal Checks: Yes
Handicapped Accessible: Yes
Bus Tours: No

Tuesday Morning
13919 Baltimore Avenue and Cypress

Directions: Take U.S. 1 South to Cypress; turn left. Store is behind the shopping complex.
Phone: (301) 953–3957 or (301) 953–7907, recording
Hours: 9:30 A.M.–6:00 P.M., Monday–Wednesday, Friday, and Saturday; 9:30 A.M.–9:00 P.M., Thursday; noon–6:00 P.M., Sunday

Credit Cards: Discover, MasterCard, Visa
Personal Checks: Yes, with proper identification
Handicapped Accessible: No
Bus Tours: Yes

LA VALE

S. Schwab Company
10 Braddock Square Shopping Center

Directions: From I–68 take the Green Street exit; turn left to Upper Potomac Industrial Park Street. Bear left across the bridge into Industrial Park. Store is the first big blue building on the left.
Phone: (301) 729–0602
Hours: 10:00 A.M.–5:00 P.M., Monday–Friday; 10:00 A.M.–4:00 P.M., Saturday
Credit Cards: Discover, MasterCard, Visa
Personal Checks: Yes
Handicapped Accessible: Yes
Bus Tours: No

OCEAN CITY

Eastern Shore Uniform Company
204 South Philadelphia Avenue

Directions: Take U.S. 50 to South Philadelphia Avenue; store is about 2 blocks on the right
Phone: (410) 546–4181
Hours: 10:00 A.M.–4:00 P.M., Monday–Saturday; open summers only (approximately May through September).
Credit Cards: Discover, MasterCard, Visa
Personal Checks: Yes
Handicapped Accessible: Yes
Bus Tours: No

Mill Outlets
7605 Coastal Highway

Directions: Take U.S. 50 to Coastal Highway; turn left at Seventy-Sixth Street.
Phone: (410) 524–6644
Hours: 9:00 A.M.–5:00 P.M., Monday–Saturday; 10:00 A.M.–6:00 P.M., Sunday
Credit Cards: MasterCard, Visa
Personal Checks: Yes
Handicapped Accessible: Yes
Bus Tours: Yes

PERRYVILLE

Perryville Outlet Center
Route 222

Directions: From I–95 take exit 93 (Route 222) east to the first traffic light; turn right, proceeding down a hill, and follow the signs
Phone: (410) 378–9399, recording
Hours: 10:00 A.M.–6:00 P.M., Sunday–Wednesday; 10:00 A.M.–8:00 P.M., Thursday–Saturday
Credit Cards: American Express, Discover, MasterCard, Visa
Personal Checks: Yes
Handicapped Accessible: Yes
Bus Tours: Yes
Food: Available
Outlets:

Adolfo II
Aileen
American Tourister
Anne Klein
Barbizon Lingerie
Bass Shoe
Book Cellar
Brass Factory

Cambridge Dry Goods
Cape Isle Knitters
Capezio
Carole Little
Corning/Revere
Etienne Aigner
Geoffrey Beene
harvé benard

He-Ro Group Outlet
J.H. Collectibles
Jones New York
Jones New York Women
Jordache
Just Kids
Kitchen Collection
Leather Loft
L'eggs/Hanes/Bali
Liz Claiborne
Maidenform
Mikasa
NCS Shoe Outlet
Nike

Paper Factory
Perfumania
Peruvian Connection
Pierre Cardin
Ribbon Outlet
Royal Robbins
Sassafras
Socks Galore & More
Sweatshirts Co.
Toys Unlimited
Van Heusen
Wallet Works
Welcome Home
Wemco

PRINCESS ANNE

Foggy Bottom
Polks Road

Directions: Take U.S. 13 south to Route 529 (Allen Road) and turn right. Go to Polks Road and turn left. Follow signs to dirt road on right to warehouse.
Phone: (410) 651–3818
Hours: 9:00 A.M. to 4:00 P.M., Monday–Friday; open Saturday April–September
Credit Cards: Discover, MasterCard, Visa
Personal Checks: Yes
Handicapped Accessible: Yes
Bus Tours: Yes

QUEENSTOWN

Bay Carpets
Routes 50 and 456

Directions: From Route 50 East, at traffic light turn left on Route 215, 2 blocks up on the right.
Phone: (410) 820–7288
Hours: 8:00 A.M.–6:00 P.M., Monday–Wednesday; 8:00 A.M.–7:00 P.M., Thursday and Friday; 9:00 A.M.–4:00 P.M., Saturday; other hours by appointment
Credit Cards: Discover, MasterCard, Visa
Personal Checks: Yes
Handicapped Accessible: Yes
Bus Tours: Yes

Chesapeake Pottery
U.S. 50 and Kirkley Road

Directions: East of Chesapeake Bay Bridge to Route 301/U.S. 50 split
Phone: (410) 827–7494
Hours: Summer hours 9:30 A.M.–6:30 P.M., Monday–Thursday; 9:30 A.M.–7:30 P.M., Friday and Saturday; 10:00 A.M.–7:30 P.M., Sunday. Shorter hours in winter; closed Christmas Day.
Credit Cards: American Express, Discover, MasterCard, Visa
Personal Checks: Yes, with proper identification
Handicapped Accessible: Yes
Bus Tours: Yes
Food: Available

Chesapeake Village at Queenstown
U.S. 50 and U.S. 301

Directions: Ten miles east of Chesapeake Bay Bridge
Phone: (410) 827–8699
Hours: 10:00 A.M.–6:00 P.M., Sunday–Wednesday; 10:00 A.M.–8:00 P.M., Thursday–Saturday

Credit Cards: Most stores accept major credit cards.
Personal Checks: Most stores accept personal checks.
Handicapped Accessible: Yes
Bus Tours: Yes. Call (800) 969–3767 for motor coach tours and incentive packages.
Food: Available
Outlets:

Adolfo II
Aileen
Argenti
Barbizon Lingerie
Bass
Book Warehouse
Bruce Alan Bags
Cape Isle Knitters
Capezio
Carole Little
Evan-Picone
Fanny Farmer
Fragrance World
Galt Sand
Generra
Gilligan & O'Malley
Gitano
Gorham
harvé benard
I.B. Diffusion

JH Collectibles
Jindo Fur
John Henry
Jones New York
Jordache
Just My Size
L'eggs/Hanes/Bali Express
Liz Claiborne
Maidenform
Nickels
Nike Outlet
9 West
Oleg Cassini
Outer Banks Apparel
Small Talk
Socks Galore & More
Van Heusen
Welcome Home
Wicker Outlet
Wildlife Treasures

Dansk
U.S. 50

Directions: Ten miles east of Chesapeake Bay Bridge
Phone: (410) 827–9220
Hours: 9:30 A.M.–6:00 P.M., Sunday–Saturday
Credit Cards: MasterCard, Visa
Personal Checks: Yes
Handicapped Accessible: Yes
Bus Tours: Yes

RANDALLSTOWN

Tuesday Morning
Brenbrook Plaza
8721 Liberty Road at Brenbrook Road

Directions: From I–695 take exit 18 (Randallstown) onto Liberty Road; store is about 2½ miles on the left.
Phone: (410) 922–6003
Hours: 9:30 A.M.–6:00 P.M., Monday–Wednesday, Friday, and Saturday; 9:30 A.M.–7:00 P.M., Thursday; noon–5:00 P.M., Sunday
Credit Cards: Discover, MasterCard, Visa
Personal Checks: Yes
Handicapped Accessible: Yes
Bus Tours: Yes

REISTERSTOWN

Hanover Shoe Store
11815 Reisterstown Road

Directions: Take I–695 to I–795 (Franklin Boulevard) to exit 7A; turn right at the second light; store is ½ block on the left
Phone: (410) 833–8612
Hours: 10:00 A.M.–9:00 P.M., Monday–Friday; 10:00 A.M.–7:00 P.M., Saturday
Credit Cards: American Express, Discover, MasterCard, Visa
Personal Checks: Yes
Handicapped Accessible: Yes
Bus Tours: Yes

ROCKVILLE

Charles P. Rogers Factory Showroom
11134 Rockville Pike

Directions: Take I–495 to Rockville Pike; store is about 7½ miles on the left
Phone: (301) 770–5900
Hours: 11:00 A.M.–8:00 P.M., Monday–Friday; 10:00 A.M.–6:00 P.M., Saturday; noon–5:00 P.M., Sunday
Credit Cards: American Express, Discover, MasterCard, Visa
Personal Checks: Yes
Handicapped Accessible: Yes
Bus Tours: No

Syms
11840 Rockville Pike

Directions: Take I–495 to Rockville Pike; proceed approximately 4 miles to the shopping center on the left
Phone: (301) 984–3335
Hours: 10:00 A.M.–9:00 P.M., Tuesday–Friday; 10:00 A.M.–6:30 P.M., Saturday; 11:30 A.M.–5:30 P.M., Sunday
Credit Cards: Syms charge only
Personal Checks: Yes, with identification
Handicapped Accessible: Yes
Bus Tours: Yes

Tuesday Morning
25 North Beall Avenue

Directions: Take I–495 to Rockville Pike; proceed approximately 8 miles to North Beall. Store is on the left.
Phone: (301) 424–2480
Hours: 9:30 A.M.–6:00 P.M., Monday–Wednesday, Friday, and Saturday; 9:30 A.M.–9:00 P.M., Thursday; noon–6:00 P.M., Sunday

Credit Cards: Discover, MasterCard, Visa
Personal Checks: Yes
Handicapped Accessible: No
Bus Tours: Yes

SALISBURY

Salisbury Pewter
Route 13 North

Directions: Take U.S. 50 to Route 13 North, and proceed about 1 mile. Store is on the right.
Phone: (410) 546–1188 or (800) 824–4708, outside Maryland
Hours: 9:00 A.M.–4:30 P.M., Monday–Friday; 10:00 A.M.–3:00 P.M., Saturday
Credit Cards: MasterCard, Visa
Personal Checks: Yes
Handicapped Accessible: Yes
Bus Tours: Yes
Notes or Attractions: Factory tours organized through Shore Hospitality (410–749–7545 or 800–654–5440)

SILVER SPRING

Wibbies
8806 Monard Drive

Directions: From I–495 take exit 31 (Georgia Avenue South); turn right at the second traffic light, onto Seminary Road. Bear left onto Brookville Road; proceed about ³/₄ mile and turn right onto Pittman Drive. Turn left onto Monard, and the store is halfway down on the left.
Phone: (301) 565–4001
Hours: 10:00 A.M.–5:00 P.M., Tuesday–Saturday
Credit Cards: Discover, MasterCard, Visa

Personal Checks: Yes, with proper identification
Handicapped Accessible: Yes
Bus Tours: No

THURMONT

Claire's Factory Store
14802 Franklinville Road

Directions: Off U.S. 15, about ¼ mile north of Thurmont, on south-bound side, in Gateway Orchid Plaza
Phone: (301) 271–2021
Hours: 10:00 A.M.–4:00 P.M., Monday; 10:00 A.M.–5:00 P.M., Tuesday–Saturday; noon–5:00 P.M., Sunday
Credit Cards: Choice, Discover, MasterCard, Visa
Personal Checks: Yes, if local; ten-dollar minimum
Handicapped Accessible: Yes
Bus Tours: Yes

TOWSON

Banister Shoes
Puttyhill Avenue (Towson Marketplace)

Directions: Take I–695 to Providence Road (exit 28). Turn left at the top of the ramp and take Providence Road to the first traffic light, Goucher Road, and turn left. Turn left at the next traffic light onto Joppa Road. Towson Marketplace is on the top of the hill on the right.
Phone: (410) 828–5356
Hours: 10:00 A.M.–9:00 P.M., Monday–Saturday; noon–5:00 P.M., Sunday
Credit Cards: American Express, Discover, MasterCard, Visa
Personal Checks: Yes
Handicapped Accessible: Yes
Bus Tours: Yes

WHEATON

Tuesday Morning
11111 Georgia Avenue

Directions: Take I–495 to the Georgia Avenue exit; proceed north to the store, which is on the right
Phone: (301) 942–1884
Hours: 9:30 A.M.–6:00 P.M., Monday–Wednesday, Friday, and Saturday; 9:30 A.M.–9:00 P.M., Thursday; noon–6:00 P.M., Sunday
Credit Cards: Discover, MasterCard, Visa
Personal Checks: Yes
Handicapped Accessible: Yes
Bus Tours: Yes

NEW JERSEY

New Jersey has no sales tax on clothing, except furs, leathers, and accessories.

1. Burlington
2. Edison
3. Fairfield
4. Flemington
5. Lafayette

6. Lambertville
7. Matawan
8. North Bergen
9. Secaucus
10. Wall Township

NEW JERSEY

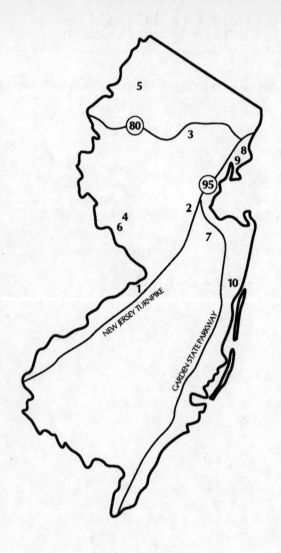

BURLINGTON

Burlington Outlet Mart
Route 130 and Salem Road

Directions: From the New Jersey Turnpike, take exit 5; turn left at Route 130. Mart is 4 blocks on the left.
Phone: (609) 386–2500
Hours: 10:00 A.M.–9:00 P.M., Monday–Friday; 10:00 A.M.–6:00 P.M., Saturday; 11:00 A.M.–6:00 P.M., Sunday
Credit Cards: MasterCard, Visa
Personal Checks: Yes
Handicapped Accessible: Yes
Bus Tours: Yes
Outlets:
Accents
Aileen
Burlington Shoe
Candle Factory
Ladies Factory Outlet

EDISON

Edison Outlet Center
Talmadge Road and Carter Drive

Directions: Take I–287 to Highway 27 South to where the highway intersects with Talmadge Road; turn west, proceeding ½ mile to Carter Drive. Turn left; the center is the third building on the left.
Phone: (212) 832–2600
Hours: 8:00 A.M.–6:00 P.M., Monday–Wednesday; 8:00 A.M.–7:00 P.M., Thursday and Friday; 9:00 A.M.–4:00 P.M., Saturday
Credit Cards: Most stores accept major credit cards.
Personal Checks: Yes
Handicapped Accessible: Yes

Bus Tours: Yes
Outlets:
Diesse Shoes
Gitano

FAIRFIELD

American Way Mall
636 Route 46 East

Directions: One-half mile from I–80, on Route 46 East
Phone: (201) 227–2228
Hours: 10:00 A.M.–9:30 P.M., Monday–Saturday; noon–5:00 P.M., Sunday
Credit Cards: Most stores accept major credit cards.
Personal Checks: Most stores accept personal checks.
Handicapped Accessible: Yes
Bus Tours: No
Food: Available
Notes or Attractions: Mixed-use mall
Outlets:
Amy Stoudt
Bare Necessities
Corner House
Designer Luggage Depot
Dress Barn
Famous Footwear
Flemington Fashion Outlet
Linens 'n Things
Manufacturer's Surplus Outlet
Old Mill
Van Heusen

FLEMINGTON

Outlets are located in several areas in and around Flemington on the highways outside town and along a number of blocks within town. A shopping/sight-seeing trolley connects the major shopping and restaurant areas and runs Tuesday through Sunday. A $1.00 fare allows you to ride all day.

Dansk Plaza
Routes 31 and 202 circle

Directions: Take I–78 to Route 31 South to junction of Route 202 (circle). Plaza is on the right.
Phone: (908) 782–7077
Hours: 10:00 A.M.–6:00 P.M., Sunday–Wednesday; 10:00 A.M.–8:00 P.M., Thursday–Saturday
Credit Cards: MasterCard, Visa
Personal Checks: Yes
Handicapped Accessible: Yes
Bus Tours: Yes
Outlets:
Chaus
Dansk
Gorham Silver
Maidenform
Marty's Shoes
Prestige Fragrance & Cosmetics

Flemington Outlet Center
Routes 31 and 202 circle

Directions: Take I–78 to Route 31 South. Outlet is on circle where routes 31 and 202 meet.
Phone: (908) 782–4100, recording
Hours: 10:00 A.M.–9:00 P.M., Monday–Friday; 10:00 A.M.–6:00 P.M., Saturday and Sunday
Credit Cards: MasterCard, Visa

Personal Checks: Yes
Handicapped Accessible: Yes
Bus Tours: Yes
Outlets:
Annie Sez
Bagtime
Bed, Bath & Beyond
Carter's Childrenswear
Dress Barn Woman
Famous Brands Housewares
Famous Footwear
Gitano
Intimate Eve
Jonathan Logan
Kitchen Place
Murray's Menswear
Noel's Hosiery Outlet
Shoe-Town
Widman Deep Discount
Windsor Shirt

Liberty Village Factory Outlets
One Church Street

Directions: Between Main Street and Route 31
Phone: (908) 782–8550
Hours: 10:00 A.M.–6:00 P.M., Sunday–Saturday,
Credit Cards: Most stores accept major credit cards.
Personal Checks: Yes
Handicapped Accessible: Yes
Bus Tours: Yes. Promotional packages available.
Additional Savings: Group discounts available
Food: Available
Notes or Attractions: New Jersey Tourist Information Center

Outlets:	Anne Klein Petites
Adrienne Vittadini ✓	Bagmakers
Aileen	Bass Shoe
Anne Klein Outlet ✓	Bentley Books

Buttons and Things
Calvin Klein Jean Outlet
Cambridge Dry Goods
Cape Isle Knitters
Capezio Factory Direct Shoes
Carole Little
Carter's Little Gallery
Coat World
Corning/Revere
Country Casuals
Crystal Works Outlet
Donna Karan
Ellen Tracy ✓
Executive Neckwear
Famous Brand Yarns
First Choice/Escada ✓
Flemington's Coat World
Gem Vault
Geoffrey Beene
Golden Talents
Happy Hatter
harvé benard
Heirloom Lace
Housewares Store

International Footwear Co.
Joan & David Shoes
Jones New York
Lady Leslie Fashions
L'eggs/Hanes/Bali
Limited Editions for Her
Lingerie Shop
9 West
Perfumania
Perry Ellis
Petals
Ribbon Outlet
Royal Doulton
Royal Grouse
Shady Lamp Shop
Socks Galore & More
Sweaters/Ski & Sport
totes
Van Heusen
Village Jewelry
Villeroy & Boch
Waterford/Wedgwood Outlet
Wathne

Pfaltzgraff Factory Outlet Store
Mine Street and Stangl Road

Directions: Take Route 202 to Flemington. At center of town turn onto Mine Street. Store is on left after 3 blocks.
Phone: (908) 782-2918
Hours: 10:00 A.M.–6:00 P.M., Sunday–Wednesday; 10:00 A.M.–8:00 P.M., Thursday–Saturday
Credit Cards: Discover, MasterCard, Visa
Personal Checks: Yes
Handicapped Accessible: Yes
Bus Tours: Yes

Wilton Armetale Factory Outlet
156 Main Street

Directions: From Route 283 get off the Mt. Joy exit and go west on Route 772. At Route 230 turn right and go through two traffic lights. Two blocks after second light turn left onto Plumb Street. Go one block and turn right onto Square Street. Store is on right side.
Phone: (908) 782–1574 or (800) 832–3149
Hours: 9:30 A.M.–5:30 P.M., Sunday–Saturday; closed Thanksgiving, Christmas, and New Year's Day.
Credit Cards: American Express, MAC, MasterCard, Visa
Personal Checks: Yes
Special Savings: Senior citizen discount available
Notes or Attractions: Bridal registry available
Handicapped Accessible: Yes
Bus Tours: Yes

LAFAYETTE

Olde Lafayette Village
I–80 exit 34B

Directions: From I–80 take exit 34B
Phone: (201) 383–8323
Hours: 10:00 A.M.–6:00 P.M., Sunday–Wednesday; 10:00 A.M.–8:00 P.M., Thursday–Saturday
Credit Cards: Discover, MasterCard, Visa
Personal Checks: Most stores accept personal checks.
Handicapped Accessible: Yes
Bus Tours: Yes
Outlets:
Aileen
Bass Shoe
Capezio
Corning/Revere
Gitano
John Henry & Friends
Van Heusen

LAMBERTVILLE

Lace Factory Outlet
287 South Main St.

Directions: Take Route 202 south from Flemington for 2 miles, to Route 179 and then to Lambertville; proceed about 2 miles. Store is ½ mile on the right after the traffic light.
Phone: (609) 397–0565
Hours: 10:00 A.M.–4:30 P.M., Monday–Sunday
Credit Cards: MasterCard, Visa
Personal Checks: Yes
Handicapped Accessible: Yes, through rear entrance
Bus Tours: Yes

MATAWAN

Marketplace Mall
Routes 34 and 9

Directions: At intersection of Routes 34 and 9, 2 miles south of Matawan
Phone: (908) 583–1507
Hours: 10:00 A.M.–6:00 P.M., Monday–Wednesday and Saturday; 10:00 A.M.–9:00 P.M., Thursday and Friday; noon–5:00 P.M., Sunday
Credit Cards: Most stores accept major credit cards.
Personal Checks: Most stores accept personal checks.
Handicapped Accessible: Yes
Bus Tours: Yes
Outlets:
Aileen
Bare Necessities
Beauty Barn
Book Stall
Calico Corners

Carter's Childrenswear
Children's Outlet
Club House
Dress Barn
Fashion Finds
Fashion Flair
Flemington Fashion Plus
Flemington Plus
Hit or Miss
L'eggs/Hanes/Bali
Leather Warehouse
Linens 'n Things
Manhattan
Marketplace Sneakers
Old Mill
Quoddy Shoes
Shoe Town
Susan Greene
Top of the Line Cosmetics
Van Heusen

NORTH BERGEN

Evan-Picone
7801 Tonnelle Avenue

Directions: From the New Jersey Turnpike, take exit 16 (Lincoln Tunnel Secaucus Patterson Plank Road) east to the third traffic light and bear left to Tonnelle Avenue (U.S. 1 and 9), going north. Drive about fifteen minutes. Store is on your left, near a Kmart, on the second floor.
Phone: (201) 869–0224
Hours: 10:00 A.M.–6:00 P.M., Monday–Wednesday, Friday, and Saturday; 10:00 A.M.–9:00 P.M., Thursday; noon–5:00 P.M., Sunday
Credit Cards: American Express, Discover, MasterCard, Visa

Personal Checks: Yes, with imprinted address
Handicapped Accessible: Yes
Bus Tours: No

SECAUCUS

More than eighty outlets operate along several streets through the Sea-caucus Outlet Center.

Note: Due to the explosive growth of outlets in this area, we were un-able to obtain complete information on the following listings by press time. Please call the individual malls and stores for current information.

Castle Road Outlet Center
600 Meadowland Parkway

Directions: From the New Jersey Turnpike, take exit 16 West (West Spur) to Route 3 East and Meadowlands Parkway.
Phone: (201) 864–7345
Hours: 10:00 A.M.–6:00 P.M., Monday–Wednesday, Friday, and Satur-day; 10:00 A.M.–9:00 P.M., Thursday; noon–5:00 P.M., Sunday
Credit Cards: Most stores accept major credit cards.
Personal Checks: Most stores accept checks with personal identification.
Handicapped Accessible: Yes
Bus Tours: Yes. Coupon books provided if notified in advance.
Outlets:
Aileen
Church's English Shoes
Cocoon Silk
Crystal Sportswear by Kobe
Danson Jewelers
Famous Footwear
Flemington Fashion Outlet
Flemington Petites
Flemington Plus
Kidrageous Children's Clothes
Kidstuff
Leather Plus

L'eggs/Hanes/Bali
Male Ego
Man's Town
Marburn Curtain Warehouse
Marty's Shoe Outlet
Oriental Rug Outlet
Paris in Secaucus Perfumes
Prato's Menswear
Shoe Town
Sleepy's Mattress Outlet
Techline Furniture
Tempo Luggage
Uniform
Unlimited Design Jewelry
Valley Fair Outlet

Designer Outlet Gallery
55 Hartz Way at Secaucus Road

Directions: From the New Jersey Turnpike, take exit 16 West (West Spur) to Route 3 East and Meadowlands Parkway. Turn left to third light; turn left and then the first right on Hartz Way.
Phone: (201) 863–9198
Hours: 10:00 A.M.–6:00 P.M., Monday–Saturday; noon–6:00 P.M., Sunday
Credit Cards: MasterCard, Visa
Personal Checks: Yes
Handicapped Accessible: Yes
Bus Tours: Yes
Outlets:
Adolfo II ✓
Andrea Carrano
Anne Klein ✓
Argenti
Carole Hockman
JH Collectibles
Jindo Outerwear

Joan & David
Jones New York
La Chine
Satchels Handbags

Harmon Cove Outlet Center

20 Enterprise Avenue North

Directions: Take the New Jersey Turnpike to Route 3 East, Meadowlands Parkway; turn left onto American Way and then left onto Enterprise Avenue N.

Phone: (201) 348–1200, extension 424 or 311

Hours: 10:00 A.M.–6:00 P.M., Monday–Saturday; 10:00 A.M.–9:00 P.M., Thursday and Friday; noon–5:00 P.M., Sunday. Some stores vary their hours. Extended holiday hours.

Credit Cards: MasterCard, Visa.

Personal Checks: Yes

Handicapped Accessible: Yes

Bus Tours: Yes

Food: Available

Outlets:

Accessories Plus
Accessories Plus II
American Tourister
Athlete's Outlet
Bally ✓
Barbizon Lingerie
Bass Shoe
Bed 'n Bath
Cambridge Dry Goods
Campus
Capezio ✓
Children's Outlet
Christian Benard ✓
Dali B
Damon Creations
Designer Luggage Depot
Emerson Radio Outlet
Executive Neckwear
Famous Brands
Fashion Flair
Flower and Plant Cove
Gabrielle
Geoffrey Beene
Gitano
Intimate Eve
Jacques Cohen, Inc.
Jonathan Logan Outlet
Kitchen Place
Maison Emanuelle
Menagerie Discount Outlet
Not Just Jeans
N.T. Tahari
Secaucus Handbag Outlet
Urban Clothing Company
Van Heusen Factory
Wholesaler's Shoe Outlet Too

Outlets at the Cove
45 Meadowlands Parkway

Directions: From the New Jersey Turnpike, take exit 16 West (West Spur) to Route 3 East and Meadowlands Parkway.
Phone: (201) 392–8700
Hours: 10:00 A.M.–6:00 P.M., Sunday–Wednesday; 10:00 A.M.–8:00 P.M., Thursday–Saturday
Credit Cards: Most stores accept major credit cards.
Personal Checks: Yes
Handicapped Accessible: Yes
Bus Tours: Yes
Outlets:
Bugle Boy
Calvin Klein
Carole Little
G. H. Bass
harvé benard
Kikit
Luggage World
9 West
Van Heusen

Additional outlets at the Secaucus Outlet Center:

Adrianna Papell
Bag City
Barbara's Outlet
Barbizon Lingerie
Burlington Coat Factory
  Warehouse
Church's English Shoes
Diane Gilman
Door Store
Enterprise Golf Outlet
European Designer Outlet
Flemington Fashion Outlet
Flemington Plus
harvé benard

Harvey Electronics
He-Ro Group Outlet
Jindo Furs
Jonathan Logan Outlet
Just Coats 'N' Swimwear
Male Ego Fashion Outlet
Mikasa
Mondi Outlet Center
NBO Warehouse Store
Outlet Store
Passport Foods Outlet
Ronlee
Sassco Fashions Outlet

WALL TOWNSHIP

Circle Factory Outlet Center
1407 West Atlantic

Directions: From Garden State Parkway take exit 98, proceeding 5 miles to the junction of Route 35 and Manasquan Court. Center is south of the traffic circle.
Phone: (908) 223–2300
Hours: 10:00 A.M.–6:00 P.M., Sunday–Wednesday; 10:00 A.M.–8:00 P.M., Thursday–Saturday
Credit Cards: MasterCard, Visa
Personal Checks: Yes
Handicapped Accessible: Yes
Bus Tours: Yes
Outlets:
Adolfo
Aileen
American Tourister
Banister Shoes
Bass Shoes
Cape Island Knitters
Cocoon Silk
Corning/Revere
Gitano
Gitano for Kids
harvé benard
Izod
Just Coats 'n Swimwear
Lechters Famous Brand Housewares
L'eggs/Hanes/Bali
Marty Shoes
Mikasa
Van Heusen

NEW YORK

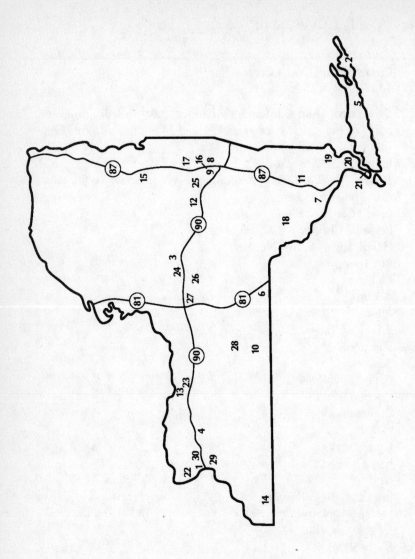

NEW YORK

1. Amherst
2. Amagansett
3. Barneveld
4. Batavia
5. Bellport
6. Binghamton
7. Central Valley
8. Cohoes
9. Colonie
10. Corning
11. Fishkill
12. Gloversville
13. Irondequoit
14. Jamestown
15. Lake George

16. Latham
17. Malta
18. Monticello
19. Mount Kisco
20. New Rochelle
21. New York City
22. Niagara Falls
23. Rochester
24. Rome
25. Schenectady
26. Sherrill
27. Syracuse
28. Watkins Glen
29. West Seneca
30. Williamsville

AMHERST

Burlington Coat Factory
1551 Niagara Falls Boulevard
Burlington Plaza

Directions: Take I–90 to Route 290 to Niagara Falls Boulevard South.
Store is ½ mile on the left.
Phone: (716) 833–0554
Hours: 10:00 A.M.–9:00 P.M., Monday–Saturday; 10:00 A.M.–6:00 P.M.,
Sunday
Credit Cards: American Express, Discover, MasterCard, Visa
Personal Checks: Yes
Handicapped Accessible: Yes
Bus Tours: Yes

AMAGANSETT

Coach Store
Main Street

Directions: From the Long Island Epxressway, take exit 70 to the end.
Take Route 111 South to Route 27 East and proceed into Amagansett.
Store is on the left side of Main Street.
Phone: (516) 267–3340
Hours: 10:00 A.M.–6:00 P.M., Sunday–Friday; 10:00 A.M.–7:00 P.M.,
Saturday
Credit Cards: American Express, MasterCard, Visa
Personal Checks: Yes, up to $250
Handicapped Accessible: No
Bus Tours: Yes

BARNEVELD

Bass Shoe
Route 12 and Mapledale Road

Directions: From I–90 take Utica exit 31; follow signs for Route 12 North. Store is 10 miles up Route 12 on the right.
Phone: (315) 896–2035
Hours: 9:00 A.M.–9:00 P.M., Monday–Saturday; 10:00 A.M.–6:00 P.M., Sunday
Credit Cards: Discover, MasterCard, Visa
Personal Checks: Yes
Handicapped Accessible: Yes
Bus Tours: Yes

Dexter Shoe Outlet Store
Route 12 and Mapledale Road

Directions: From I–90 take Utica exit 31; follow signs for Route 12 North. Store is 10 miles up Route 12.
Phone: (315) 896–6177
Hours: 10:00 A.M.–6:00 P.M., Monday–Thursday; 10:00 A.M.–8:00 P.M., Friday and Saturday; 10:00 A.M.–5:00 P.M., Sunday
Credit Cards: MasterCard, Visa
Personal Checks: Yes
Handicapped Accessible: Yes
Bus Tours: Yes

BATAVIA

Melton Clothing Company
56 Harvester Avenue

Directions: From the New York Thruway, take the Batavia exit to the traffic light and turn left onto Route 98; proceed to Route 5 and make a left. Stay on Route 5 through the city to Harvester Avenue; turn right. Store is on the right, about halfway down the block.

Phone: (716) 343–8750

Hours: 10:00 A.M.–9:00 P.M., Monday–Saturday; 10:00 A.M.–5:00 P.M., Sunday

Credit Cards: Discover, MasterCard, Visa

Personal Checks: Yes, with identification

Handicapped Accessible: Former factory with freight elevators for wheelchairs; advance notice required for that use. Aisles are crowded.

Bus Tours: Yes

BELLPORT

Bellport Outlet Center

Route 27 (Sunrise Highway)

63, 5, 3 mi

Directions: Take the Long Island Expressway to exit 64, Sunrise Highway. Go east to exit 56, Station Road. *Rt 27.*

Phone: (516) 286–3872

Hours: 10:00 A.M.–9:00 P.M., Monday–Saturday; 11:00 A.M.–6:00 P.M., Sunday

Credit Cards: MasterCard, Visa

Personal Checks: Yes

Handicapped Accessible: Yes

Bus Tours: Yes

Outlets:

Bass Shoe	Leather Loft
Cape Isle Knitters	L'eggs/Hanes/Bali
Carole Little	Maidenform
Crazy Horse	Nike
Crystal Works	9 West
Fragrance World	North Face
Galt Sand	Oneida *(516) 286 0197*
Geoffrey Beene	Pierre Cardin
Jones New York	Van Heusen
Jordache	Welcome Home

Naturalizer

140

BINGHAMTON

Barb Bees Factory Outlet
156 Court Street

Directions: Take I–81 to downtown Binghamton to Court and Carol streets in the middle of town
Phone: (607) 722–7732
Hours: 11:00 A.M.–3:00 P.M., Monday–Saturday
Credit Cards: Discover only
Personal Checks: Yes
Handicapped Accessible: Yes
Bus Tours: Yes

Binghamton Knitting Company, Inc.
11 Alice Street

Directions: Take I–81 to downtown Binghamton to Court and Alice streets
Phone: (607) 722–6941
Hours: 9:00 A.M.–4:00 P.M., Monday–Friday; 9:00 A.M.–noon, Saturday
Credit Cards: MasterCard, Visa
Personal Checks: Yes
Handicapped Accessible: No
Bus Tours: Yes

Fashion Flair
1144 Front Street

Directions: From I–81 take exit 6; turn left at bottom of ramp. Store is ⅛ mile on the left-hand side of the road.
Phone: (607) 723–6064
Hours: 10:00 A.M.–6:00 P.M., Monday–Wednesday and Saturday; 10:00 A.M.–9:00 P.M., Thursday and Friday; noon–5:00 P.M., Sunday
Credit Cards: American Express, Discover, MasterCard, Visa

Personal Checks: Yes
Handicapped Accessible: Yes
Bus Tours: Yes

Aunt Mary's Yarn, Needleworks, and Crafts
4700 Vestal Parkway East, Route 434

Directions: From Route 17 take exit 71 south (Route 201 South). Follow Route 201 to traffic circle. Take first right off traffic circle and follow signs for Route 434 East. Store is three traffic lights down Route 434 on south side (Vestal Plaza).
Phone: (607) 797–8086
Hours: 10:00 A.M.–9:00 P.M., Monday–Saturday; noon–5:00 P.M., Sunday
Credit Cards: Discover, MasterCard, Visa
Personal Checks: Local only
Handicapped Accessible: Yes
Bus Tours: Yes

CENTRAL VALLEY

Woodbury Commons Factory Outlets
Route 32

Directions: From the New York Thruway, take exit 16; turn right after the toll booth
Phone: (914) 928–7467, administrative office
Hours: January–June, 10:00 A.M.–6:00 P.M., Monday–Saturday; 11:00 A.M.–6:00 P.M., Sunday. May–December, 10:00 A.M.–9:00 P.M., Thursday–Saturday
Credit Cards: American Express, MasterCard, Visa at most stores
Personal Checks: Yes, at most stores
Handicapped Accessible: Yes
Bus Tours: Yes. Coupon discount booklet available.
Special Savings: Look for shopping guide for maps, savings, and coupons
Food: Food court

Outlets:
Accessory Factory
Adidas Outlet
Adolfo II
Adrienne Vittadini
Aileen
American Tourister
Anne Klein Outlet
Anne Klein Petites
Bagmakers
Banister Shoes
Bass Shoe Outlet
Bear Mountain Books
Boston Trader Kids
Boston Traders
Calvin Klein
Cambridge Dry Goods
Cape Isle Knitters
Carlos Falchi
Carole Hockman Lingerie
Carole Little
Carter's Childrenswear
Champion Hanes Activewear
Chaus
Clifford Michael
Cole-Haan
Corning/Revere
Crazy Horse
Crystal Works
Dansk
Delta Hosiery Outlet
Donna Karan
Ellen Tracy
Eric Allen
Espirit
Etienne Aigner
Famous Brand Yarns
Fashion Flair

First Choice/Escada
Flemington's Coat World
From Me to You
Gitano
Gucci
harvé benard
He-Ro Group Outlet
Housewares Store
International Clothing Company
International Footwear
In-Wear Matinique
Jessica McClintock
Jindo Furs
Joan & David Outlet
Jones New York—Women
Jones New York—Sport, Misses
  & Petites
Kenar-Nicole Matthews
Lady Leslie Fashions
L'eggs/Hanes/Bali
Leslie Fay
Liz Claiborne
Lots of Linens
Maidenform
Manhattan
Mark Cross
Moda Fashion Apparel
Mondi
Nautica
Oneida Silver
Paper Outlet
Petals
Prestige Fragrance & Cosmetics
Ribbon Outlet
Rodier Paris
Rosenbaum Jewelry
Royal Doulton Shop
Royal Grouse II

Russ Togs
Sergio Valenti
Shady Lamp Shop
Socks Galore & More
Socks Plus
Special Seasons
Sports & Sorts
Sweaters Ski & Sport Outlet
Tahari

Tapemeasure
TieLand
Toy Liquidators
Unisa
Vakko
Van Heusen
Wallet Works
Westport Ltd.

COHOES

Cohoes Commons
55 Mohawk Street

Directions: I–87, west on Route 7 to Cohoes
Phone: (518) 235–8717, recording
Hours: 10:00 A.M.–6:00 P.M., Sunday–Wednesday; 10:00 A.M.–8:00 P.M., Thursday–Saturday
Credit Cards: MasterCard, Visa
Personal Checks: Yes
Handicapped Accessible: Yes
Bus Tours: Yes
Outlets:
American Tourister
Dansk
Escada
L'eggs/Hanes/Bali
Polo/Ralph Lauren

COLONIE

Fashion Flair
Wolf Road Shoppers Park

Directions: From I–87 South, take exit 4; turn right and proceed for about ½ mile. Store is on the left.
Phone: (518) 459–5917
Hours: 10:00 A.M.–9:00 P.M., Monday–Friday; 10:00 A.M.–6:00 P.M., Saturday; noon–5:00 P.M., Sunday
Credit Cards: American Express, MasterCard, Visa
Personal Checks: Yes
Handicapped Accessible: Yes
Bus Tours: Yes

CORNING

Corning Store
114 Pine Street

Directions: From U.S. 15 take Route 17 East to Pine Street
Phone: (607) 962–1545
Hours: 9:00 A.M.–6:00 P.M.; Monday–Wednesday, Friday, and Saturday; 9:00 A.M.–8:00 P.M., Thursday; noon–6:00 P.M., Sunday
Credit Cards: Discover, MasterCard, Visa
Personal Checks: Yes
Handicapped Accessible: Yes
Bus Tours: Yes
Notes or Attractions: Tour the Corning Glass Center and the Steuben Glass Factory (607–974–8271). Open 9:00 A.M.–5:00 P.M., Monday–Sunday; closed Thanksgiving Day, December 24–December 25, and January 1. From U.S. 15 take Route 17 East and follow signs. Fees are $6.00 for adults, $5.00 for seniors, $4.00 for children six to fourteen, and free for children under six; families pay $14.00 maximum, and students and AAA members receive 10 percent discount. Group tour information: (607) 974–2000.

Fieldcrest Cannon
21 West Market

Directions: From U.S. 15 take Route 17 East to West Market.
Phone: (607) 936–6371
Hours: 9:00 A.M.–8:00 P.M., Monday–Friday; 9:00 A.M.–6:00 P.M., Saturday; noon–5:00 P.M., Sunday
Credit Cards: MasterCard, Visa
Personal Checks: Yes
Handicapped Accessible: Yes
Bus Tours: Yes

Van Heusen Factory Store
54 East Market

Directions: From U.S. 15 take Route 17 East to East Market
Phone: (607) 962–6579
Hours: 10:00 A.M.–5:00 P.M., Monday–Wednesday and Saturday; 10:00 A.M.–6:00 P.M., Thursday and Friday, noon–5:00 P.M., Sunday
Credit Cards: Discover, MasterCard, Visa
Personal Checks: Yes
Handicapped Accessible: Yes
Bus Tours: Yes

FISHKILL

Fishkill Outlet Village
Route 9 and I-84

Directions: Take I–84 to U.S. 9; follow to intersection with Route 52.
Phone: (914) 897–3135
Hours: 10:00 A.M.–6:00 P.M., Sunday–Wednesday; 10:00 A.M.–8:00 P.M., Thursday–Saturday
Credit Cards: Most stores accept major credit cards.
Personal Checks: Yes

Handicapped Accessible: Yes
Bus Tours: Yes
Outlets:
Aileen
American Tourister
Banister Shoes
Bass Shoe
Cape Isle Knitters
Corning/Revere
Geoffrey Beene
Gitano
Hathaway
Jonathan Logan
Leather Loft
London Fog
Olga/Warner
Polly Flinders
Prestige Fragrance and Cosmetics Inc.
Socks Galore & More
Swank
Van Heusen
Welcome Home

GLOVERSVILLE

Gloversville is known as the birthplace of the nation's leather industry.

Heacock's Deerskin Factory Store
112 North Arlington Avenue

Directions: Route 30A to State Street; turn left onto State to Bleeker and turn left to right on Grand Street to Arlington Avenue.
Phone: (518) 725–5423
Hours: May–December only; call for hours
Credit Cards: MasterCard, Visa

Personal Checks: Yes
Handicapped Accessible: No
Bus Tours: Yes, small ones

Perrella Factory Outlet (B & G Leathers)
17 Foster Street

Directions: From Route 30A turn left onto King's Row Avenue, proceeding to Eighth Avenue East. Turn left, proceeding to Foster Street; turn right and the building is on the left.
Phone: (518) 725–2315
Hours: 10:00 A.M.–5:00 P.M., Monday–Friday; 10:00 A.M.–2:00 P.M., Saturday. Extended hours in November and December.
Credit Cards: No
Personal Checks: Yes
Handicapped Accessible: Yes
Bus Tours: Yes

Rubin Gloves Factory Store
51 East Fulton Street

Directions: From Route 30A turn left onto King's Row Avenue, proceeding to Eighth Avenue East. Turn left onto East Fulton Street.
Phone: (518) 725–7138
Hours: Open only November through Christmas—10:00 A.M.–4:30 P.M., Monday–Friday; 10:00 A.M.–3:00 P.M., Saturday
Credit Cards: No
Personal Checks: Yes
Handicapped Accessible: No
Bus Tours: Yes

St. Thomas Inc.
St. Thomas Place

Directions: Take Route 30A north past the Holiday Inn on the right-hand side; the traffic light at the next block is Harrison Street. Turn left on Harrison and go to the end, to South Main Street. Turn right onto South Main and proceed to Spring Street. Look for the big gray building behind the park.

Phone: (518) 725–3115
Hours: 10:00 A.M.–4:00 P.M., Monday–Friday
Credit Cards: MasterCard, Visa ($50 minimum)
Personal Checks: Yes
Handicapped Accessible: No
Bus Tours: Yes

Taylor Made Products
167 North Main Street

Directions: Take Route 30A north past the Holiday Inn on the right-hand side; the traffic light at the next block is Harrison Street. Turn left on Harrison and go to the end, to North Main Street. Turn left and proceed along North Main Street until you come to the store.

Phone: (518) 725–2624
Hours: 8:00 A.M.–5:00 P.M., Monday–Friday; 9:00 A.M.–1:00 P.M., Saturday
Credit Cards: Discover, MasterCard, Visa
Personal Checks: Yes
Handicapped Accessible: Yes
Bus Tours: Yes

Vertucci Glove
16–18 Mill Street

Directions: Take Route 30A north to Harrison Street. Turn left; go to the end, to South Main Street. Turn right and proceed down South Main to Mill Street.

Phone: (518) 725–3725
Hours: Labor Day through Christmas, 8:00 A.M.–4:00 P.M., Monday–Friday; 9:00 A.M.–4:00 P.M., Saturday
Credit Cards: No
Personal Checks: Yes
Handicapped Accessible: No
Bus Tours: No

IRONDEQUOIT

Burlington Coat Factory
Culver Ridge Plaza

Directions: Take Route 590 north to the Ridge Road exit; turn left and drive for 2 blocks. Store is on the right.
Phone: (716) 342–1230
Hours: 10:00 A.M.–9:30 P.M., Monday–Saturday; 11:00 A.M.–6:00 P.M., Sunday
Credit Cards: American Express, Discover, MasterCard, Visa
Personal Checks: Yes
Handicapped Accessible: Yes
Bus Tours: Yes

JAMESTOWN

Burlington Coat Factory
832 Foote Avenue (Route 60 South)
Culver Ridge Plaza

Directions: Take Route 590 north to Ridge Road exit. Turn left and the store is on the right in two blocks.
Phone: (716) 342–1230
Hours: 10:00 A.M.–9:30 P.M., Monday–Saturday; 11:00 A.M.–6:00 P.M., Sunday
Credit Cards: American Express, Discover, MasterCard, Visa
Personal Checks: Yes
Handicapped Accessible: Yes
Bus Tours: Yes

Champion Factory Outlet
832 Foote Avenue

Directions: Route 60 south to Foote Avenue

Phone: (716) 488–9344
Hours: 10:00 A.M.–9:00 P.M., Monday–Saturday; noon–5:00 P.M., Sunday
Credit Cards: Discover, MasterCard, Visa
Personal Checks: Yes
Handicapped Accessible: Yes
Bus Tours: Yes

LAKE GEORGE

A number of outlet and retail stores and malls flank that portion of Route 9 between Glens Falls and Lake George referred to as the Million Dollar Half Mile.

Adirondack Factory Outlet Mall
Route 9

Directions: Take I–87 to exit 20. Turn right into center to blue building.
Phone: (518) 793–2161, recording
Hours: Summer hours 9:30 A.M.–9:00 P.M.,Monday–Saturday; 10:00 A.M.–6:00 P.M., Sunday. Winter hours 9:30 A.M.–6:00 P.M., Monday–Wednesday; 9:30 A.M.–9:00 P.M., Thursday–Saturday; 10:00 A.M.–5:00 P.M., Sunday.
Credit Cards: American Express, MasterCard, Visa (some accept Discover)
Personal Checks: Yes, with identification
Handicapped Accessible: Yes
Bus Tours: Yes
Notes or Attractions: Days Inn adjacent
Outlets:
Aileen
Barbizon Lingerie
Black Sheep featuring Woolrich
Book Warehouse
Bugle Boy

Champion Factory
Clock Center
Converse
Corning/Revere
Izod/Gant
Kitchen Collection
Lots of Linens
Manhattan
Polly Flinders
Swank
Sweaters, Ski & Sport
totes/Sunglass World
Toy Liquidators
U.S.A. Classic

French Mountain Commons
Route 9

Directions: Take I–87 to exit 20. Go left onto Route 9. Mall is within ¹/₂ mile.
Phone: (518) 792–1483
Hours: Summer hours 9:30 A.M.–8:00 P.M., Monday–Saturday; 10:00 A.M.–5:00 P.M., Sunday. Winter hours 10:00 A.M.–6:00 P.M., Monday–Wednesday and Saturday; 10:00 A.M.–9:00 P.M., Thursday and Friday; noon–5:00 P.M., Sunday.
Credit Cards: All major
Personal Checks: With address imprinted and proper identification
Handicapped Accessible: Yes
Bus Tours: Yes
Food: Available
Outlets:
Country Road Australia
Damon/Enroe
Fieldcrest Cannon
Hushpuppies Factory Direct
Jonathan Logan
Lady Leslie

9 West
Oneida
Pfaltzgraff
Pier 1 Imports
Reebok
Welcome Home

Lake George Plaza Outlet Center
Route 9

Directions: Take I–87 to exit 20. Proceed on Route 9. Center is on the right.
Phone: (518) 798–7234
Hours: Summer hours 9:30 A.M.–8:00 P.M., Monday–Saturday; 10:00 A.M.–5:00 P.M., Sunday. Winter hours 10:00 A.M.–6:00 P.M., Monday–Wednesday and Saturday; 10:00 A.M.–9:00 P.M., Thursday and Friday; noon–5:00 P.M., Sunday.
Credit Cards: Discover, MasterCard
Personal Checks: Yes, with driver's license
Handicapped Accessible: Yes
Bus Tours: Yes
Outlets:
Anne Klein
Crazy Horse
Dansk
Etienne Aigner
Geoffrey Beene
Gilligan & O'Malley
harvé benard
London Fog
Micki Designer Separates
Nautica

Log Jam Factory Stores
Route 9

Directions: Take I–87 to exit 19 and proceed 4 to 5 miles on Route 9. Outlet center is on right next to Log Jam Restaurant.
Phone: (603) 778–8484, New Hampshire management office
Hours: 9:30 A.M.–9:00 P.M., Monday–Saturday; 10:00 A.M.–6:00 P.M., Sunday
Credit Cards: Most stores accept major credit cards.
Personal Checks: Most stores accept personal checks.
Handicapped Accessible: Yes
Bus Tours: Yes
Outlets:
Banister Shoes
Carter's Childrenswear
Famous Brands Housewares
Gitano
Leather Loft
L'eggs/Hanes/Bali
Maidenform
Perfumania
Ribbon Outlet
Richard Roberts Jewelers
Sportshoe Center
Table de France Outlets, Inc.
Westport Ltd.

LATHAM

Burlington Coat Factory
Routes 9 and 155

Directions: From I–87 take exit 7 to intersection of Routes 9 and 155.
Phone: (518) 783–0465
Hours: 10:00 A.M.–9:00 P.M., Monday–Saturday; 11:00 A.M.–6:00 P.M., Sunday
Credit Cards: American Express, Discover, MasterCard, Visa

Personal Checks: Yes
Handicapped Accessible: Yes
Bus Tours: Yes

Dunham Footwear
Route 9, 898 New Loudon Road

Directions: From I–87 take exit 7 and go left at the traffic light. Store is the second building on the right, 1/4 mile from the Latham Circle.
Phone: (518) 785–8366
Hours: 9:00 A.M.–9:00 P.M., Monday–Friday; 9:00 A.M.–8:00 P.M., Saturday; 11:00 A.M.–5:00 P.M., Sunday
Credit Cards: American Express, Discover, MasterCard, Visa
Personal Checks: Yes
Handicapped Accessible: Yes
Bus Tours: Yes

Latham Outlet Mall
400 Old Loudon Road

Directions: Off I–87, exit 7, at the intersection of Routes 9 and 9R
Phone: (518) 785–8200
Hours: 10:00 A.M.–6:00 P.M., Sunday–Thursday; 10:00 A.M.–9:00 P.M., Friday and Saturday
Credit Cards: MasterCard, Visa
Personal Checks: Most stores accept personal checks.
Handicapped Accessible: Yes
Bus Tours: Yes
Outlets:
harvé benard
La Chine Classics
Lenox Crystal & China
Nettle Creek
Oneida Ltd.
Statuary
Van Heusen

MALTA

Saratoga Village Factory Outlets
100 Saratoga Village Boulevard

Directions: From I–87 take exit 12
Phone: (518) 899–2000
Hours: 10:00 A.M.–6:00 P.M., Monday–Saturday; noon–5:00 P.M., Sunday (May through December, until 9:00 P.M. Thursday and Friday)
Credit Cards: Most stores accept major credit cards.
Personal Checks: Yes
Handicapped Accessible: Yes
Bus Tours: Yes
Special Savings: Group discounts available.
Food: Available
Outlets:

Adidas Outlet
Adrienne Vittadini
Aileen
Banister Shoes
Bass Shoe
Bruce Alan Bags, Etc.
Bugle Boy
Cambridge Dry Goods
Cape Isle Knitters
Carol Little
Carter's Childrenswear
Coat World
Corning/Revere
Crazy Horse
Diane Freis
Ellen Tracy

Fashion Flair
Gitano Warehouse Clearance
   Center
Housewares Store
Joan & David Outlet
Jones New York
L'eggs/Hanes/Bali
Lots of Linens
Prestige Fragrance & Cosmetics
Royal Doulton
Sergio Valente
Sweaters, Ski & Sport
Toy Liquidators
Van Heusen
Wallet Works

MONTICELLO

Apollo Plaza Manufacturers Outlet Center
East Broadway

Directions: From Route 17 take exit 106
Phone: (914) 794–2010
Hours: Labor Day through Memorial Day, 10:00 A.M.–7:00 P.M., Monday–Saturday; 11:00 A.M.–5:00 P.M., Sunday; plus extended winter holiday hours. Memorial Day through Labor Day, 10:00 A.M.–9:00 P.M., Monday–Saturday; 10:00 A.M.–6:00 P.M., Sunday. Closed Thanksgiving, Christmas, New Year's Day, and Easter.
Credit Cards: Most stores accept major credit cards.
Personal Checks: Most stores accept personal checks.
Handicapped Accessible: Yes
Bus Tours: Yes
Notes or Attractions: Near Catskill Mountains resorts
Outlets:

Aileen Factory Outlet
American Tourister
Banister Shoes
Barbizon Lingerie
Bass
Big Ben Jewelers
Carter's Childrenswear
Corning/Revere
Damon Shirts
Fashion Flair/Izod
Fieldcrest Cannon
Gitano
harvé benard
Hathaway Olga/Warner

Jonathan Logan Outlet
Kitchen Collection
Leslie Fay
Little Red Shoe House
London Fog
Manhattan
Mothercare
Names for Dames featuring
    Adolfo
Socks Plus
Top of the Line Cosmetics
Toy Liquidators
Van Heusen
Westport LTD.

MOUNT KISCO

Dansk Factory Outlet
14 South Moger Avenue

Directions: From Saw Mill Parkway, Mount Kisco exit, take Route 133 East into Mount Kisco; right onto South Moger Avenue. Store is on the right side.
Phone: (914) 666–6616
Hours: 9:30 A.M.–6:00 P.M., Monday–Wednesday, Friday, and Saturday; 9:30 A.M.–8:00 P.M., Thursday; 11:00 A.M.–5:00 P.M., Sunday
Credit Cards: MasterCard, Visa
Personal Checks: Yes
Handicapped Accessible: Yes
Bus Tours: Yes

Mount Kisco Outlet Mall
Saw Mill River Parkway

Directions: Take Saw Mill River Parkway to the Kisco Avenue exit; turn left onto Kisco and left again at the first traffic light
Phone: (914) 666–2942
Hours: 10:00 A.M.–9:00 P.M., Monday–Friday; 10:00 A.M.–6:00 P.M., Saturday; noon–5:00 P.M., Sunday
Credit Cards: Most stores accept major credit cards
Personal Checks: Yes
Handicapped Accessible: Yes; elevators and handicapped parking.
Bus Tours: Yes, if notified in advance. Special side parking lot for buses.

Outlets:

Aileen	Gentlemen's Wearhouse
Bass Shoe	Geoffrey Beene
Bugle Boy	Old Mill
By the Yard	Royal Book Outlet
Cape Isle Knitters	Socks Galore & More
Capezio	Toy Liquidators
E. K. Bags	Van Heusen
Famous Brands	Welcome Home
Housewares Outlet	Westchester Apparel
Famous Footwear	World Fare Trading

NEW ROCHELLE

Bally
One Bally Place

Directions: From I–95 North take exit 16; bear left and turn right at the stop sign; go under the bridge. Stay in the right-hand lane to Huguenot Street, and the next street is Bally.
Phone: (914) 576–3230
Hours: 10:00 A.M.–8:00 P.M., Monday–Friday; 10:00 A.M.–6:00 P.M., Saturday; noon–5:00 P.M., Sunday
Credit Cards: American Express, MasterCard, Visa
Personal Checks: Yes
Handicapped Accessible: Yes
Bus Tours: Yes

Lillian Vernon
549 Main Street

Directions: From I–95 North take exit 15 to Main Street
Phone: (914) 636–4294
Hours: 10:00 A.M.–6:00 P.M., Monday–Saturday
Credit Cards: American Express, Diners Club, Discover, MasterCard, Visa
Personal Checks: Yes
Handicapped Accessible: Yes
Bus Tours: Yes

NEW YORK CITY

Fur Vault
41 W. Fifty-Seventh Street

Directions: Between Fifth Avenue and Avenue of the Americas
Phone: (212) 754–1177

Hours: 10:00 A.M.–6:30 P.M., Monday–Saturday; noon–5:00 P.M., Sunday
Credit Cards: American Express, Diners Club, Discover, MasterCard, Visa
Personal Checks: Yes
Handicapped Accessible: Yes
Bus Tours: Yes

Soho Mill Outlet
490 Broadway

Directions: Between Broome and Spring streets
Phone: (212) 226–8040
Hours: 10:00 A.M.–6:00 P.M., Monday–Wednesday; 10:00 A.M.–7:00 P.M., Thursday and Friday; 11:00 A.M.–7:00 P.M., Saturday; 11:00 A.M.–6:00 P.M., Sunday
Credit Cards: American Express, MasterCard, Visa
Personal Checks: Yes
Handicapped Accessible: Yes
Bus Tours: No

NIAGARA FALLS

Niagara Factory Outlet Mall
1900 Military Road

Directions: Take I–190 to Route 62 East; turn left onto Military Road
Phone: (716) 297–2022
Hours: 10:00 A.M.–9:00 P.M., Monday–Saturday; 10:00 A.M.–5:00 P.M., Sunday
Credit Cards: Most stores accept major credit cards.
Personal Checks: Most stores accept personal checks.
Handicapped Accessible: Yes
Bus Tours: Yes
Food: Available
Notes or Attractions: Currency exchange

Outlets:

Aileen
Banister Shoes
Bare Necessities
Bass Shoes
Benetton
Booksellers Warehouse
Calvin Klein
Caron Yarn
Corning/Revere
Danskin Outlet
Famous Footwear
Fanny Farmer
Fashion Factory
Fashion Shoe Outlet
Freddy's Discount Drugs
harvé benard
Hit or Miss
Jaeger Outlet
Kitchen Place
L'eggs/Hanes/Bali
Linens 'n Things
Mikasa
Nautica
Old Mill Outlet
OshKosh B'Gosh
Paper Outlet
Pfaltzgraff
Polo/Ralph Lauren
Royal Doulton
Ruff Hewn
Shoeworks
SneaKee Feet
Swank Outlet
Top of the Line Cosmetics
totes
Van Heusen
Warehouse
Welcome Home

Rainbow Centre Factory Outlet

302 Rainbow Boulevard North

Directions: One hundred yards from Rainbow Bridge and ½ block from Niagara Falls in downtown Niagara

Phone: (716) 285–9758 or (716) 285–5525, information booth

Hours: 10:00 A.M.–9:00 P.M., Monday–Saturday; 11:00 A.M.–6:00 P.M., Sunday (winter, noon–5:00 P.M.)

Credit Cards: Most stores accept major credit cards.

Personal Checks: Most stores accept personal checks.

Handicapped Accessible: Yes

Bus Tours: Yes

Food: Available

Notes or Attractions: Shopping and hotel packages available. Enclosed walkway to Radisson and Hilton hotels; other hotels nearby.

Outlets:

Athlete's Den Outlet
Bass Shoe Outlet
Bleyle
Boston Traders Outlet
Burlington Coat Factory
Candy Barrel Outlet
Claire's Outlet Boutique
Deb Fashion Outlet
Esprit Outlet
Fowler's Chocolate Factory
Gitano Warehouse Clearance
    Center
Green Onion Kitchen Shoppe
JH Collectibles
Jindo Furs
Kay Bee Toys
Land & Seas
Leatherland
Leather Loft

London Fog
Morey's Jewelers
Payless ShoeSource
Polo/Ralph Lauren
Ports of the Orient
Potpourri
Prestige Fragrance and Cosmetics
Radio Shack
Remembrance Shoppe
Rings N' Things
Rite-Aid
Secaucus Handbags
Sheri's Moccasin Outlet
Socks Galore & More
Sunglasses Outlet
U.S.A. Outlet
Van Heusen
Waldenbooks
Watch Outlet

ROCHESTER

Burlington Coat Factory
South Town Plaza
3333 West Henrietta Road

Directions: Take I–390 North to Jefferson Road (Route 252 West) to Route 50. Store is on the southwest corner of Routes 252 and 50.
Phone: (716) 292–5110
Hours: 10:00 A.M.–9:00 P.M., Monday–Saturday; 11:00 A.M.–6:00 P.M., Sunday
Credit Cards: American Express, Discover, MasterCard, Visa
Personal Checks: Yes, with identification
Handicapped Accessible: Yes
Bus Tours: Yes

Panorama Outlet Mall
1601 Penfield Road

Directions: Take I–490 to the Penfield Road exit. Turn left at the light at the bottom of the ramp. Drive 3½ miles to plaza on the right.
Phone: (716) 586–3992 or (716) 586–3135
Credit Cards: Most stores accept major credit cards.
Personal Checks: Yes
Handicapped Accessible: Yes
Bus Tours: No
Notes or Attractions: This mall has some two dozen factory outlets and an additional four dozen retail stores, theaters, and restaurants
Outlets:
Aileen
Banister Shoes
Bare Necessities
Booksellers Warehouse
Dress Barn
Endicott Johnson
Famous Footwear
Fanny Farmer
Fashion Bug
Hit or Miss
Linens 'n Things
$9.99 Stockroom
She House
Shoe Works
Sneakee Feet
Van Heusen
Windsor Shirt Outlet

ROME

Corning/Revere Store
100 S. James Street

Directions: From the New York Thruway, take exit 31 to Liberty Plaza

Phone: (315) 337–7828
Hours: 9:00 A.M.–5:00 P.M., Monday–Saturday
Credit Cards: Discover, MasterCard, Visa
Personal Checks: Yes
Handicapped Accessible: Yes
Bus Tours: Yes

SCHENECTADY

Champion Factory Outlet
Crosstown Plaza

Directions: Route 7 at Watt Street
Phone: (518) 381–4186
Hours: 10:00 A.M.–9:00 P.M., Monday–Saturday; noon–5:00 P.M., Sunday
Credit Cards: Discover, MasterCard, Visa
Personal Checks: Yes, with driver's license
Handicapped Accessible: Yes; handicapped dressing room.
Bus Tours: Yes

Newberry Knitting Co., Inc.
1420 Curry Road

Directions: From I–890 take the Chrysler Avenue exit to the traffic light. Turn left onto Altamont Avenue and proceed to Curry Road. Store is on the left.
Phone: (518) 355–1630
Hours: 9:00 A.M.–4:00 P.M., Monday–Friday; 10:00 A.M.–1:00 P.M., Saturday
Credit Cards: MasterCard, Visa
Personal Checks: Yes
Handicapped Accessible: Steps
Bus Tours: Yes

SHERRILL

Oneida Silversmiths
Sherrill Road

Directions: From Route 5 turn left at Sherrill Road; stay to your right at the Y, and turn left at the next left. Store is on the right-hand side in the shopping plaza.
Phone: (315) 361–3661
Hours: 9:00 A.M.–5:30 P.M., Monday–Saturday; noon–5:00 P.M., Sunday
Credit Cards: MasterCard, Visa
Personal Checks: Yes, with proper identification
Handicapped Accessible: Yes
Bus Tours: Yes

SYRACUSE

Syracuse China
2301 Teall Avenue

Directions: From I–690 take the Teall Avenue exit. Store is on your left.
Phone: (315) 455–5818
Hours: 9:00 A.M.–9:00 P.M., Monday–Friday; 9:00 A.M.–5:00 P.M., Saturday; 11:00 A.M.–5:00 P.M., Sunday
Credit Cards: Discover, MasterCard, Visa
Personal Checks: Yes
Handicapped Accessible: Yes
Bus Tours: Yes

WATKINS GLEN

Famous Brands
412 N. Franklin Street

Directions: Take Route 14 toward Montour Falls. Store is on the right-hand side, on North Franklin, about 3 miles before Watkins Glen.
Phone: (607) 535–4952
Hours: 9:00 A.M.–5:30 P.M., Monday–Wednesday and Saturday; 9:00 A.M.–9:00 P.M., Thursday and Friday; 11:00 A.M.–5:00 P.M., Sunday
Credit Cards: Discover, MasterCard, Visa
Personal Checks: Yes; must be from New York State banks
Handicapped Accessible: Yes
Bus Tours: Yes

WEST SENECA

Burlington Mall
1881 Ridge Road

Directions: Take I–90 to the Ridge Road exit to the mall
Phone: (716) 675–4394
Hours: 10:00 A.M.–9:00 P.M., Monday–Saturday; 11:00 A.M.–5:00 P.M., Sunday
Credit Cards: MasterCard, Visa
Personal Checks: Yes
Handicapped Accessible: Yes
Bus Tours: Yes
Food: Available on both sides of Ridge Road
Outlets:
Burlington Coat Factory
Champion
Famous Footwear
Fashion Bug Plus
Freddy's Discount Drugs

Hit or Miss
Kids Port USA
Linens 'n Things
Madd Maxx
N.W.S. Electronics Outlet
Old Mill
Shoe Town
Van Heusen

WILLIAMSVILLE

Transitown Plaza
4175 Transit Road

Directions: From the New York Thruway, take exit 49 (Transit Road), and turn left. Store is in plaza about ½ mile down the road on the right-hand side.
Phone: (716) 633–5266
Hours: 10:00 A.M.–9:00 P.M., Monday–Saturday; some stores open noon–5:00 P.M. on Sunday
Credit Cards: Most stores accept major credit cards.
Personal Checks: Yes
Handicapped Accessible: Yes
Bus Tours: Yes
Notes or Attractions: Mixed-use mall
Outlets:
Champion
Fashion Flair
Van Heusen

PENNSYLVANIA

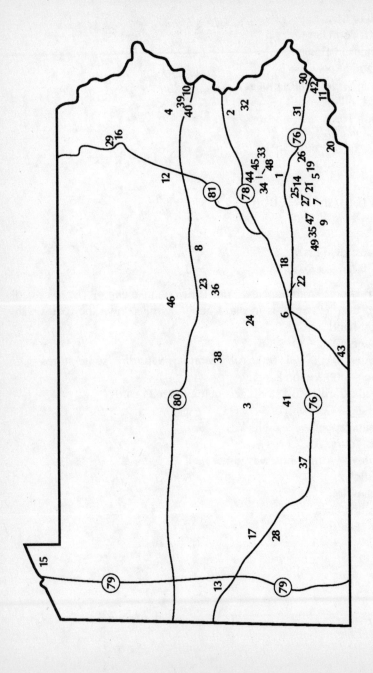

PENNSYLVANIA

In Pennsylvania there is no tax on clothing and shoes.

1. Adamstown
2. Allentown
3. Altoona
4. Bartonsville
5. Bird-in-Hand
6. Carlisle
7. Columbia
8. Danville
9. East Prospect
10. East Stroudsburg
11. Eddyston
12. Edwardsville
13. Ellwood City
14. Ephrata
15. Erie
16. Eynon
17. Greensburg
18. Harrisburg
19. Intercourse
20. Kennett Square
21. Lancaster
22. Lemoyne
23. Lewisburg
24. Lewistown
25. Lititz
26. Morgantown
27. Mount Joy
28. Mount Pleasant
29. Olyphant
30. Philadelphia
31. Phoenixville
32. Quakertown
33. Reading
34. Robesonia
35. Ronks
36. Shamokin Dam
37. Somerset
38. State College
39. Stroudsburg
40. Tannersville
41. Three Springs
42. Upper Darby
43. Waynesboro
44. West Lawn
45. West Reading
46. Williamsport
47. Wrightsville
48. Wyomissing
49. York

ADAMSTOWN

George W. Bollman & Co. Inc.
Direct Factory Outlet
Route 272 and Willow Street

Directions: From the Pennsylvania Turnpike take exit 21 to Route 272 North (right); store is 3 miles down, on the right-hand side
Phone: (215) 484–4615
Hours: 9:00 A.M.–5:00 P.M., Monday–Friday; 9:00 A.M.–4:00 P.M., Saturday; noon–4:00 P.M., Sunday
Credit Cards: MAC, MasterCard, Visa
Personal Checks: No
Handicapped Accessible: Yes
Bus Tours: Yes

ALLENTOWN

Astor Swimwear Outlet
1710 MacArthur Road

Directions: From the Pennsylvania Turnpike take exit 22 (MacArthur Road) to the jug handle past Lehigh Valley Mall on the right. Take the jug handle all the way around to the store, which is on the southbound side.
Phone: (215) 439–8791
Hours: 10:00 A.M.–5:00 P.M., Monday–Wednesday and Saturday; 10:00 A.M.–9:00 P.M., Thursday and Friday; 11:00 A.M.–4:00 P.M., Sunday
Credit Cards: MasterCard, Visa
Personal Checks: Yes
Handicapped Accessible: Yes
Bus Tours: Yes

ALTOONA

Benzel's Pretzel
5200 Sixth Avenue

Directions: From the Pennsylvania Turnpike take the Bedford exit (Route 22 North) to Sixth Avenue and Fifty-Second Street
Phone: (814) 942–5062
Hours: 9:00 A.M.–5:00 P.M., Monday–Friday; 9:00 A.M.–1:00 P.M., Saturday
Credit Cards: No
Personal Checks: Yes
Handicapped Accessible: Yes
Bus Tours: Yes
Notes or Attractions: Factory tour

Warnaco Outlet
El Dorado Plaza
Sixth Avenue

Directions: From the Pennsylvania Turnpike take the Bedford exit (Route 22 North) to Sixth Avenue and Fifty-Second Street
Phone: (814) 942–2240
Hours: 10:00 A.M.–8:00 P.M., Monday–Saturday; noon–5:00 P.M., Sunday
Credit Cards: American Express, MasterCard, Visa
Personal Checks: Yes
Handicapped Accessible: Yes; wheelchair ramp available at far end of the parking lot
Bus Tours: Yes

BARTONSVILLE

American Candle
Route 611

Directions: From I–80 take exit 46 North; turn left, and go ½ mile. Store is on the left.
Phone: (717) 629–3388
Hours: 9:30 A.M.–5:30 P.M., Sunday–Thursday; 9:30 A.M.–9:00 P.M., Friday and Saturday
Credit Cards: American Express, Diner's Club, Discover, MasterCard, Visa
Personal Checks: Yes, with driver's license and two credit cards.
Handicapped Accessible: Yes
Bus Tours: Yes

BIRD-IN-HAND

Kindermart
Route 340 and Maple Avenue

Directions: Take Route 30 to Route 340 East for 4 miles, going under the railroad bridge. Store is in Farmers' Market, on the right side of the road.
Phone: (717) 397–5385
Hours: 9:00 A.M.–5:00 P.M., Monday–Thursday; 8:30 A.M.–5:30 P.M., Friday and Saturday
Credit Cards: Discover, MasterCard, Visa
Personal Checks: Yes
Handicapped Accessible: Yes
Bus Tours: Yes

Susquehanna Glass
Box 150, Route 340

Directions: Take Route 30 to Route 340 East for 4 miles, going under the railroad bridge. Store is in Farmers' Market, on the right side of the road.

Phone: (717) 393–5670
Hours: 9:00 A.M.–5:00 P.M., Monday–Saturday
Credit Cards: MasterCard, Visa
Personal Checks: Yes
Handicapped Accessible: Yes
Bus Tours: Yes

CARLISLE

Butcher Block
MJ Carlisle Mall
Noble Boulevard

Directions: From I–81 take exit 14; turn left and proceed to the traffic light; turn left again and proceed to MJ Carlisle Mall
Phone: (717) 243–1990
Hours: 10:00 A.M.–9:00 P.M., Monday–Saturday; noon–5:00 P.M., Sunday
Credit Cards: MasterCard, Visa
Personal Checks: Yes
Handicapped Accessible: Yes
Bus Tours: Yes

COLUMBIA

Columbia Garment Co.
304 Union Street

Directions: Take Route 30 East to the Columbia exit (south). Turn right onto Linden Street. Turn left onto Third Street and drive 7 blocks to the corner of Third and Union.
Phone: (717) 684–2306
Hours: 9:00 A.M.–4:00 P.M., Monday–Friday; 8:00 A.M.–1:00 P.M., Saturday

Credit Cards: MasterCard, Visa
Personal Checks: Yes
Handicapped Accessible: Entrance has two steps.
Bus Tours: Yes

Susquehanna Glass Outlet and Clearance Center
731 Avenue H

Directions: From Route 30 take the Third Street exit; turn right onto Third Street, proceeding to the second traffic light, Locust Street. Turn left and proceed to Seventh Street; turn right, and go up the alley in the middle of the block.
Phone: (717) 684–2155
Hours: 10:00 A.M.–5:00 P.M., Monday–Saturday
Credit Cards: MasterCard, Visa
Personal Checks: Yes
Handicapped Accessible: Yes, with some assistance
Bus Tours: Yes, if notified in advance

DANVILLE

Danville Factory Outlet
327 Ferry Street

Directions: Take I–83 to Routes 11 and 15 to Danville. Go to the third traffic light and turn right onto Ferry Street. Turn right into Cole's Hardware parking lot. Store is across the street.
Phone: (717) 275–3410
Hours: 10:00 A.M.–5:00 p.m, Monday–Thursday and Saturday; 10:00 A.M.–6:00 P.M., Friday
Credit Cards: MasterCard, Visa
Personal Checks: Yes
Handicapped Accessible: Yes
Bus Tours: Yes

EAST PROSPECT

East Prospect Factory Outlet
16 W. Maple Street

Directions: From I–83 North take exit 7 (East Prospect). Drive for 12 miles to the center of the town, Maple Street.
Phone: (717) 252–4075
Hours: 10:00 A.M.–5:00 P.M., Monday–Friday; 9:00 A.M.–4:00 P.M., Saturday. Extended hours in summer.
Credit Cards: MasterCard, Visa
Personal Checks: Yes
Handicapped Accessible: Yes
Bus Tours: Yes

EAST STROUDSBURG

Dollar Save Outlet
Business Route 209 and Route 447 South

Directions: Take I–80 to exit 52 east. Turn left at Route 447. Drive about 2½ miles to end of road.
Phone: (717) 421–5379
Hours: 10:00 A.M.–5:00 P.M., Monday–Saturday; 11:00 A.M.–5:00 P.M., Sunday
Credit Cards: Discover, MasterCard, Visa
Personal Checks: Yes
Handicapped Accessible: Yes, some steps
Bus Tours: No

Foxmoor Factory Outlets
Route 209

Directions: From I–80, take exit 52 to Route 209 North, Marshalls Creek

Phone: (717) 223–8706
Hours: 10:00 A.M.–6:00 P.M., Sunday–Wednesday; 10:00 A.M.–8:00 P.M., Thursday–Saturday
Credit Cards: Most stores accept major credit cards
Personal Checks: Yes
Handicapped Accessible: Yes
Bus Tours: Yes
Outlets:
Arrow
Bon Worth
Book Warehouse
Bugle Boy
Cami'z
Capezio
Fragrance Cove
Lots of Linens
Westport Ltd

Pocono Candle Shop
Directions: Take I–80 to exit 48, Business Route 209 east (Main Street); proceed to 9th and turn right.
Phone: (717) 421–1832
Hours: 10:00 A.M.–5:00 P.M., Sunday–Saturday
Credit Cards: MasterCard, Visa
Personal Checks: Yes
Handicapped Accessible: Yes
Bus Tours: Yes

EDDYSTON

Scotfoam Corporation (Foamex)
1500 East Second Street
Directions: Take I–95 North to exit 6, Avenue of the States. Turn right at the first traffic light; proceed to the second traffic light and turn left onto 9th Street. Turn right at the first traffic light to Eddystone Avenue;

proceed to 2nd Street (dead end) and turn left. Drive past the stop sign to the second building on the left.
Phone: (215) 876–6212
Hours: 8:30 A.M.–4:15 P.M., Tuesday–Friday; 8:30 A.M.–3:00 P.M., Saturday
Credit Cards: MasterCard, Visa
Personal Checks: Yes
Handicapped Accessible: Yes
Bus Tours: Yes

EDWARDSVILLE

C. A. Reed
Gateway Shopping Center

Directions: Off Route 309
Phone: (717) 283–1918
Hours: 9:00 A.M.–5:00 P.M., Monday–Saturday
Credit Cards: No
Personal Checks: Yes
Handicapped Accessible: Yes
Bus Tours: Yes

Rolane Factory Outlet
300 Wilkes-Barre Township Boulevard

Directions: From I–81 take the Mount Top–Blackman Street exit, bearing right to Route 309. Go past three traffic lights and past Cole Street. Store is on the left.
Phone: (717) 822–1785
Hours: 10:00 A.M.–5:30 P.M., Monday–Thursday and Saturday; 10:00 A.M.–8:30 P.M., Friday; noon–5:00 P.M., Sunday
Credit Cards: Discover, MasterCard, Visa
Personal Checks: Yes
Handicapped Accessible: Yes
Bus Tours: Yes

Flemington Fashion Outlet
West Side Mall

Directions: From I–81 take the Wilkes-Barre exit to Route 115, toward Wilkes-Barre, to the bypass. Take the Kingston exit; then turn left. Turn right at the second light and proceed to Wyoming Avenue. Turn left onto Wyoming Avenue and drive to Northampton Street; turn left and proceed to the store.
Phone: (717) 283–0890
Hours: 10:00 A.M.–9:00 P.M., Monday–Saturday; noon–5:00 P.M., Sunday
Credit Cards: MasterCard, Visa
Personal Checks: Yes
Handicapped Accessible: Yes
Bus Tours: No

ELLWOOD CITY

Airway Luggage Outlet
1000 Beaver Avenue

Directions: From the Pennsylvania Turnpike take exit 2 (Beaver Valley North) to the second traffic light, Route 351. Take Route 351 for 2 miles, to the Morrow Ford garage; make a left turn and drive to the back of the building.
Phone: (412) 758–9030
Hours: 9:00 A.M.–6:00 P.M., Monday–Saturday
Credit Cards: No
Personal Checks: Yes
Handicapped Accessible: Yes
Bus Tours: Yes

EPHRATA

Cobbler's Factory Outlet
514 North Reading Road

Directions: Off Route 272, 1½ miles north of Ephrata
Phone: (717) 733–1005
Hours: 9:00 A.M.–5:00 P.M., Monday–Thursday and Saturday; 9:00 A.M.–9:00 P.M., Friday; noon–4:00 P.M., Sunday
Credit Cards: MasterCard, Visa
Personal Checks: Yes
Handicapped Accessible: Yes
Bus Tours: Yes

LMC Factory Store
978 East Main Street

Directions: From the Pennsylvania Turnpike take exit 21 onto Route 222 South. Drive to the first exit, Route 322 East. Store is on the left-hand side of the road.
Phone: (717) 738–2026
Hours: 9:30 A.M.–4:00 P.M., Monday–Friday; 9:30 A.M.–2:00 P.M., Saturday
Credit Cards: MasterCard, Visa
Personal Checks: Yes, local only
Handicapped Accessible: No
Bus Tours: Yes

ERIE

Blair New Process Company
3016 W. Lake Road

Directions: Take I–79 to the West Twelfth Street exit; go west to fourth

traffic light, Route 832. Turn right and proceed to first traffic light, West Eighth Street. Turn left, and store is 800 feet down, on right-hand side of street.
Phone: (814) 838–6541
Hours: 9:00 A.M.–6:00 P.M., Monday–Saturday
Credit Cards: MasterCard, Visa
Personal Checks: Yes
Handicapped Accessible: Yes
Bus Tours: Yes

Erie Center Factory Outlet Mall
1638 Peach Street

Directions: Take I–90 to the Peach Street North exit to Eighteenth Street
Phone: (814) 454–4541
Hours: 10:00 A.M.–6:00 P.M., Sunday–Wednesday; 10:00 A.M.–8:00 P.M., Thursday–Saturday
Credit Cards: Most stores accept major credit cards.
Personal Checks: Yes
Handicapped Accessible: Yes
Bus Tours: Yes
Outlets:
Draperies, Etc.
$9.99 Storeroom
Paper Factory
Van Heusen

EYNON

London Fog Factory Outlet
Route 6

Directions: From the Scranton-Carbondale Highway, turn west onto Providence Road. Turn right on Albright and turn right on Grove Street (Route 6).
Phone: (717) 876–5611

Hours: 11:00 A.M.–9:00 P.M., Monday–Saturday; 11:00 A.M.–6:00 P.M., Sunday
Credit Cards: MasterCard, Visa
Personal Checks: Yes
Handicapped Accessible: Yes
Bus Tours: Yes

GREENSBURG

Westmoreland Outlet World
Donohoe Road

Directions: Take Route 30 to Westmoreland Outlet World
Phone: (412) 837–8810
Hours: 10:00 A.M.–9:00 P.M., Monday–Saturday; noon–5:00 P.M., Sunday
Credit Cards: Most stores accept major credit cards.
Personal Checks: Yes
Handicapped Accessible: Yes
Bus Tours: Yes
Food: Available
Outlets:
Art and Frame Outlet
Beer Arena
Lighthouse Factory Outlet
O'Furniture
Wholesale Stores Incorporated
World of Values

HARRISBURG

Branded Shoe Outlet
Colonial Park Plaza
Route 22 and Colonial Road

Directions: Take I–83 to the Colonial Park exit. Turn right onto Colonial Road. Proceed to plaza on right.

Phone: (717) 545–5238
Hours: 10:00 A.M.–9:00 P.M., Monday–Saturday; noon–5:00 P.M., Sunday
Credit Cards: Discover, MasterCard, Visa
Personal Checks: Yes
Handicapped Accessible: Yes
Bus Tours: Yes

Cobbler's Factory Outlet
17 Kline Village

Directions: Take Route 322 to Paxtang Avenue North to Market Street
West to North Twenty-Fifth Street
Phone: (717) 234–0446
Hours: 10:00 A.M.–6:00 P.M., Monday–Saturday
Credit Cards: MasterCard, Visa
Personal Checks: Yes
Handicapped Accessible: No
Bus Tours: No

INTERCOURSE

Old Candle Barn Outlet
Route 340

Directions: On Route 340, Main Street
Phone: (717) 768–3231
Hours: 8:00 A.M.–5:00 P.M., Monday–Saturday
Credit Cards: No
Personal Checks: No
Handicapped Accessible: Yes
Bus Tours: Yes

KENNETT SQUARE

Bostonian Factory Outlet
741 W. Cypress Street

Directions: Take I–95 to Route 52 North to Route 1 South for about 2 miles, to the Kennett Square exit. Turn left at the fourth traffic light, onto West Cypress Street.
Phone: (215) 444–3759
Hours: 10:00 A.M.–6:00 P.M., Monday–Wednesday and Saturday; 10:00 A.M.–9:00 P.M., Thursday and Friday; noon–5:00 P.M., Sunday
Credit Cards: Discover, MasterCard, Visa
Personal Checks: Yes
Handicapped Accessible: Yes
Bus Tours: Yes

LANCASTER

Astor Swimwear Outlet
1461 Manheim Pike

Directions: Take Route 283 to Route 72 (Manheim Pike). Outlet is on the left.
Phone: (717) 299–4315
Hours: 10:00 A.M.–5:00 P.M., Monday–Wednesday and Saturday; 10:00 A.M.–9:00 P.M., Thursday and Friday; 11:00 A.M.–4:00 P.M., Sunday
Credit Cards: MasterCard, Visa
Personal Checks: Yes
Handicapped Accessible: Yes
Bus Tours: No

Black & Decker Reconditioned Outlet
118 Keller Avenue

Directions: From Route 30 take the Fruitville Pike exit. Turn left at the

bottom of the ramp. Drive through two more traffic lights, and turn left on Keller Avenue. Store is on the right-hand side.
Phone: (717) 393–5251
Hours: 8:00 A.M.–5:00 P.M., Monday–Friday; 9:00 A.M.–noon, Saturday
Credit Cards: Discover, MasterCard, Visa
Personal Checks: Yes
Handicapped Accessible: Yes, with assistance
Bus Tours: No

The Braun Company
2298 Willow Street Pike

Directions: From Route 30 take the Route 222 South exit to the brick Cape Cod building on the right-hand side
Phone: (717) 464–3378
Hours: 10:00 A.M.–6:00 P.M., Monday–Wednesday, Friday, and Saturday; 10:00 A.M.–8:00 P.M., Thursday
Credit Cards: Discover, MasterCard, Visa
Personal Checks: Yes
Handicapped Accessible: Yes
Bus Tours: No

Charles Chips
1008 Ivy Drive

Directions: From Route 30 take the Mountville exit; turn left and proceed for about 1 mile to the traffic light, turning onto Stony Battery Road. Store is in a little white barn in a driveway on the left, across from the Four Seasons sporting complex.
Phone: (717) 898–2945
Hours: 9:00 A.M.–5:00 P.M., Monday–Friday; 9:00 A.M.–noon, Saturday
Credit Cards: No
Personal Checks: Yes, local only
Handicapped Accessible: No
Bus Tours: No

Fashion Flair
1929 Lincoln Highway East

Directions: Take Route 462 east to Lincoln Highway East
Phone: (717) 393–9332
Hours: 9:30 A.M.–9:00 P.M., Monday–Saturday; noon–5:00 P.M., Sunday
Credit Cards: American Express, Discover, MasterCard, Visa
Personal Checks: Yes, with driver's license
Handicapped Accessible: Yes
Bus Tours: Yes

Lancaster Outlet City
Lancaster Outlet City Drive

Directions: Off Route 30, 4 miles east of Lancaster, on the right
Phone: (717) 392–7202, recording
Hours: 10:00 A.M.–9:00 P.M., Monday–Saturday; noon–5:00 P.M., Sunday; closed Easter, Thanksgiving, Christmas, and New Year's Day.
Credit Cards: MasterCard, Visa
Personal Checks: Yes, with proper identification
Handicapped Accessible: Yes
Bus Tours: Yes
Food: Available
Outlets:
Aileen
All-in-One Linens
Annie Sez
Argo
Bauer's Shoe Outlet
Cambridge Dry Goods
Delta Hosiery Outlet
Flemington Fashion Outlet
Flemington Fashion Outlet Plus
H. L. Miller Tops & Tees
International Footwear
Manhattan
Murray's Menswear
Pottery Factory Outlet

RockBottom Jeans
Shap's
Sweater Mill
Touch of Class
Windsor Shirt Company

Lancaster Pottery & Glass Outlet
2335 Lincoln Highway East

Directions: Route 30 East
Phone: (717) 299–6835
Hours: 9:00 A.M.–9:00 P.M., Monday–Saturday; 9:00 A.M.–6:00 P.M., Sunday
Credit Cards: Discover, MasterCard, Visa
Personal Checks: Yes, with driver's license
Handicapped Accessible: Yes
Bus Tours: Yes

Quality Centers
Routes 30 and 896

Directions: On left-hand side of the road at Routes 30 and 896.
Phone: (717) 299–1949
Hours: April–December, 9:30 A.M.–9:00 P.M., Monday–Saturday; 11:00 A.M.–5:00 P.M., Sunday. January–March, 9:30 A.M.–6:00 P.M., Monday–Saturday; noon–5:00 P.M., Sunday.
Credit Cards: MasterCard, Visa
Personal Checks: Yes
Handicapped Accessible: Yes
Bus Tours: Yes
Outlets:
Delta Hosiery Mill Outlet
Fanny Farmer
Fieldcrest Canon
Gold Exchange
Manhattan
Mikasa

Royal Doulton
Top of the Line
Villeroy & Boch
Waterford Wedgwood

Rockvale Square Factory Outlet Village
35 S. Willowdale Drive

Directions: Off Route 30 East and Route 896
Phone: (717) 293–9595
Hours: March 16–December 31, 9:30 A.M.–9:00 P.M., Monday–Saturday; noon–5:00 P.M., Sunday. January 1–March 15, 10:00 A.M.–6:00 P.M., Monday–Saturday; noon–5:00 P.M., Sunday.
Credit Cards: Most stores accept major credit cards.
Personal Checks: Most stores accept personal checks.
Handicapped Accessible: Yes
Bus Tours: Yes
Food: Available. Ten buildings, with double-decker shuttle-bus service; 113-unit Rockvale Village Inn (717–293–9500)
Outlets:

Building 1
Corning-Revere
Dress Barn
Dress Barn Woman
Eagle's Eye
Factory Linens
Jonathan Logan Outlet
L'eggs/Hanes/Bali
Little Red Shoe House
Neiss Collectibles
Petals
Pewtarex Store
Ribbon Outlet
Susquehanna Glass

Building 2
American Tourister
Banister Shoes

Famous Brands Housewares
  Outlet
Fashion Flair
Geoffrey Beene
Kitchen Collection
Oneida
Toy Liquidators
Van Heusen
VIP Outlet Center minimall
Warnaco

Building 3
Aileen
Aunt Mary's Yarns
Bon Worth
Brassworks
Executive Neckwear
Leather Loft

13

Names for Dames
  featuring Adolfo
Paper Factory
Pfaltzgraff
Prestige Fragrance & Cosmetics
QVC Network
Wallet Works

Building 4
Bargain Sneakers
Bass Shoe
Bruce Alan Bags, Etc.
Cape Isle Knitters
Champion Activewear Outlet
Crazy Horse
Evan-Picone
harvé benard
Just Coats N' Swimwear
Just My Size
Kids Barn
Knittery
Maidenform
Nettle Creek
Reed & Barton
Regal Outlet Store
Socks Galore & More
Sports Wearhouse
Sweaters & Ski & Sportswear
Welcome Home
Wicker Unlimited

Building 5
Hamilton Watch & Clock Shoppe
Kinder Bin
LF Factory Outlet

Building 6
Lenox Shop

Building 7
Bag & Baggage Luggage and
  Handbag
Barbizon
Book Warehouse
Cambridge Dry Goods
Footfactory
Gitano
Lady Leslie
Linens 'n Things
Mushroom
Music Den
Nilani
$9.99 Stockroom
Norty's
Town & Country Menswear
Val Mode Lingerie

Building 8
Bugle Boy
Dansk
Farah
London Fog Outlet
Windsor Shirt

Building 9
Reading China & Glass

Building 10
Specials, Exclusively Levi Strauss
  & Co.

totes Warehouse Store
220 Centerville Road

Directions: From Route 30 West take the Centerville exit; store is to the left as you come off the ramp
Phone: (717) 299–6526
Hours: 9:30 A.M.–5:30 P.M., Monday–Thursday and Saturday; 9:30 A.M.–8:00 P.M., Friday; noon–5:00 P.M., Sunday
Credit Cards: Discover, MasterCard, Visa
Personal Checks: Yes
Handicapped Accessible: Yes
Bus Tours: Yes

LEMOYNE

Cobbler's Factory Outlet
1004 Market Street

Directions: Take I–83 to U.S. 15 North to Market Street East; store is on the right
Phone: (717) 737–8425
Hours: 9:00 A.M.–5:00 P.M., Monday, Tuesday, Friday, and Saturday; 9:00 A.M.–8:00 P.M., Wednesday
Credit Cards: MasterCard, Visa
Personal Checks: Yes
Handicapped Accessible: Yes
Bus Tours: Yes, if notified in advance

LEWISBURG

Peddler's Wagon
Brookpark Farm
RD 2, Route 45 West

Directions: Take Route 45 West out of Lewisburg for 1 mile. Outlet is on the right.

Phone: (717) 524–7869
Hours: 10:00 A.M.–6:00 P.M., Monday–Thursday; 10:00 A.M.–8:00
P.M., Friday and Saturday; 11:00 A.M.–5:00 P.M., Sunday
Credit Cards: MasterCard, Visa
Personal Checks: Yes
Handicapped Accessible: Yes
Bus Tours: Yes
Food: Available

Rug Outlet
Brookpark Farm
RD 2, Route 45

Directions: Take Route 45 West out of Lewisburg for 1 mile. Outlet is
on the right.
Phone: (717) 524–9494
Hours: 9:00 A.M.–6:00 P.M., Monday–Saturday; 11:00 A.M.–5:00 P.M.,
Sunday. (Hours are approximate.)
Credit Cards: MasterCard, Visa
Personal Checks: Yes
Handicapped Accessible: Yes
Bus Tours: Yes

LEWISTOWN

Cobbler's Factory Outlet
1100 W. Fourth Street

Directions: Take Highway 22 West to Route 622; store is on the left
Phone: (717) 242–2030
Hours: 10:00 A.M.–6:00 P.M., Monday–Thursday and Saturday; 10:00
A.M.–8:00 P.M., Friday; noon–4:00 P.M., Sunday
Credit Cards: No
Personal Checks: Yes
Handicapped Accessible: Yes
Bus Tours: Yes

LITITZ

Wilbur Chocolate Factory Outlet
46 Broad Street

Directions: Take Route 501 north to Lititz to Broad Street
Phone: (717) 626–1131
Hours: 10:00 A.M.–5:00 P.M., Monday–Saturday
Credit Cards: No
Personal Checks: Yes
Handicapped Accessible: No
Bus Tours: Yes

MORGANTOWN

Manufacturers Outlet Mall
Exit 22 at the Pennsylvania Turnpike

Directions: Off the Pennsylvania Turnpike, at exit 22; follow signs to mall.
Phone: (215) 286–2000
Hours: 10:00 A.M.–9:00 P.M., Monday–Saturday; noon–5:00 P.M., Sunday
Credit Cards: Most stores accept major credit cards.
Personal Checks: Most stores accept personal checks.
Handicapped Accessible: Yes; carts available
Bus Tours: Yes
Food: Food court
Notes and Attractions: Hotel attached to mall
Outlets:

Aileen	Beauty Scenter
All-in-One Linen	Caroline's Treasure
Bag & Baggage Luggage and Handbag Outlet	Cluett Peabody
	Crib
Bauer Shoes	Delta Hosiery

Famous Brands Housewares
Flemington Fashion Outlet
Flemington Fashion Outlet Plus
Foot Factory
Genesco
Golden Chain Gang
Hanes Activewear
IZOD-Lacoste
Johnston & Murphy
Judy Bond Blouses
Kidstuff
Lechters Inc.
L'eggs/Hanes/Bali
Little Red Shoe House
Londontowne
Madran Tools

Manhattan
Maxine's Books
Munsingwear
Norty's
Old Mill Ladies Sportswear
Paper Outlet
Princess Gardner
Ship 'n Shore
Specials, Exclusively Levi Strauss
    & Co.
Sweater Mill
totes
Val Mode Lingerie
Van Heusen
VIP Yarn
Wallpaper Outlet

MOUNT JOY

Wilton Armetale Factory Outlet
Plumb and Square Streets

Directions: One block south of Route 230 (West Main Street)
Phone: (717) 653–5595 or (800) 348–7184
Hours: 9:30 A.M.–5:30 P.M., Monday–Saturday; closed Thanksgiving, Christmas, New Year's Day.
Credit Cards: American Express, MasterCard, Visa
Personal Checks: Yes
Handicapped Accessible: Yes
Bus Tours: Yes
Special Savings: Senior citizen discount available
Notes or Attractions: Bridal registry available

MOUNT PLEASANT

Lenox Crystal Clearance Center
Lenox Road

Directions: Off Route 31 East
Phone: (412) 547–9555
Hours: 9:00 A.M.–6:00 P.M., Monday–Sunday
Credit Cards: Discover, MasterCard, Visa
Personal Checks: Yes
Handicapped Accessible: Yes
Bus Tours: Yes

OLYPHANT

Fashion Flair
Scranton-Carbondale Highway (Route 6)

Directions: From I–81 take the Scranton-Carbondale Highway exit (Route 6). Store is on the right, about 3 miles down the road.
Phone: (717) 489–1622
Hours: Winter hours 10:00 A.M.–5:30 P.M., Monday–Wednesday and Saturday; noon–5:30 P.M., Sunday. Summer hours 10:00 A.M.–9:00 P.M., Monday–Friday.
Credit Cards: American Express, Discover, MasterCard, Visa
Personal Checks: Yes
Handicapped Accessible: Yes
Bus Tours: Yes

PHILADELPHIA

Elkay Factory Outlet
Caster and Erie Streets

Directions: Take I–95 to the Alleghany Road exit. Follow Alleghany Road to Frankfurt Avenue and turn left. Turn left again on Caster Avenue. Cross Kensington Avenue. Outlet is on the left in the middle of the block.
Phone: (215) 533–9775
Hours: 10:00 A.M.–5:00 P.M., Monday–Wednesday and Saturday; 10:00 A.M.–8:00 P.M., Thursday and Friday
Credit Cards: MasterCard, Visa
Personal Checks: No
Handicapped Accessible: No
Bus Tours: No

Elkay Factory Outlet
44 West Chelton Avenue

Directions: Germantown Avenue and Green Street in downtown Philadelphia
Phone: (215) 849–3890
Hours: 9:30 A.M.–5:30 P.M., Monday–Saturday
Credit Cards: MasterCard, Visa
Personal Checks: No
Handicapped Accessible: No
Bus Tours: No

Fabric Factory Outlet
1536 Wadsworth Avenue

Directions: Take Roosevelt Boulevard to Adams Avenue West to the end; turn right onto Tacony Creek Parkway, to the first traffic light. Then turn left on Cheltenham Avenue, driving for about 4 miles to Wadsworth; turn left. Go 2 blocks; store is on the left.

Phone: (215) 247–1155
Hours: 9:00 A.M.–6:00 p.m, Monday, Tuesday, Thursday, and Saturday; 9:00 A.M.–9:00 P.M., Wednesday and Friday; noon–5:00 P.M., Sunday
Credit Cards: MasterCard, Visa
Personal Checks: Yes
Handicapped Accessible: Yes
Bus Tours: Yes

Franklin Mills
Franklin Mills Circle

Directions: Follow I–95 to PA 63 right off Woodhaven Road.
Phone: (215) 632–1700
Hours: 10:00 A.M.–9:30 P.M., Monday–Saturday; 11:00 A.M.–6:00 P.M., Sunday
Credit Cards: Most stores accept major credit cards.
Personal Checks: Most stores accept personal checks.
Handicapped Accessible: Yes
Bus Tours: Yes, promotional packages available
Food: Available
Notes or Attractions: One of the largest outlet malls in the country. Also has stores and boutiques and several large anchor department stores. Hourly baby-sitting at YMCA Kids Corner, Auction Court. Strollers, wheelchairs, and shopping carts are available at each entrance.
Outlets (Numbers refer to locations in building):

American Tourister, 1540	Best of Times, 1264
Amy Stoudt, 1233	Big & Tall, 1441
Ann Taylor, 1600	Bijou Catrin, 1701
The Answer, 1428	Bloomingdale's Outlet, 1887
Artist's Outlet, 1819	Bostonian Shoe, 1253
Athlete's Foot, 1109	Brass Factory, 1260
Bally Outlet, 1543	Briefcase Unlimited, 1358
Banister Shoes, 1608	Bugle Boy, 1575
Bear Mountain Books, 1101	Camera Shop, 1700
Bed, Bath & Beyond, 1417	Canadian's Outlet, 1449

Canterbury of New Zealand, 1491
Cargo, 1472
Chico's Outlet, 1698
Children's Bootery, 1370
Children's Outlet, 1442
Coat Factory, 1842
Colors by Alexander Julian, 1548
Contemporary Man, 1225
Corner House, 1336
Dazzles, 1208
Delta Hosiery, 1454
Designer Luggage Depot, 1805
Designer Yarns, 1425
Diamonds Unlimited, 1580
Dress Barn, 1400
Dress Barn Woman, 1878
Everything's a $1.00, 1808
Executive Neckwear, 1301
Famous Brands Outlet, 1790
Famous Footwear, 1464
Fan Fever, 1206
Fashion Factory, 1886
Filene's Basement, 1477
Flemington Fashion, 1282
Forever Accessory, 1912
Formal Celebration, 1116
Garage, 1434
Georgiou, 1601
Guess, 1629
Hamilton Luggage, 1392
Handbag Company Outlet, 1785
Helen's Handbags, 1519
Intimate Eve, 1318
Jewel Master, 1562
Jewelry Outlet, 1509
Jewelry Vault, 177
J. C. Penney Outlet

J. G. Hook, 1621
Jordache Outlet, 1667
Just Kids, 1834
Kid's Barn, 1406
Kidswear, 1134
Kitchen Place, 1245
Lady Footlocker Outlet, 1870
Leather and Fur, 1801
Leather Gallery, 1823
Maidenform, 1685
Marty's Shoes, 1800
Merit Outlet, 1707
Merry-Go-Round Outlet, 1862
Middishade Factory Stockroom, 1651
National Locker Room, 1883
$9.99 Stockroom, 1259
9 West Outlet, 1659
No Nonsense, 1157
Not Just Barrettes, 1307
Original I. Goldberg, 1811
Pacific Party Co., 1782
Palace Music Outlet, 1133
Parade of Shoes, 1117
Payless Shoes, 1901
Perfumania, 1586
Petite Shop Outlet, 1219
Phar-Mor
Philly Fever, 1504
Plumm's Outlet, 1218
Portraits Plus, 1165
Ports of the World, Anchor
Prestige Fragrance and
   Cosmetics, 1497
Price Jewelers, 1239
PUMA, 1643
Rack Room, 1395
Radio Shack, 1693

Radio Shack, 1186
Reading China and Glass
Record World, 1894
Remington Factory Outlet, 1347
Ritz Camera, 1272
Royal Jewelers, 1369
Saks Fifth Avenue Clearinghouse, 1618
Sam Goody, 1744
S & K Menswear, 1384
Sears Outlet, Anchor
Secaucus Handbags, 1260
Shades of America, 1365
Small Delights, 1718
Sneakee Feet, 1743
Spain's Hallmark, 1300
Specials, Exclusively by Levi Strauss & Co., 1346

Spiegel Outlet, Anchor
Splash Creations, 1767
Square Circle, 1173
Sunday Best, 1827
T. Edwards/Brooks Outlet, 1405
TJ Maxx, 1634
Top of the Line Cosmetics, 1387
Toy Liquidators, 1735
Toytown, 1420
Toy Works, 1161
United Shoe Outlet, 1553
Van Heusen Outlet, 1535
Wallach's Outlet store, 1281
Westport, Ltd, 1635
Whims, 1289
Windsor Shirt Co., 1818
Youngworld, 1678

Summerdale Mills Fabric Outlet
8101 Frankford Avenue

Directions: From I–95 take the Cottman Avenue exit; turn right at the first traffic light, onto State Road. Turn left onto Rhawn Street; then right onto Frankford Avenue. Store is on the right.
Phone: (215) 335–9494
Hours: 10:00 A.M.–6:00 P.M., Monday, Tuesday, and Thursday–Saturday; 10:00 A.M.–9:00 P.M., Wednesday
Credit Cards: Discover, MasterCard, Visa
Personal Checks: Yes
Handicapped Accessible: Yes
Bus Tours: Yes

Thos. David Factory Store
401 Race Street

Directions: I–95, to Center City on Market Street, two blocks north to Race Street. Store is between 4th and 5th streets.

Phone: (215) 922–4659
Hours: 10:00 A.M.–6:00 P.M., Monday–Saturday
Credit Cards: American Express, Discover, MasterCard, Visa
Personal Checks: Yes
Handicapped Accessible: Yes
Bus Tours: Yes

Thos. David Factory Store
3500 Scotts Lane

Directions: Take I–76 North toward Valley Forge to Kelly Drive. Turn right and then turn left onto Scotts Lane. Store is on the right.
Phone: (215) 843–3155
Hours: 10:00 A.M.–5:00 P.M., Thursday–Monday
Credit Cards: American Express, Discover, MasterCard, Visa
Personal Checks: Yes
Handicapped Accessible: No
Bus Tours: Yes

Thos. David Factory Store
10175 Northeast Avenue

Directions: I–95, Woodhaven exit Route 1 south. Turn right on Red Lion road, travel 3 traffic lights and turn right on Northeast Avenue.
Phone: (215) 677–7390
Hours: 10:00 A.M.–5:00 P.M., Thursday–Monday,
Credit Cards: American Express, Discover, MasterCard, Visa
Personal Checks: Yes
Handicapped Accessible: No
Bus Tours: Yes

Windsor Shirt Company
Sixteenth and Walnut Streets

Directions: Downtown Philadelphia
Phone: (215) 546–1010

Hours: 9:30 A.M.–6:00 P.M., Monday–Friday; 9:30 A.M.–5:30 P.M., Saturday; 11:00 A.M.–5:00 P.M., Sunday
Credit Cards: American Express, Discover, MasterCard, Visa
Personal Checks: Yes
Handicapped Accessible: Yes
Bus Tours: No

PHOENIXVILLE

Kimberton Outlet
Walnut and Lincoln Streets

Directions: Take Route 23 to Lincoln Street and turn right. Continue for 7 blocks to Walnut Street.
Phone: (215) 933–8987
Hours: 9:30 A.M.–5:00 P.M., Monday–Friday; 10:00 A.M.–5:00 P.M., Saturday
Credit Cards: MasterCard, Visa
Personal Checks: Yes
Handicapped Accessible: No
Bus Tours: No

QUAKERTOWN

Stockroom/Evan-Picone
Route 663

Directions: From the Pennsylvania Turnpike northeast extension, take exit 32; turn left at the light and store is on the right, about 2 miles down the road.
Phone: (215) 536–4833
Hours: 10:00 A.M.–6:00 P.M., Monday–Wednesday; 10:00 A.M.–9:00 P.M., Thursday and Friday; 10:00 A.M.–5:30 P.M., Saturday; noon–5:00 P.M., Sunday

Credit Cards: American Express, Discover, MasterCard, Visa
Personal Checks: Yes
Handicapped Accessible: No
Bus Tours: No

READING

Astor Swimwear Outlet
1722 North 10th Street

Directions: Take Ninth Street out of town; store is at Exeter and North Tenth Streets.
Phone: (215) 929–3322
Hours: Open April through Labor Day, 10:00 A.M.–5:00 P.M., Monday–Saturday. (Call for evening hours.)
Credit Cards: MasterCard, Visa
Personal Checks: Yes, with driver's license
Handicapped Accessible: Yes
Bus Tours: No

The Big Mill
Eighth and Oley Streets

Directions: Take the Pennsylvania Turnpike to Buttonwood; then turn left on Sixth Street and proceed to Oley Street.
Phone: (215) 378–9100
Hours: 9:30 A.M.–6:00 P.M., Monday–Wednesday; 9:30 A.M.–8:00 P.M., Thursday–Saturday; 11:00 A.M.–5:00 P.M., Sunday
Credit Cards: Most stores accept major credit cards.
Personal Checks: Most stores accept personal checks.
Handicapped Accessible: Yes; with some difficulty
Bus Tours: Yes
Special Savings: Call for free coupons
Food: Available

Outlets:
Adolfo Sport/Collectibles II
Chaus
Children's Mill Inc.
Custom Sportswear
Delta Hosiery Mill Outlet
Gitano Warehouse Clearance Center
Intimate Eve
Jordache and Shoe Town
Just'a Sweet Shoppe
Kids, ETC
Manhattan
Paldies Young Men's Clothing
Petticoat Corner
PUMA USA
Stone Mountain Handbags
Top of the Line Cosmetics

Down East Factory Outlet
916 N. Ninth Street

Directions: Take the Pennsylvania Turnpike to Buttonwood; then turn right on Ninth Street.
Phone: (215) 372–1144
Hours: 9:30 A.M.–5:30 P.M., Monday–Saturday; noon–5:00 P.M., Sunday
Credit Cards: MasterCard, Visa
Personal Checks: Yes
Handicapped Accessible: No
Bus Tours: Yes

Outlets on Hiesters Lane
755 Hiesters Lane

Directions: Drive north on Park Road from Vanity Fair; turn right onto the Route 422 bypass (Eleventh Street exit). Turn right at the traffic light to Hiesters Lane. Center is on the left, 2 blocks down the road.
Phone: (215) 921–9394 or (215) 921–8910

Hours: Summer: 9:30 A.M.–5:30 P.M., Monday–Thursday and Saturday; 9:30 A.M.–8:00 P.M., Friday; noon–5:00 P.M., Sunday. Call for winter hours.
Credit Cards: Most stores accept major credit cards.
Personal Checks: Yes
Handicapped Accessible: Yes
Bus Tours: Yes
Outlets:
All-in-One Linen
Burlington Coat Factory
Flemington Fashion Outlet
Flemington Fashion Outlet Plus
Marty's Shoe Outlet
Mikasa
Snack Factory
Sweater Mill
Sweets Streets

Reading Outlet Center
801 North Ninth Street

Directions: Downtown Reading at North Ninth and Douglas streets.
Phone: (215) 373–5495
Hours: 9:00 A.M.–6:00 P.M., Monday–Wednesday; 9:00 A.M.–8:00 P.M., Thursday–Saturday; 11:00 A.M.–5:00 P.M., Sunday
Credit Cards: Most stores accept major credit cards.
Personal Checks: Most stores accept personal checks.
Handicapped Accessible: Yes
Bus Tours: Yes
Special Savings: Call for free discount coupons
Notes or Attractions: More than seventy manufacturers' outlets in seven buildings within 2 city blocks. Look for Reading Outlet Center brochure for maps and coupons.

Building 1
Allen Edmonds
Bag and Baggage
Beauty Scenter
Best Things
Bostonian Shoe
Bubbles & Scents
Bugle Boy
Carole Hockman Lingerie
Carter's Childrenswear
Clothes Out Closet
Coach Factory Store
Famous Brands Housewares
Farah Factory Clearance Store
Flemington Fashion
Fragrance Cove
Frisco Blues
harvé benard
Izod/Evan-Picone Warehouse
    Sale
Jaeger
Joan & David
John Henry & Friends
Kids Creation
Kitchen Collection Closeout Store
L'eggs/Hanes/Bali
London Fog
Nautica
Norty's Clearance
Old Mill Sportswear
Polo/Ralph Lauren
Quality Discount Apparel
Reading Christmas Outlet
Ruff Hewn
T. H Mandy Outlet Women's
    Fashions
totes
Touch of Gold Jewelry

Trader Kids
Van Heusen Clearance Center
Wallet Works
Whims Sarah Coventry

Building 2
Clifford & Wills
J. Crew

Building 3
Brassworks
Dooney & Bourke
Fanny Farmer
Timberland

Building 4
Evan-Picone
Gant
Gilligan & O'Malley
Hartstrings
Heirlooms
Leather Loft
Leslie Fay
Liz Claiborne
Sunglass World

Building 5
Corning/Revere
Kitchen Collection
Toy Liquidators

Building 6
Bass Shoes
Crazy Horse
Time World
Van Heusen

Building 7
The Gap

Building 8
Rawlings Sport Goods

ROBESONIA

Robesonia Outlet Center
Route 422 East

Directions: Off Route 422, east of Reading
Phone: (215) 693–3144
Hours: 9:30 A.M.–8:30 P.M., Monday–Friday; 9:00 A.M.–6:00 P.M., Saturday; 11:00 A.M.–5:00 P.M., Sunday
Credit Cards: Discover, MasterCard, Visa
Personal Checks: Yes
Handicapped Accessible: Yes
Bus Tours: Yes, small tours
Outlets:
Aunt Mary's Yarns
Bag Outlet
Branded Shoe Outlet
Gloray Knitting Mills sweater
Ocello Sportswear
Paper Outlet
Rolane Hosiery
VIP Mill Store

RONKS

Crazy Horse
34 South Willowdale Drive

Directions: From I–83 take the Route 30 exit east; store is on the right
Phone: (717) 293–0814
Hours: 9:30 A.M.–9:00 P.M., Monday–Saturday; noon–5:00 P.M., Sunday
Credit Cards: MasterCard, Visa
Personal Checks: Yes
Handicapped Accessible: Yes
Bus Tours: Yes

Izod
2819 Lincoln Highway

Directions: From I–83 take the Route 30 exit east; store is on the right
Phone: (717) 687–0405
Hours: 9:00 A.M.–6:00 P.M., Sunday–Thursday; 9:00 A.M.–9:00 P.M.,
Friday and Saturday
Credit Cards: American Express, Discover, MasterCard, Visa
Personal Checks: Yes
Handicapped Accessible: Yes
Bus Tours: Yes

SHAMOKIN DAM

C.A. Reed
Routes 11 and 15

Directions: U.S. 15 and Route 11 at Shamokin Dam
Phone: (717) 743–6704
Hours: 9:00 A.M.–5:00 P.M., Monday–Wednesday and Saturday; 9:00
A.M.–9:00 P.M., Friday
Credit Cards: No
Personal Checks: Yes
Handicapped Accessible: Yes
Bus Tours: Yes

Pennsylvania House Furniture Factory Outlet
Orchard Hills Plaza

Directions: Routes 11 and 15
Phone: (717) 743–2800
Hours: 10:00 A.M.–5:00 P.M., Tuesday–Saturday; 1:00 P.M.–5:00 P.M.,
Sunday
Credit Cards: MasterCard, Visa
Personal Checks: Yes
Handicapped Accessible: Yes
Bus Tours: Yes

SOMERSET

Georgian Place
Route 601 North

Directions: Off the Pennsylvania Turnpike, at exit 10 (Highway 601 North)
Phone: (814) 445–3325
Hours: 10:00 A.M.–9:00 P.M., Monday–Saturday; 11:00 A.M.–6:00 P.M., Sunday and holidays
Credit Cards: Most stores accept major credit cards.
Personal Checks: Yes, with two forms of identification.
Handicapped Accessible: Yes
Bus Tours: Yes, promotional packages available
Food: Available
Notes or Attractions: Baby-stroller rental; banking facilities
Outlets:

Aileen
American Tourister
Banister
Barbizon
Bentwood Company
Book Warehouse
Brands Factory Outlet
Brass Works
Cape Isle Knitters
Carter's Childrenswear
Corning/Revere
Crystal Works
Fashion Jewelry Exchange
Fieldcrest Cannon Factory
Formfit Outlet
Fragrance World, Inc.
Gitano
Great Outdoor Clothing Co.
harvé benard

Jonathan Logan Outlet
Jones New York Women
Jordache
Kitchen Collection
Leslie Fay Outlet
Manhattan
Micki Designer Separates
Nickels Company Store
Oneida Silver
Paper Factory
Pierre Cardin
Ribbon Outlet
Stone Mountain Handbag
Sweatshirt Company
Ties & More
Toy Liquidators
Van Heusen
Wallet Works
Welcome Home

STATE COLLEGE

Fashion Flair
2101 S. Atherton Street

Directions: From Route 322 proceed through Boalsburg to Atherton and then to South Atherton Street; Hills Plaza is on the right.
Phone: (814) 238–7324
Hours: 10:00 A.M.–9:00 P.M., Monday–Friday; 10:00 A.M.–8:00 P.M., Saturday; noon–5:00 P.M., Sunday
Credit Cards: American Express, Discover, MasterCard, Visa
Personal Checks: Yes
Handicapped Accessible: Yes
Bus Tours: Yes

STROUDSBURG

Pocono Outlet Complex
Ninth and Ann Streets

Directions: From I–80 take exit 48 to Business Route 209; proceed to Ninth Street and turn right onto Ann Street
Phone: (717) 424–6050
Hours: 10:00 A.M.–6:00 P.M., Sunday–Wednesday; 10:00 A.M.–8:00 P.M., Thursday–Saturday
Credit Cards: Most stores accept major credit cards.
Personal Checks: No
Handicapped Accessible: Yes
Bus Tours: Yes
Outlets:

Alexander's Shoe Outlet	B & J Children's Outlet
American Candle	Buffalo Mills Outlet
American Pottery & Glass	Buffalo's Added Touch Boutique
American Ribbon Manufacturers	Candle Towne U.S.A

China Plus
Country Cheese 'N Jam
   Gift Outlet
Crazy Franks Accessory Outlet
Designer Wholesale Outlet
Elegant Boutique
Heritage Shop
Hi-Tec Outlet
International Boutique, Inc.
International Lingerie, Cosmetics,
   & Children's Wear
Kandy Korner

Maternity with Love
Party II
Pocono Candle Shop
Pocono Kitchen & Curtain
Pocono Linen Outlet
Pocono Odd-Lot Outlet
Pocono Toy Outlet
Potting Shed
Prancing Pony
Run of the Mill
Stationery Outlet
Stroud Handbag Outlet

TANNERSVILLE

Crossings Outlet Square
285 Crossings Factory Stores

Directions: Off I–80, at exit 45
Phone: (717) 629–4650
Hours: 10:00 A.M.–9:00 P.M., Monday–Saturday; 11:00 A.M.–6:00 P.M.,
Sunday
Credit Cards: Most stores accept major credit cards.
Personal Checks: Most stores accept personal checks.
Handicapped Accessible: Yes
Bus Tours: Yes
Food: Available
Outlets:

Adolfo
Aileen
American Tourister
Anne Klein
Bagmakers
Banister/Capezio
Bass
Book Cellar

Cape Isle Knitters
Carole Little
Carter's Childrenswear
Dansk
Etienne Aigner
Gitano
harvé benard
Home Again

Izod/Gant
Jones New York
Kitchen Collection
L'eggs/Hanes/Bali
London Fog
Maidenform
Napier
Nautica
Oneida (717) 629-3888
Perfumania
Pfaltzgraff

Pierre Cardin
Reebok
Socks Galore & More
Sports Warehouse
Springmaid Wamsutta
Sweatshirt Co.
totes/Sunglass World
Toy Liquidators
Van Heusen
Westport/Dress Barn

THREE SPRINGS

Colonial Wood Benders, Inc.
Rio Grande and Sugar Streets

Directions: Take the Pennsylvania Turnpike to exit 14; turn left at end of ramp onto Route 275. Drive to first light and turn left onto Route 641 to "T." Turn onto Route 522 to traffic light, then onto Route 994 into sharp right-hand bend. Take first right street to white stone block building on right.
Phone: (814) 448–3300
Hours: 8:00 A.M.–5:00 P.M., Monday–Friday
Credit Cards: MasterCard, Visa
Personal Checks: Yes
Handicapped Accessible: Yes
Bus Tours: No

UPPER DARBY

Middishade Factory Stockroom
38 South 69th Street

Directions: Take Market Street out of Philadelphia to the end; turn left, and Middishade is the sixth store on the left

Phone: (214) 734–0130
Hours: 10:00 A.M.–7:00 P.M., Monday–Thursday; 10:00 A.M.–9:00 P.M., Friday; 10:00 A.M.–8:00 P.M., Saturday; noon–5:00 P.M., Sunday
Credit Cards: American Express, Discover, MAC, MasterCard, Visa
Personal Checks: Yes
Handicapped Accessible: Yes
Bus Tours: No

WAYNESBORO

Waynesboro Factory Outlet Barn
Walnut Street

Directions: From I–81 take the Greencastle exit, and drive east on Route 16 to Waynesboro; turn right on Walnut Street and proceed to East Third Street.
Phone: (301) 486–2484, Maryland rental agency
Hours: 10:00 A.M.–8:30 P.M., Monday and Friday; 10:00 A.M.–5:00 P.M., Tuesday–Thursday and Saturday; 1:00 P.M.–5:00 P.M., Sunday
Credit Cards: Most stores accept major credit cards.
Personal Checks: Yes
Handicapped Accessible: Yes
Bus Tours: Yes
Food: Available
Notes or Attractions: Some stores are in the barn; some are across from it
Outlets:
Bag & Baggage Luggage and Handbag Outlet
Carter's Childrenswear
Corning Factory Store
Delta Hosiery
Freeman Shoes
Jeans N' Things
Lancaster Lingerie Outlet
Palm Beach Mill Outlet
Quoddy Crafted Shoes Factory Direct Stores

Sheet & Towel Outlet
United Shoe Outlet
Van Heusen

WEST LAWN

Astor Swimwear Outlet
2501 Penn Avenue

Directions: From the Reading Vanity Fair outlet, take Penn Avenue to the store.
Phone: (215) 678–3737
Hours: April through Labor Day, 10:00 A.M.–5:00 P.M., Monday–Saturday; call for evening hours
Credit Cards: MasterCard, Visa
Personal Checks: Yes
Handicapped Accessible: Yes
Bus Tours: Yes

WEST READING

Reading China & Glass
739 Reading Avenue

Directions: Take Route 422 to the West Reading exit; turn right at the end of the ramp, and then turn right on Seventh Street and proceed to Reading Avenue
Phone: (215) 378–5285 or (800) 747–RCAG ext. 7224
Hours: 9:00 A.M.–9:00 P.M., Monday–Friday; 9:00 A.M.–6:00 P.M., Saturday; 11:00 A.M.–5:00 P.M., Sunday
Credit Cards: American Express, MasterCard, Visa
Personal Checks: Yes
Handicapped Accessible: Yes
Bus Tours: Yes

WILLIAMSPORT

C. A. Reed
416 West Third Street

Directions: Drive west on West Third Street to Center Street. Store is at that intersection.
Phone: (717) 323–2796
Hours: 9:00 A.M.–5:00 P.M., Monday–Thursday and Saturday; 9:00 A.M.–7:00 P.M., Friday
Credit Cards: No
Personal Checks: Yes, over ten dollars
Handicapped Accessible: No
Bus Tours: Yes

Cobbler's Factory Outlet
Memorial Avenue and Cemetery Street

Directions: Take Route 15 to Memorial Avenue East to Cemetery Street. Store is in the Weldon Building.
Phone: (717) 326–5777
Hours: 9:00 A.M.–5:00 P.M., Monday–Thursday and Saturday; 9:00 A.M.–8:00 P.M., Friday; noon–4:00 P.M., Sunday
Credit Cards: MasterCard, Visa
Personal Checks: Yes
Handicapped Accessible: Yes
Bus Tours: Yes

Fashion Flair
471 Hepburn Street
Hepburn Center

Directions: Route 15 north to Williamsport to Market Street Bridge to business district (left-hand lane) to third traffic light Little League Boulevard and turn left to Hepburn. Store is on the corner.
Phone: (717) 326–3844

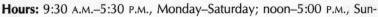

Hours: 9:30 A.M.–5:30 P.M., Monday–Saturday; noon–5:00 P.M., Sunday
Credit Cards: American Express, Discover, MasterCard, Visa
Personal Checks: Yes
Handicapped Accessible: Yes
Bus Tours: Yes

Weldon Factory Salesroom
Memorial Avenue and Cemetery Street

Directions: Take Route 15 North to Williamsport. Turn left at 4th Street and drive about 5 minutes to Cemetery Street. Turn right to salesroom.
Phone: (717) 326–0691
Hours: 9:00 A.M.–5:00 P.M., Monday–Thursday and Saturday; 9:00 A.M.–8:00 P.M., Friday; noon–4:00 P.M., Sunday
Credit Cards: Discover, MasterCard, Visa
Personal Checks: Yes
Handicapped Accessible: Yes
Bus Tours: Yes

WRIGHTSVILLE

John Wright Warehouse
North Front Street

Directions: Take the Route 30 bypass to the Wrightsville exit; drive south to Route 462. Turn left, and drive to Front Street; turn left and proceed to store, which is on the right.
Phone: (717) 252–2519
Hours: 9:00 A.M.–5:00 P.M., Monday–Saturday; noon–5:00 P.M., Sunday
Credit Cards: American Express, Discover, MasterCard, Visa
Personal Checks: Yes
Handicapped Accessible: Yes

Tours: Yes
d: Available
tes or Attractions: Stephan Bahn Winery and a restaurant on site

WYOMISSING

Baby's Outlet
828 Penn Avenue

Directions: Take Route 30 East to Route 222 North to Route 22 West; take the West Reading exit (Penn Avenue). Store is across from the Vanity Fair Factory Outlet.
Phone: (215) 372–8781
Hours: 10:00 A.M.–5:30 P.M., Monday, Wednesday, and Saturday; 10:00 A.M.–8:00 P.M., Tuesday, Thursday, and Friday; noon–5:00 P.M., Sunday
Credit Cards: Discover, MAC, MasterCard, Visa
Personal Checks: Yes
Handicapped Accessible: Yes
Bus Tours: Yes

Danskin Factory Outlet
350 North Park Road

Directions: Two blocks from the Vanity Fair Factory Outlet
Phone: (215) 374–6231
Hours: 9:00 A.M.–9:00 P.M., Monday–Friday; 9:00 A.M.–6:00 P.M., Saturday; noon–5:00 P.M., Sunday
Credit Cards: MasterCard, Visa
Personal Checks: Yes
Handicapped Accessible: Yes
Bus Tours: Yes

Glen-Gery Brick Factory Outlet
1166 Spring Street

Directions: Take Route 422 West to the Bern Road exit and stay to

your right; drive past one traffic light and take the next left, onto Bern Road. Store is on the right.
Phone: (215) 372–7826
Hours: 9:00 A.M.–5:00 P.M., Monday–Friday
Credit Cards: No
Personal Checks: Yes, with identification
Handicapped Accessible: No
Bus Tours: Yes, if notified in advance

Vanity Fair Factory Outlet
Hill Avenue and Park Road

Directions: From Route 30 East drive to Route 222 North to Route 22 West. Take the West Reading exit (Penn Avenue). The outlet is 1 mile on the right.
Phone: (215) 378–0408
Hours: 9:00 A.M.–9:00 P.M., Monday–Friday; 9:00 A.M.–6:00 P.M., Saturday (extended Saturday hours during fall); noon–5:00 P.M., Sunday
Credit Cards: Discover, MasterCard, Visa
Personal Checks: Yes
Handicapped Accessible: Yes
Bus Tours: Yes
Notes or Attractions: Shops are in a number of colored buildings (Brown, Orange, Big Blue, Green, Big Red, Gold, Purple, Navy, and Turquoise)
Outlets:

American Tourister	Freeman Shoes
Black & Decker	Handmade Quilts
Bollman Hats	Instant Decor
Boston Traders	Jewelry Outlet
Cambridge Dry Goods	Jonathan Logan Outlet
Canterbury of New Zealand	Kitchen Linens Etc.
Carpet Factory Outlet	Kuppenheimer Men's Clothier
Carter's Childrenswear	Laura Ashley
Eagles Eye	Leather Gallery
Electronics Outlet	L. L. Bean
Evan-Picone	Mushroom Factory Store
Fieldcrest Cannon Factory	Nanny's Shoppe

North Face
Oneida
Oxford Brands Ltd.
Paper Factory
Pol-O-Craft
Prestige Fragrance and Cosmetics
Reading Bag Company
Reading China and Glass
Royal Robbins

Sunglass World
Supply Outlet for Lovable Pets
TC Sports
totes
Van Heusen
VF Clearance
VF Factory Outlet
Windsor Shirt Company
Your Toy Center

YORK

Classic Caramel Company
231 W. College Avenue

Directions: Take the Franklin Street exit off I–30 and turn right onto West Princess Street. Proceed to William Penn High School and drive into the alley on the left.
Phone: (717) 845–8342 or (717) 843–0921
Hours: 9:00 A.M.–4:00 P.M., Monday–Friday; 9:00 A.M.–1:00 P.M., Saturday
Credit Cards: No
Personal Checks: No
Handicapped Accessible: Yes
Bus Tours: Yes

Meadowbrook Outlet Village
2901 Whiteford Road

Directions: Mount Zion Road exit off Route 30
Phone: (717) 755–0899
Hours: 10:00 A.M.–9:00 P.M., Monday–Saturday; noon–5:00 P.M., Sunday
Credit Cards: Most stores accept major credit cards.
Personal Checks: Most stores accept personal checks.

Handicapped Accessible: Yes
Bus Tours: Yes
Food: Available; picnic area
Outlets:
Banister Shoes
Bass Shoes
Crazy Horse
Danskin
Delta Hosiery
Doe-Spun
Hamilton Watch & Clock Shoppe
harvé benard
Izod
Jonathan Logan
Knittery
Leather Loft
Manhattan
Petals
Pewtarex Factory
Pfaltzgraff
Prestige Fragrance & Cosmetics, Inc
Ribbon Outlet
Toys Unlimited
Uddermost

Office Furniture Outlet
519 N. Franklin Street

Directions: Take Sherman Street from Route 30 for about 1 mile and turn right at the Mini Market. You'll be on York Street. Take York to North Franklin Street and turn right. Store is at a dead end.
Phone: (717) 848–2900
Hours: 8:30 A.M.–5:00 P.M., Monday–Friday; 10:00 A.M.–1:00 P.M., Saturday
Credit Cards: MasterCard, Visa
Personal Checks: Yes
Handicapped Accessible: No
Bus Tours: Yes

Pewtarex Factory Outlet Stores
722 W. Market Street

Directions: Take Route 30 to Route 74 to West Market Street
Phone: (717) 848–1859
Hours: 9:30 A.M.–5:30 P.M., Monday–Friday; 9:30 A.M.–3:00 P.M., Saturday
Credit Cards: Discover, MasterCard, Visa
Personal Checks: Yes
Handicapped Accessible: No
Bus Tours: Yes

Stauffer's Nut, Candy, Cookies
375 S. Belmont Street

Directions: Take Route 30 to Route 74 to West Market Street; turn right and proceed to South Belmont Street
Phone: (717) 848–6630
Hours: 9:00 A.M.–5:00 P.M., Monday–Thursday; 7:00 A.M.–5:00 P.M., Friday; 9:00 A.M.–3:00 P.M., Saturday
Credit Cards: No
Personal Checks: Yes
Handicapped Accessible: Yes
Bus Tours: Yes

VIRGINIA

1. Alexandria
2. Bailey's Crossroads
3. Blacksburg
4. Blackstone
5. Danville
6. Fairfax
7. Falls Church
8. Fort Chiswell
9. Fredericksburg
10. Herndon
11. Lightfoot
12. Lynchburg
13. Manassas
14. Mechanicsville
15. Norge
16. Roanoke
17. Rocky Mount
18. South Boston
19. Springfield
20. Vienna
21. Virginia Beach
22. Waynesboro
23. Williamsburg
24. Woodbridge
25. Wytheville

VIRGINIA

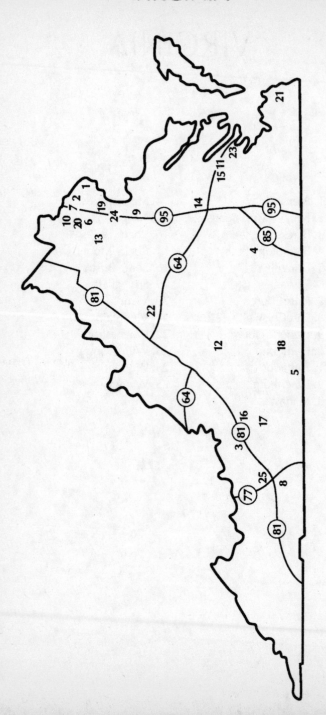

ALEXANDRIA

Rack Room Shoes
Landmark Plaza
6198–A Little River Turnpike

Directions: From I–395 take exit 3B West (Duke Street) and drive to the first shopping center on your right
Phone: (703) 941–6261
Hours: 10:00 A.M.–9:00 P.M., Monday–Saturday; noon–5:00 P.M., Sunday
Credit Cards: American Express, Discover, MasterCard, Visa
Personal Checks: Yes
Handicapped Accessible: Yes
Bus Tours: Yes

Tuesday Morning
6464A Lincolnia

Directions: Off Columbia Pike, past Bailey's Crossroad, about 1½ miles on the left-hand side of the road, in Barcroft Plaza Shopping Center
Phone: (703) 941-7512 or (703) 941-7511, recording
Hours: 9:30 A.M.–6:00 P.M., Monday, Wednesday, Friday, and Saturday; 9:30 A.M.–9:00 P.M., Thursday; noon–6:00 P.M., Sunday
Credit Cards: Discover, MasterCard, Visa
Personal Checks: Yes
Handicapped Accessible: Yes
Bus Tours: Yes

BAILEY'S CROSSROADS

Rack Room Shoes
Leesburg Pike Shopping Center

Directions: From I–395 take the King Street exit toward Falls Church.

Store is across the street from the Skyline Mall.
Phone: (703) 931–6318
Hours: 10:00 A.M.–9:00 P.M., Monday–Saturday; noon to 5:00 P.M., Sunday
Credit Cards: American Express, Discover, MasterCard, Visa
Personal Checks: Yes
Handicapped Accessible: Yes
Bus Tours: Yes

BLACKSBURG

Virginia Apparel Outlet
1301 S. Main Street

Directions: Take I–81 to exit 118 to the Route 460 bypass, which merges into Route 460 (business route). Stay to the right, and take the Downtown Traffic exit to South Main Street. Store is behind Hardees, on the right.
Phone: (703) 961–2889
Hours: 10:00 A.M.–5:00 P.M., Monday–Saturday
Credit Cards: Discover, MasterCard, Visa
Personal Checks: Yes, with identification
Handicapped Accessible: Yes
Bus Tours: Yes

BLACKSTONE

Virginia Apparel Outlet
101 S. Main Street

Directions: Take Route 40 to the first traffic light in Blackstone and turn left. Store is on the corner of Main and East Broad.
Phone: (804) 292–1489
Hours: 10:00 A.M.–5:00 P.M., Monday–Saturday

Credit Cards: Discover, MasterCard, Visa
Personal Checks: Yes, with identification
Handicapped Accessible: Yes
Bus Tours: Yes

DANVILLE

Dan River Outlet
1001 West Main Street

Directions: Take Route 29 south to Park Avenue and turn left. Follow to the end of the street and turn left onto West Main Street. Turn right for ½ mile; store is on the left.
Phone: (804) 799–7205
Hours: 8:00 A.M.–5:00 P.M., Monday–Friday; 9:00 A.M.–5:00 P.M., Saturday
Credit Cards: MasterCard, Visa
Personal Checks: Yes
Handicapped Accessible: Yes
Bus Tours: Yes

Tultex Mill Outlet
3300 Riverside Drive
Riverside Shopping Center

Directions: From Route 29 South take Route 58 West (Riverside Drive). Store is on the right.
Phone: (804) 793–5446
Hours: 10:00 A.M.–6:00 P.M., Monday–Saturday
Credit Cards: MasterCard, Visa
Personal Checks: Yes
Handicapped Accessible: Yes
Bus Tours: Yes

FAIRFAX

Wibbies Factory Outlet

3158 Spring Street

Directions: Take U.S. 50 West from Fairfax Circle for 1 block; turn right on Spring Street. Drive to the top of the hill and turn left. Store is on the right, in a business park.
Phone: (703) 385–5451
Hours: 10:00 A.M.–5:00 P.M., Tuesday–Saturday
Credit Cards: Discover, MasterCard, Visa
Personal Checks: Yes, with proper identification
Handicapped Accessible: Yes
Bus Tours: Yes, with advance notice

Outlet Mall at Fairfax

10710 Lee Highway

Directions: Take I–66 West to Route 123 South; turn right onto Route 50 and drive west for about 2 blocks.
Phone: (703) 591–8082
Hours: 10:00 A.M.–9:30 P.M., Monday–Saturday; 10:00 A.M.–6:00 P.M., Sunday
Credit Cards: MasterCard, Visa
Personal Checks: Yes
Handicapped Accessible: Yes
Bus Tours: Yes
Outlets:
Aileen
Delta Hosiery
Dress Barn
Hamilton Luggage & Handbags
Hit or Miss
Linens 'n things
Sam's Tailoring
Shoe Town

Pfaltzgraff Factory Stores
10334 Main Street

Directions: From Route 50 take Chain Bridge Road to Main Street and turn left. Store is on the left in 2 blocks.
Phone: (703) 591–6141
Hours: 10:00 A.M.–9:00 P.M., Monday–Friday; 10:00 A.M.–6:00 P.M., Saturday; noon–5:00 P.M., Sunday. Closed Easter, Thanksgiving, Christmas, and New Year's Day.
Credit Cards: Discover, MasterCard, Visa
Personal Checks: Yes
Handicapped Accessible: Yes
Bus Tours: Yes

Tuesday Morning
3025–29 Nutley Street

Directions: Take Route 50 South to Nutley Street, turn right, and drive for 2 blocks. Store is on the right, in the Pan Am Shopping Center.
Phone: (703) 280–2130
Hours: 9:30 A.M.–6:00 P.M., Monday, Wednesday, Friday, and Saturday; 9:30 A.M.–9:00 P.M., Thursday; noon–6:00 P.M., Sunday
Credit Cards: Discover, MasterCard, Visa
Personal Checks: Yes
Handicapped Accessible: Yes
Bus Tours: Yes

FALLS CHURCH

Syms
1000 E. Broad Street

Directions: From I–495 and Route 50 East, turn left on South Street and drive to Hillwood; make a right turn into the parking lot.
Phone: (703) 241–8500

Hours: 10:00 A.M.–9:00 P.M., Tuesday–Friday; 10:00 A.M.–6:30 P.M., Saturday; 11:30 A.M.–5:30 P.M., Sunday
Credit Cards: Syms Charge
Personal Checks: Yes
Handicapped Accessible: Yes
Bus Tours: Yes

FORT CHISWELL

Factory Merchants Fort Chiswell Mall
Factory Merchants Drive

Directions: Take I–81 to exit 80. Mall is right at exit on Route 77.
Phone: (703) 637–6214
Hours: 9:00 A.M.–9:00 P.M., Monday–Saturday; noon–6:00 P.M., Sunday
Credit Cards: Most stores accept major credit cards.
Personal Checks: Most stores accept personal checks.
Handicapped Accessible: No
Bus Tours: Yes
Notes or Attractions: U.S. Forest Service Regional Visitor Center (703–637–6766)
Outlets:

Aileen	Izod/Gant
Arrow	Kitchen Collection
Banister Shoes	Leather Loft
Bass Shoes	L'eggs/Hanes/Bali
Black & Decker	Little Red Shoe House
Bon Worth	London Fog
Book Warehouse	Manhattan
Bugle Boy	Ribbon Outlet
Campus Factory Outlet	Socks Galore & More
Corning/Revere	Toys Unlimited
Fragrance World	Van Heusen
Full Size Fashions	Wallet Works
Genesco	Welcome Home
Gitano	

FREDERICKSBURG

Massaponax Outlet Center
904 Princess Anne Street

Directions: Off I–95, exit 126, at U.S. 1
Phone: (703) 373–8853
Hours: 10:00 A.M.–6:00 P.M., Monday–Saturday; noon–5:00 P.M., Sunday
Credit Cards: Most stores accept major credit cards.
Personal Checks: Most stores accept personal checks.
Handicapped Accessible: Yes, elevators available
Bus Tours: Yes
Outlets:

Aileen
Bass
Book Cellar
Bruce Alan Bags
Cape Isle Knitters
Corning/Revere
Delta Hosiery
Gitano
harvé benard
Jordache
Kitchen Collection
Manhattan
Napier
Old Mill

Olga/Warner's
Oneida
Paper Factory
Perfumania
Rack Room
S & K Menswear
Springmaid/Wamsutta
TH Mandy Outlet
Toy Liquidators
USA Classics
Van Heusen
Welcome Home
Westport Ltd.

HERNDON

Tuesday Morning
Herndon Centre
492 Elden Street

Directions: From I–495 take the Dulles Toll Roll exit to the Reston exit; turn right onto Reston Parkway. Proceed for five traffic lights and turn left onto Route 606, driving to the Herndon town line. Drive for four traffic lights to Herndon Centre; the shopping center is on the right.

Phone: (703) 471-7532 or (703) 471-5571, recording
Hours: 9:30 A.M.–6:00 P.M., Monday, Wednesday, Friday, and Saturday; 9:30 A.M.–9:00 P.M., Thursday; noon–6:00 P.M., Sunday
Credit Cards: Discover, MasterCard, Visa
Personal Checks: Yes
Handicapped Accessible: Yes
Bus Tours: Yes

LIGHTFOOT

Williamsburg Outlet Mall
6401 Richmond Road

Directions: From I–64 take exit 234 (Route 60) to Richmond Road
Phone: (804) 565–0732 or (804) 565–3378
Hours: 9:00 A.M.–9:00 P.M., Monday–Saturday; 9:00 A.M.–6:00 P.M., Sunday
Credit Cards: Most stores accept major credit cards.
Personal Checks: Most stores accept personal checks.
Handicapped Accessible: Yes
Bus Tours: Yes
Food: Available
Outlets:

All American	Cape Isle Knitters
Barbizon Fine Lingerie	Champion Hanes Activewear
Bass	Children's Outlet
Bon Worth	Diamonds Unlimited
Book Hutch	Dress Barn
Bruce Alan Bags, Etc.	Dress Barn Woman
Burlington Brands	Executive Neckwear

Famous Footwear
Famous Galleries of
   Williamsburg
Frugal Franks
Fuller Brush
General Shoe Factory
   to You Shoes
Gold 'n Things Jewelry
Hit or Miss
Islandgear
Jewelry Connection
Just My Size
Kids Wearhouse
Kitchen Place
L'eggs/Hanes/Bali
Linens 'n Things
London Fog
Mercantile
$9.99 Stockroom

Old Mill
Paper Factory
Prestige Fragrance and Cosmetics
Rack Room
Regal Ware
Russell Jerzees Outlet
S & K Famous Brand Menswear
Secaucus Handbags Outlet
Socks Galore & More
Solid Brass Inc.
Specials, Exclusively Levi Strauss
   & Co.
Sunshades
Swank
totes
Toy Liquidators
Welcome Home
Whims

Williamsburg Pottery
Route 60

Directions: From I–64 take exit 234 and go south on Route 646
Phone: (804) 564–3326
Hours: 9:00 A.M.–7:00 P.M., Sunday–Saturday
Credit Cards: MasterCard, Visa
Personal Checks: Yes, with picture identification and credit card
Handicapped Accessible: Yes
Bus Tours: Yes
Outlets:
Ann-Michele Originals
Aunt Mary's Yarns
Banister Shoes
Black & Decker Tools
Cabin Creek Furniture
Carter's Childrenswear

Fashion Flair
Fieldcrest-Cannon
Kid City
Manhattan
Manufacturer's Shoe Outlet
Oneida Silversmiths
Paul Revere Shoppe
Pfaltzgraff Pottery Outlet
Prestige Fragrance & Cosmetics
Rolane
Salt Glaze Pottery
totes
Van Heusen
Wallet Works
Westport Ltd.

LYNCHBURG

Tultex Mill Outlet
3225 Old Forest Road

Directions: From Route 29 take Route 501 to Old Forest Road
Phone: (804) 385–6477
Hours: 10:00 A.M.–6:00 P.M., Monday–Saturday
Credit Cards: MasterCard, Visa
Personal Checks: Yes
Handicapped Accessible: Yes; ramp at the end of the sidewalk
Bus Tours: Yes

MANASSAS

Rack Room Shoes
8377 Sudley Road

Directions: Take I–66 West to the Route 234 South exit. Store is in the Manaport Plaza on the left, across the street from the Manassas Mall.

Phone: (703) 361–0363
Hours: 10:00 A.M.–9:30 P.M., Monday–Saturday; noon–6:00 P.M., Sunday
Credit Cards: American Express, Discover, MasterCard, Visa
Personal Checks: Yes
Handicapped Accessible: Yes
Bus Tours: Yes
Tuesday Morning
Sudley Manor Square Shopping Center
7827 Sudley Road

Directions: Take I–66 West to Route 234 South to the fourth traffic light; turn left, getting into the immediate right-hand lane toward Kmart, and proceed to the store
Phone: (703) 361–8890
Hours: 9:30 A.M.–6:00 P.M., Monday–Wednesday, Friday, and Saturday; 9:30 A.M.–9:00 P.M., Thursday; noon–6:00 P.M., Sunday
Credit Cards: Discover, MasterCard, Visa
Personal Checks: Yes
Handicapped Accessible: Yes
Bus Tours: Yes

MECHANICSVILLE

Imp Pedlar (C & J Clark)
6559 Mechanicsville

Directions: Take I–295 to Route 360 to Mechanicsville, proceeding about 1 ½ miles on Route 360 to the store, which is located in Hanover Village Shopping Center, on the right-hand side of the road
Phone: (804) 730–2016
Hours: 10:00 A.M.–9:00 P.M., Monday–Saturday; 10:00 A.M.–5:30 P.M., Sunday
Credit Cards: MasterCard, Visa
Personal Checks: Yes
Handicapped Accessible: Yes
Bus Tours: Yes

NORGE

Aileen
7463 Richmond Road

Directions: From I–64 take exit 55A (Route 60) to Richmond Road
Phone: (804) 564–0332
Hours: 9:00 A.M.–7:00 P.M., Monday–Saturday; 9:00 A.M.–5:00 P.M., Sunday
Credit Cards: MasterCard, Visa
Personal Checks: Yes
Handicapped Accessible: Yes
Bus Tours: Yes

ROANOKE

Rack Room Shoes
Celebration Station

Directions: From I–81 take the Airport exit to the first traffic light and turn left. Turn right at Herronimus parking lot.
Phone: (703) 366–5174
Hours: 10:00 A.M.–9:00 P.M., Monday–Saturday; 1:00 P.M.–6:00 P.M., Sunday
Credit Cards: American Express, Discover, MasterCard, Visa
Personal Checks: Yes
Handicapped Accessible: Yes
Bus Tours: Yes

Tultex Mill Outlet
5327 Williamson Road

Directions: From I–81 take the Airport exit; drive past Cross Roads Mall, and turn left onto Williamson Road. In about 4 blocks, store is on the right.

Phone: (703) 362–4949
Hours: 9:30 A.M.–6:00 P.M., Monday–Saturday; 1:00 P.M.–5:00 P.M.,
Sunday
Credit Cards: MasterCard, Visa
Personal Checks: Yes
Handicapped Accessible: Yes
Bus Tours: Yes

ROCKY MOUNT

Virginia Apparel Outlet
721 N. Main Street

Directions: Take Route 220 South out of Roanoke to the Rocky
Mount Business exit. Proceed for 1.2 miles; store is on the right.
Phone: (703) 483–8266
Hours: 10:00 A.M.–5:00 P.M., Monday–Saturday
Credit Cards: Discover, MasterCard, Visa
Personal Checks: Yes, with identification
Handicapped Accessible: Yes
Bus Tours: Yes

SOUTH BOSTON

Tultex Mill Outlet
Hupps Mill Plaza

Directions: Take Route 360 South to Cavalier Road and make a right
turn. Drive 2 miles to Hupps Mill Plaza, on the left.
Phone: (804) 575–5597
Hours: 9:30 A.M.–6:00 P.M., Monday–Saturday
Credit Cards: MasterCard, Visa
Personal Checks: Yes
Handicapped Accessible: Yes
Bus Tours: Yes

SPRINGFIELD

Lamp Factory Outlet
6396 Springfield Plaza

Directions: Take I–95 to the Springfield exit (Route 644 West). Turn right, into Springfield Plaza.
Phone: (703) 569–5330
Hours: 10:00 A.M.–9:00 P.M., Monday–Saturday; noon–5:00 P.M., Sunday
Credit Cards: American Express, Discover, MasterCard, Visa
Personal Checks: Yes
Handicapped Accessible: Yes
Bus Tours: Yes

Talbots Surplus Store
6814 Old Springfield Plaza

Directions: Take I–95 to the Springfield exit (Route 644 West). Turn right, into Springfield Plaza.
Phone: (703) 644–5115
Hours: 9:30 A.M.–8:00 P.M., Monday–Friday; 9:00 A.M.–6:00 P.M., Saturday; noon–5:00 P.M., Sunday
Credit Cards: American Express, Diner's Club, MasterCard, Talbots, Visa
Personal Checks: Yes
Handicapped Accessible: Yes
Bus Tours: No

VIENNA

Tuesday Morning
136 Maple Avenue West
Vienna Shopping Center

Directions: From I–495 take Route 123 to Maple Avenue West. Store is on the left, in the back of the shopping center.

Phone: (703) 938–6707
Hours: 9:30 A.M.–6:00 P.M., Monday–Wednesday, Friday, and Saturday; 9:30 A.M.–9:00 P.M., Thursday; noon–6:00 P.M., Sunday
Credit Cards: Discover, MasterCard, Visa
Personal Checks: Yes
Handicapped Accessible: No
Bus Tours: Yes

VIRGINIA BEACH

Great American Outlet Mall
3750 Virginia Beach Boulevard

Directions: Take the Virginia Beach–Norfolk Expressway to the Rosemont Road exit to Route 58 (Virginia Beach Boulevard)
Phone: (804) 463–8665
Hours: 10:00 A.M.–9:00 P.M., Monday–Saturday; 12:30 P.M.–5:30 P.M., Sunday
Credit Cards: Most stores accept major credit cards.
Personal Checks: Most stores accept local checks.
Handicapped Accessible: Yes
Bus Tours: Yes, promotional packages available
Food: Available
Outlets:
Acme Boot Village
Aileen
All Sorts of Sports
Banister Shoes
Bare Necessities
Bugle Boy Outlet
Dress Barn
Dress Barn Woman
Famous Footwear
Fashion Flair
Fieldcrest Cannon

Fine Jewelry by Solange
Gitano
Jewelry Connection
Kids City
Kidsfeet
Kids Port USA
Kitchen Place
Leather Loft
$9.99 Stockroom
Old Mill
Paper Factory
Rack Room Shoes
Stormcrow Leather
Sunshades LTD.
Top of the Line Cosmetics
Toy Liquidators

Lillian Vernon
4000 Virginia Beach Boulevard

Directions: Take the Virginia Beach–Norfolk Expressway to exit 4 (Rosemont Road). Turn left on Virginia Beach Boulevard. Store is on the right.
Phone: (804) 463–7451
Hours: 10:00 A.M.–9:00 P.M., Monday–Friday; 10:00 A.M.–6:00 P.M., Saturday
Credit Cards: American Express, Diner's Club, Discover, MasterCard, Visa
Personal Checks: Yes
Handicapped Accessible: Yes
Bus Tours: Yes

Lucia . . . That's Me!
2720 N. Mall Drive

Directions: Take the Virginia Beach–Norfolk Expressway to exit 4 (Rosemont Road). Turn left on Virginia Beach Boulevard and proceed to the Lynnhaven North Shopping Center.

Phone: (804) 431–1931
Hours: 10:00 A.M.–9:00 P.M., Monday–Saturday; noon–5:00 P.M., Sunday
Credit Cards: MasterCard, Visa
Personal Checks: Yes, with proper identification
Handicapped Accessible: Yes
Bus Tours: Yes

WAYNESBORO

Waynesboro Village Factory Outlets
601 Shenandoah Drive, Box 1B

Directions: Take exit 94 off I–64, complex is at the southeast intersection of I–64 and Route 340
Phone: (703) 942–2320, administration office, or (703) 942-2302, information center
Hours: 10:00 A.M.–6:00 P.M., Monday–Saturday; 12:30 P.M.–5:30 P.M., Sunday
Credit Cards: Most stores accept major credit cards.
Personal Checks: Yes
Handicapped Accessible: Yes
Bus Tours: Yes
Notes and Attractions: Antique barn; Shenandoah Valley Crafters Cooperative
Outlets:
Aileen Ladies Sportswear
American Tourister
Banister Shoes
Barbizon Lingerie
Bass
Bugle Boy
Christmas Goose Collectibles
Corning/Revere
Dansk
Donnkenny

Gitano Kids
Gitano Warehouse Clearance Center
Housewares Store
Jonathan Logan Outlet
Leather Loft
L'eggs/Hanes/Bali
Liz Claiborne
London Fog
Manhattan
Paper Factory
Petal Pushers
Prestige Fragrance & Cosmetics
Ribbon Outlet
Royal Doulton
Sweaters, Ski & Sport
Toy Liquidators
Van Heusen
Westport Ltd.

WILLIAMSBURG

Berkeley Commons Outlet Center
5699 Richmond Road

Directions: From I–64 take exit 234; and follow east Route 60 and proceed 2 miles to the center, on the right
Phone: (804) 565–0702, recording
Hours: June through December, 9:00 A.M.–9:00 P.M., Sunday–Saturday. January and February, 9:00 A.M. to 6:00 P.M., Monday–Saturday; 10:00 A.M.–6:00 P.M., Sunday. March through May, 9:00 A.M.–9:00 P.M., Monday–Saturday; 10:00 A.M.–8:00 P.M., Sunday
Credit Cards: Most stores accept major credit cards.
Personal Checks: Most stores accept personal checks.
Handicapped Accessible: Yes
Bus Tours: Yes; promotional packages available
Food: Available

Outlets:
Aca Joe
Adolfo II
Anne Klein Outlet
Bass Shoe
Book Cellar
Brass Factory
Calvin Klein
Capezio
Carole Little
Carroll Reed
Carter's
Crystal Works
Designer Jewelry
Eddie Bauer
Etienne Aigner
Evan-Picone
Geoffrey Beene
Gilligan & O'Malley
Gitano
Gitano Kids
Hamilton Luggage & Handbags
harvé benard
He-Ro Group

I.B. Diffusion
J. Crew
J. G. Hook
JH Collectibles
Jones NY
Jordache
Kitchen Collection
Liz Claiborne
Lucia . . . That's Me!
Maidenform
Members Only
Mikasa
Nike
9 West
Pierre Cardin
Ribbon Outlet
Royal Doulton
Socks Galore & More
Stone Mountain Handbags
Top of the Line Cosmetics
Van Heusen/Bass
Welcome Home
Windsor Shirt Company

Carolina Furniture
5425 Richmond Road

Directions: From I–64 take exit 234 (Route 60 West) to Richmond Road
Phone: (804) 565–3000 or (800) 582–8916, Virginia only
Hours: 9:00 A.M.–6:00 P.M., Monday–Thursday and Saturday; 9:00 A.M.–9:00 P.M., Friday; 1:00 P.M.–6:00 P.M., Sunday
Credit Cards: MasterCard, Visa
Personal Checks: Yes
Handicapped Accessible: Yes; aisles are tight, however
Bus Tours: Yes

Patriot Plaza
3032 Richmond Road

Directions: From I–64 take exit 55A (Route 60 West) to Richmond Road
Phone: Call individual stores.
Hours: 9:00 A.M.–9:00 P.M., Monday–Saturday; 10:00 A.M.–6:00 P.M., Sunday
Credit Cards: MasterCard, Visa
Personal Checks: Yes
Handicapped Accessible: Yes
Bus Tours: Yes
Outlets:
American Tourister
Dansk
Gorham
Leather Loft
Nettle Creek
Towle/1690 House
Villeroy & Boch
WestPoint Pepperell

Williamsburg Outlet Shops
6536 Richmond Road

Directions: From I-64 take exit 234 (Route 60 West) to Richmond Road
Phone: (804) 229–7480
Hours: 10:00 A.M.–9:00 P.M., Monday–Saturday; 11:00 A.M.–6:00 P.M., Sunday
Credit Cards: Most stores accept major credit cards.
Personal Checks: Yes, local checks only
Handicapped Accessible: Yes
Bus Tours: Yes
Outlets:
Book Warehouse
Carpet & Rug Outlet
Christmas Mouse

Imp Pedlar
Iva's
Lightfoot Manor
Pinehurst Lingerie
Tanner Dress Shop
20 and Under
Williamsburg Shirt Company

Williamsburg Soap & Candle Company
7521 Richmond Road

Directions: From I–64 take exit 231 (Highway 607 to Norge) to Route 60. Store is on the left.
Phone: (804) 564–3354
Hours: 9:00 A.M.–5:00 P.M., Sunday–Saturday. Later hours in summer; closed Thanksgiving, Christmas, and New Year's Day.
Credit Cards: MasterCard, Visa
Personal Checks: Yes
Handicapped Accessible: Yes
Bus Tours: Yes

WOODBRIDGE

Potomac Mills
2700 Potomac Mills Circle

Directions: From I–95 take exit 156, Dale City; follow signs
Phone: (703) 643–1770 or (703) 490–5948
Hours: 10:00 A.M.–9:30 P.M., Monday–Saturday; 11:00 A.M.–6:00 P.M., Sunday
Credit Cards: Most stores accept major credit cards.
Personal Checks: Most stores accept personal checks.
Handicapped Accessible: Yes
Bus Tours: Yes
Food: Food court

Notes or Attractions: Outlets and off-price stores in a very long building divided into neighborhoods. Days Inn adjacent (703–494–4433).

Neighborhood 1
Cargo Factory Outlet
Everything's A Dollar
J.C. Clinton's
Kid City
Lamp Factory Outlet
New York Electronics
9.99 Stockroom
9 West
Piece Goods Shop
Swank Factory Store
Toy Liquidators
Waccamaw
Woodward & Lothrop Outlet
    Center

Neighborhood 2
American Tourister
Carter's Childrenswear
Coat World
Compare Menswear by Ted Louis
Designer Yarns
L. J.'s Fashions
T.H. Mandy
The Warehouse
Waxie Maxie Warehouse Store

Neighborhood 3
Books-A-Million
Jewelry Vault
Just Kids Outlet Store
Newport Sportswear
Rack Room Branded Shoes
Sassafras
Secaucus Handbags

Shoe Town Outlet
Sneakee Feet

Neighborhood 4
Benetton Outlet
L'eggs/Hanes/Bali Factory Outlet

Neighborhood 5
Daffy's Clothing Bargains
    for Millionaires
Intimate Eve
Jewelry Outlet
Jordache
Nike Outlet
Price Jewelers
RW's Sweater Outlet
S & K Brand Menswear

Neighborhood 6
The Answer
Banister Shoes
Bugle Boy Outlet
Contemporary Man
Linens 'n Things
Manhatten Factory Outlet
Merry Go Round Outlet
Specials, Exclusively Levi Strauss
Webster Warehouse
Westport Ltd.

Neighborhood 7
Best Jewelry
Brass Factory Outlet
Cambridge Dry Goods
Claires Outlet Boutique
Dress Barn
Executive Neckwear

Fashion Express
Hamilton Luggage
Hamrick's
International Diamond Cutters
  Exchange
Maidenform Outlet
Paper Factory
Pro Image
Remington Factory Outlet
Ritz Camera & Video
  Outlet Center
Ross Dress For Less
Square Circle

Neighborhood 8

Cosmetics & Sculptured Nails
Dina's Discount Boutique
Famous Brands Housewares
Hahn's Shoes Outlet
IKEA
Lee Winter
Macy's Specialty Stores
Men's Market
Oriental Weavers
Prestige Fragrances & Cosmetics
Sears Outlet
Unisa
Windsor Shirt Co.
Young Land

Neighborhood 9

Books-A-Million Annex
Calvin Klein
Carole Hochman Lingerie
Chico's
Delta Hosiery
Dollar Bills
Eddie Bauer Outlet
First Choice
Georgetown Leather
  Design Outlet
Guess? Factory Store
Hilda of Iceland
Kids Barn
Lady Footlocker Outlet
Laura Ashley
Lillian Vernon
Mondi
No Nonsense
Nordstrom Rack
Phil's Shoes
Rowe Showplace Gallery
Sterling Super Optical
Top of the Line Cosmetics
Toy Works
Van Heusen Factory Store
Whims Sarah Coventry Outlet

Tuesday Morning

Prince William Plaza II
14344 Jefferson Davis Highway at Belair Road

Directions: Take I–95 to exit 156 and drive south on Jefferson Davis Highway for about 3 miles.
Phone: (703) 494–1215
Hours: 9:30 A.M.–6:00 P.M., Monday–Wednesday, Friday, and Saturday; 9:30 A.M.–9:00 P.M., Thursday; noon–6:00 P.M., Sunday

Credit Cards: Discover, MasterCard, Visa
Personal Checks: Yes
Handicapped Accessible: Yes
Bus Tours: Yes

WYTHEVILLE

Wicker Basket Outlet
Route 2, Box 236A

Directions: Take exit 77 off I-81. Outlet is visible from the highway.
Phone: (703) 228–6030
Hours: 10:00 A.M.–8:00 P.M., Monday–Saturday; 10:00 A.M.–6:00 P.M., Sunday
Credit Cards: MasterCard, Visa
Personal Checks: Yes
Handicapped Accessible: Yes
Bus Tours: Yes

Wythe Shopping Plaza
922 E. Main Street

Directions: Take I–81 to exit 73. Plaza is right at the exit, on Route 77.
Phone: None
Hours: 9:00 A.M.–6:00 P.M., Monday–Thursday and Saturday; 9:00 A.M.–9:00 P.M., Friday; noon–5:00 P.M., Sunday
Credit Cards: MasterCard, Visa
Personal Checks: Yes
Handicapped Accessible: Yes
Bus Tours: Yes
Outlets:
Bag & Baggage of Virginia
Burlington Clothing Outlet
London Fog
Van Heusen

WEST VIRGINIA

1. Ceredo
2. Ellenboro
3. Franklin
4. Martinsburg
5. Milton

6. New Martinsville
7. Princeton
8. Star City
9. Wheeling
10. Williamstown

WEST VIRGINIA

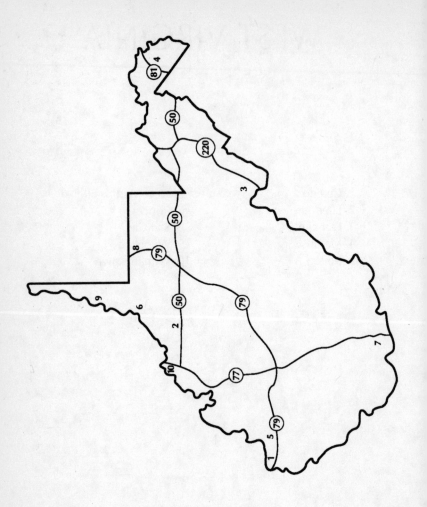

CEREDO

Pilgrim Glass Corporation
Airport Road and Walker's Branch

Directions: From Huntington, take I–64 West to Kenova, exit 1. Turn left at bottom of the ramp. Turn left at stop sign. Factory is at the end of the road.
Phone: (304) 453–3553
Hours: 9:00 A.M.–5:00 P.M., Monday–Saturday
Credit Cards: MasterCard, Visa
Personal Checks: Yes
Handicapped Accessible: Yes
Bus Tours: Yes

ELLENBORO

Mid-Atlantic Glass Company
Old U.S. Route 50

Directions: From I–79 take the Clarksburg exit and drive west on Route 50 for about 40 miles to the Ellenboro-Harrisville exit. Turn right and go across a little bridge. Turn right again and go up the road about ½ mile. Store is on the right.
Phone: (304) 869–3351
Hours: 8:00 A.M.–5:00 P.M., Monday–Friday; 9:00 A.M.–3:00 P.M., Saturday
Credit Cards: MasterCard, Visa
Personal Checks: Yes
Handicapped Accessible: No
Bus Tours: Yes

FRANKLIN

Hanover Shoe Store
Route 220

Directions: Take Route 220 South out of Franklin for 3 miles. Factory is on the left.
Phone: (304) 358–2335
Hours: 9:30 A.M.–5:00 P.M., Monday–Saturday
Credit Cards: American Express, Discover, MasterCard, Visa
Personal Checks: Yes
Handicapped Accessible: Yes
Bus Tours: Yes

MARTINSBURG

Blue Ridge Outlet Center
315 West Stephens Street

Directions: From I–81 take exit 13 East onto King Street. Turn right on Queen Street and proceed to Stephens Street.
Phone: (800) 445–3993 or (304) 261–SHOP (7467)
Hours: 10:00 A.M.–6:00 P.M., Monday–Wednesday and Saturday; 10:00 A.M.–9:00 P.M., Thursday and Friday; 11:00 A.M.–5:00 P.M., Sunday. Closed Easter, Thanksgiving, and Christmas; extended hours during some seasons.
Credit Cards: MasterCard, Visa
Personal Checks: Yes
Handicapped Accessible: Yes
Bus Tours: Yes
Food: Available

Outlets:
Berkeley Building:
Anne Klein
Banister Shoes
Barbizon
Boston Traders
Brass Works
Corning/Revere
Factory Linens
Fashion Flair
Fuller Brush
Gold-N-Silver
Just My Size
Leather Loft
L'eggs/Hanes/Bali
Manhattan
Nike
Paper Factory
Perfumania
Petals
Ribbon Outlet
Robert Scott & David Brooks
Royce Hosiery
Silver Sky Jewelry
Socks Galore & More
totes/Sunglass World
Van Heusen
Wallet Works
Warnaco

Crawford Building:
Polo/Ralph Lauren
West Virginia Fine Glass

Dunn Building:
Amity
Bass Shoe
Benetton
CrazyHorse
Euro Collections
Etienne Aigner
Evan Picone/Gant
Georgetown Leather Design
Hanes Activewear
Head over Heels
J. Crew
Nautica
Pfaltzgraff
Ruff Hewn
Specials, Exclusively by Levi
    Strauss

Clock Building:
Book Warehouse
Carter's Childenswear
Dan River
Generra
Gorham
London Fog
Toy Liquidators

Tanger Factory Stores
Viking Way

Directions: From I–81 take exit 13 (King Street) and proceed to Viking Way

Phone: (304) 263–5187 or (304) 263–6255

Hours: 10:00 A.M.–9:00 P.M., Monday–Saturday; 11:00 A.M.–6:00 P.M., Sunday

Credit Cards: Most stores accept major credit cards.
Personal Checks: Most stores accept personal checks.
Handicapped Accessible: Yes
Bus Tours: Yes
Food: Available
Notes or Attractions: Sheraton Hotel adjacent
Outlets:
American Tourister
Cape Isle Knitters
Eagle's Eye
Geoffrey Beene
JH Collectibles
Liz Claiborne
Oneida
OshKosh B'Gosh
Reebok
Van Heusen

Rolane Factory Outlet
230 Porter Avenue

Directions: From I–81 take the King Street exit to Porter Avenue and turn right. Store is on the left.
Phone: (304) 263–8888
Hours: 10:00 A.M.–5:30 P.M., Monday–Thursday and Saturday; 10:00 A.M.–8:30 P.M., Friday; noon–5:00 P.M., Sunday
Credit Cards: Discover, MasterCard, Visa
Personal Checks: Yes
Handicapped Accessible: Yes
Bus Tours: Yes

MILTON

Blenko Glass Company, Inc.
Box 67
Fairground Road

Directions: Take I–64 to exit 28, Milton. Go left and proceed to traffic light. Turn right. At next traffic light turn left; follow signs to outlet.
Phone: (304) 743–9081
Hours: 8:00 A.M.–4:00 P.M., Monday–Saturday; noon–4:00 P.M., Sunday
Credit Cards: American Express, Discover, MasterCard, Visa
Personal Checks: Yes
Handicapped Accessible: No
Bus Tours: Yes

NEW MARTINSVILLE

Viking Glass Company (Dalzell Viking)
802 Parkway

Directions: Turn west on Parkway. Go to first light south of Ohio Route 7 bridge. Go right on First Street. Store is next to factory.
Phone: (304) 455–2900
Hours: 9:00 A.M.–5:00 P.M., Monday–Saturday; noon–5:00 P.M., Sunday
Credit Cards: MasterCard, Visa
Personal Checks: Yes, with identification
Handicapped Accessible: Yes, through rear entrance
Bus Tours: Yes
Notes and Attractions: Tours of hand-crafted glassworks conducted Monday through Friday from 9:15 to 10:30 A.M. and from 1:15 to 3:30 P.M.

PRINCETON

Tultex Mill Outlet
1119 C Stafford Drive

Directions: Take Route 460 to the traffic light with the sign indicating DOWNTOWN PRINCETON; go to the next traffic light and turn right. Then turn into the Princeton Shopping Center parking lot.
Phone: (304) 425–8448
Hours: 10:00 A.M.–6:00 P.M., Monday–Saturday
Credit Cards: MasterCard, Visa
Personal Checks: Yes
Handicapped Accessible: Yes
Bus Tours: Yes

STAR CITY

Gentile Glass Company
425 Industrial Avenue

Directions: I–79, exit 155 to routes 17 and 19 southeast, to bridge and traffic light. Turn left. Go 1 block to stop sign and turn left. Go 1 block to 425 Industrial Avenue.
Phone: (304) 599–2750
Hours: 8:00 A.M.–3:30 P.M., Monday–Friday; 8:00 A.M.–noon, Saturday
Credit Cards: No
Personal Checks: Yes
Handicapped Accessible: No
Bus Tours: Yes

WHEELING

Fostoria Glass Factory Outlet
769 National Road

Directions: From I–70 take exit 2 to National Road
Phone: (304) 233–3035
Hours: 9:00 A.M.–5:00 P.M., Sunday–Friday; 9:00 A.M.–8:00 P.M., Saturday
Credit Cards: MasterCard, Visa
Personal Checks: Yes
Handicapped Accessible: Yes
Bus Tours: Yes

WILLIAMSTOWN

Fenton Art Glass Company
420 Caroline Avenue

Directions: Take I–77 to Route 31/14
Phone: (304) 375–7772
Hours: September through May, 8:00 A.M.–5:00 P.M., Monday–Saturday. June through August, 8:00 A.M.–8:00 P.M., Monday–Friday; 8:00 A.M.–5:00 P.M., Saturday.
Credit Cards: Discover, MasterCard, Visa
Personal Checks: Yes
Handicapped Accessible: Yes
Bus Tours: Yes, if notified in advance
Special Savings: Annual February sale at gift shop
Notes or Attractions: Free forty-minute guided tours are available weekdays from 8:40 to 10:00 A.M. and from 11:20 A.M. to 2:20 P.M. Museum with small admission charge.

PRODUCT INDEX

Lady Footlocker Outlet, 49
L. L. Bean, 52
Marketplace Sneakers, 55
National Locker Room, 58
Nautica, 58
Nike, 59
North Face, 60
Ocello Sportswear, 65
Rawlings Sport Goods, 70
Reebok, 70
Russell Jerzees, 74
Sneakee Feet, 77
Sports & Sorts, 78
Sports Fans, 79
Sportshoe Center, 79
Sports Wearhouse, 79
Sweater, Ski & Sport, 81
Sweatshirt Company, 82

Books and Records
Bear Mountain Books, 7
Bentley Books, 8
Book Cellar, 10
Book Hutch, 10
Books-a-Million, 11
Booksellers Warehouse, 11
Book Stall, 11
Book Warehouse, 11
Maxine's Books, 55
Record World, 70
Royal Book Outlet, 73
Waldenbooks, 88

Candles, Soaps
American Candle, 3
Candle Factory, 14
Candle Towne U.S.A., 14
Old Candle Barn Outlet, 61
Pocono Candle Shop, 67
Welcome Home, 89

Williamsburg Soap & Candle
  Company, 92

**China, Clocks, Cookware, Crystal,
Dinnerware, Gifts, Glass, Watches**
American Pottery & Glass, 3
Blenko Glass Company, Inc., 10
Brass Factory, 11
Brass Works, 11
Chesapeake Pottery, 17
China Plus, 18
Clock Center, 19
Corning/Revere, 21
Country Cheese 'N Jam Gift Outlet,
  22
Dansk Factory Outlet, 23
Fenton Art Glass Outlet, 31
Fostoria Glass Factory Outlet, 32
Fuller Brush, 34
Gentile Glass Company, 35
Gorham, 37
Hamilton Watch & Clock Shoppe,
  38
Lancaster Pottery & Glass Outlet, 49
Lenox Crystal & China, 51
Lillian Vernon, 51
Mid-Atlantic Glass Company, 56
Mikasa Factory Store, 57
Oneida, 61
Pewtarex Factory Outlet Stores, 65
Pfaltzgraff, 65
Pilgrim Glass Corporation, 66
Reading China & Glass, 70
Reed & Barton, 70
Royal Doulton, 73
Salisbury Pewter, 74
Salt Glaze Pottery, 74
Solid Brass Inc., 78
Susquehanna Glass, 81
Syracuse China Factory Outlet, 82

Clothing, Women's

Noel's Hosiery, 60
No Nonsense, 60
Royce Hosiery, 73
Socks Galore & More, 77
Socks Plus, 78

Sporting Goods, Skiwear, Outdoor Gear, and Accessories
Adidas Outlet, 1
All Sorts of Sports, 2
Enterprise Golf Outlet, 28
Original I. Goldberg, 62
Philly Fever, 66
Pro Image, 69
Rawlings Sport Goods, 70
Sweater Mill, 81
Sweater, Ski & Sport, 81
Sweatshirt Company, 82

Sunglasses
J. C. Clintons, 43
Sunday Best, 80

Sunglass Outlet, 80
Sunglass World, 81
Sunshades, 81
totes, 84

Tools
Black & Decker, 9
Madran Tools, 53

Toys, Games, Crafts
Kay Bee Toys, 46
Pocono Toy Outlet, 67
Toy Liquidators, 85
Toys Unlimited, 85
Toy Works, 85
Your Toy Center, 92

Wood Products
Colonial Wood Benders, Inc., 21
Door Store, 26
Handmade Quilts , 39

OUTLET INDEX

Aca Joe
VA: Williamsburg, 239

Accents
NJ: Burlington, 123

Accessories Plus
NJ: Secaucus, 133

Accessories Plus II
NJ: Secaucus, 133

Accessory Factory
NY: Central Valley, 143

Acme Boot Village
VA: Virginia Beach, 235

Adidas Outlet
NY: Central Valley, 143
NY: Malta, 156

Adolfo
NJ: Wall Township, 135
PA: Tannersville, 208

Adolfo II
MD: Perryville, 112

American Tourister
DE: Rehoboth Beach, 96
MD: Chester, 102
MD: Perryville, 112
NJ: Secaucus, 113
NJ: Wall Township, 135
NY: Central Valley, 143
NY: Cohoes, 144
NY: Fishkill, 147
NY: Monticello, 157
PA: Lancaster, 187
PA: Philadelphia, 195
PA: Somerset, 206
PA: Tannersville, 208
PA: Wyomissing, 215
VA: Waynesboro, 237
VA: Williamsburg, 240
VA: Woodbridge, 242
WV: Martinsburg, 250

Amity
WV: Martinsburg, 249

Amy Stoudt
NJ: Fairfield, 124
PA: Philadelphia, 195

Andrea Carrano
NJ: Secaucus, 132

Anne Klein
MD: Perryville, 112
NJ: Flemington, 126
NJ: Secaucus, 132
NY: Central Valley, 143
NY: Lake George, 153
PA: Tannersville, 208
VA: Williamsburg, 239
WV: Martinsburg, 249

Anne Klein Petites
NJ: Flemington, 126
NY: Central Valley, 143

Annie Sez
NJ: Flemington, 126
PA: Lancaster, 185

Ann-Michele Originals
VA: Lightfoot, 229

Ann Taylor
PA: Philadelphia, 195

The Answer
PA: Philadelphia, 195
VA: Woodbridge, 242

Argenti
MD: Queenstown, 115
NJ: Secaucus, 132

Argo Factory Store
PA: Lancaster, 185

Arrow
PA: East Stroudsburg, 176
VA: Fort Chiswell, 226

Art and Frame Outlet
PA: Greensburg, 181

Artist's Outlet
PA: Philadelphia, 195

Astor Swimwear Outlet
PA: Allentown, 170
PA: Lancaster, 183
PA: Reading, 200
PA: West Lawn, 211

Barbizon Lingerie
MD: Perryville, 112
MD: Queenstown, 115
NJ: Secaucus (2), 133
NY: Lake George, 151
NY: Monticello, 157
PA: Lancaster, 188
PA: Somerset, 206
VA: Lightfoot, 228
VA: Waynesboro, 237
WV: Martinsburg, 249

Bare Necessities
NJ: Fairfield, 124
NJ: Matawan, 129
NY: Niagara Falls, 161
NY: Rochester, 163
VA: Virginia Beach, 235

Bargain Sneaker
MD: Annapolis, 101
PA: Lancaster, 188

Bass Shoes
DE: Rehoboth Beach, 96
MD: Annapolis, 101
MD: Perryville, 112
MD: Queenstown, 115
NJ: Flemington, 126
NJ: Lafayette, 128
NJ: Secaucus (2), 133, 134
NJ: Wall Township, 135
NY: Barneveld, 139
NY: Bellport, 140
NY: Central Valley, 143
NY: Fishkill, 147
NY: Malta, 156
NY: Monticello, 157
NY: Mt. Kisco, 158

NY: Niagara Falls (2), 161, 162
PA: Lancaster, 188
PA: Reading, 203
PA: Tannersville, 208
PA: York, 217
VA: Fort Chiswell, 226
VA: Fredericksburg, 227
VA: Lightfoot, 228
VA: Waynesboro, 237
VA: Williamsburg, 239
WV: Martinsburg, 249

Bauer Shoes
PA: Lancaster, 185
PA: Morgantown, 191

Bay Carpets
MD: Queenstown, 114

Bear Mountain Books
NY: Central Valley, 143
PA: Philadelphia, 195

Beauty Barn
NJ: Matawan, 129

Beauty Scenter
PA: Morgantown, 191
PA: Reading, 203

Bed 'n Bath
NJ: Secaucus, 133

Bed, Bath & Beyond
NJ: Flemington, 126
PA: Philadelphia, 195

Beer Arena
PA: Greensburg, 181

Book Cellar
MD: Perryville, 112
PA: Tannersville, 208
VA: Fredericksburg, 227
VA: Williamsburg, 239

Book Hutch
VA: Lightfoot, 228

Books-A-Million
VA: Woodbridge, 242, 243

Booksellers Warehouse
NY: Niagara Falls, 161
NY: Rochester, 163

Book Stall
NJ: Matawan, 129

Book Warehouse
DE: Rehoboth Beach, 96
MD: Queenstown, 115
NY: Lake George, 151
PA: East Stroudsburg, 176
PA: Lancaster, 188
PA: Somerset, 206
VA: Fort Chiswell, 226
VA: Williamsburg, 240
WV: Martinsburg, 249

Bostonian Factory Outlet
PA: Kennett Square, 183
PA: Philadelphia, 195
PA: Reading, 203

Boston Trader Kids
NY: Central Valley, 143

Boston Traders
NY: Central Valley, 143
NY: Niagara Falls, 162

PA: Wyomissing, 215
WV: Martinsburg, 249

Branded Shoe Outlet
PA: Harrisburg, 181
PA: Robesonia, 204

Brands Factory Outlet
PA: Somerset, 206

Brass Factory
MD: Perryville, 112
PA: Philadelphia, 195
VA: Williamsburg, 239
VA: Woodbridge, 242

Brass Works
PA: Lancaster, 187
PA: Reading, 203
PA: Somerset, 206
WV: Martinsburg, 249

The Braun Company
PA: Lancaster, 184

Briefcase Unlimited
PA: Philadelphia, 195

Bruce Alan Bags
MD: Queenstown, 115
NY: Malta, 156
PA: Lancaster, 188
VA: Fredericksburg, 227
VA: Lightfoot, 228

Bubbles & Scents
PA: Reading, 203

Buffalo Mills Outlet
PA: Stroudsburg, 207

Cami'z
PA: East Stroudsburg, 176

Campus Factory Outlet
NJ: Secaucus, 133
VA: Fort Chiswell, 226

Canadian's Outlet
PA: Philadelphia, 195

Candle Factory
NJ: Burlington, 123

Candle Towne U.S.A
PA: Stroudsburg, 207

Candy Barrel Outlet
NY: Niagara Falls, 162

Candy Kitchen
DE: Rehoboth Beach, 96

Canterbury of New Zealand
PA: Philadelphia, 196
PA: Wyomissing, 215

Cape Craft
MD: Annapolis, 101

Cape Isle Knitters
DE: Rehoboth Beach, 96
MD: Annapolis, 101
MD: Perryville, 112
MD: Queenstown, 115
NJ: Flemington, 127
NJ: Wall Township, 135
NY: Bellport, 140
NY: Central Valley, 143
NY: Fishkill, 147

NY: Malta, 156
NY: Mt. Kisco, 158
PA: Lancaster, 188
PA: Somerset, 206
PA: Tannersville, 208
VA: Fredericksburg, 227
VA: Lightfoot, 228
WV: Martinsburg, 250

Capezio
DE: Rehoboth Beach, 96
MD: Perryville, 112
MD: Queenstown, 115
NJ: Flemington, 127
NJ: Lafayette, 128
NJ: Secaucus, 133
NY: Mt. Kisco, 158
PA: East Stroudsburg, 176
VA: Williamsburg, 239

C.A. Reed
PA: Edwardsville, 177
PA: Shamokin Dam, 205
PA: Williamsport, 212

Cargo Factory Outlet
PA: Philadelphia, 196
VA: Woodbridge, 242

Carlos Falchi
NY: Central Valley, 143

Carole Hockman Lingerie
NJ: Secaucus, 132
NY: Central Valley, 143
PA: Reading, 203
VA: Woodbridge, 243

Carole Little
MD: Perryville, 112

Chico's Outlet
PA: Philadelphia, 196
VA: Woodbridge, 243

Children's Bootery
PA: Philadelphia, 196

Children's Mill Factory Outlet Inc.
PA: Reading, 201

Children's Outlet
NJ: Matawan, 130
NJ: Secaucus, 133
PA: Philadelphia, 196
VA: Lightfoot, 228

China Plus
MD: Laurel, 110
PA: Stroudsburg, 208

Christian Benard
NJ: Secaucus, 133

Christmas Goose
VA: Waynesboro, 237

Christmas Mouse
VA: Williamsburg, 240

Christmas Tree Hill
DE: Rehoboth Beach, 97

Church's English Shoes
NJ: Secaucus, 131

Claire's Factory Store
MD: Thurmont, 119

Claire's Outlet Boutique
NY: Niagara Falls, 162
VA: Woodbridge, 242

Classic Caramel Company
PA: York, 215

Clifford & Wills
PA: Reading, 203

Clifford Michael
NY: Central Valley, 143

Clock Center
NY: Lake George, 152

Clothes Out Closet
PA: Reading, 203

Clothes Outlet
MD: Cockeysville, 103

Club House
NJ: Matawan, 130

Cluett Apparel
PA: Morgantown, 191

Coach Factory Store
NY: Amagansett, 138
PA: Reading, 203

Coat Factory
PA: Philadelphia, 196

Coat World
NJ: Flemington, 127
NY: Malta, 156
VA: Woodbridge, 242

Cobbler's Factory Outlet
PA: Ephrata, 179
PA: Harrisburg, 182
PA: Lemoyne, 189
PA: Lewistown, 190
PA: Williamsport, 212

Creative Impressions Art
DE: Rehobeth Beach, 96

Crib
PA: Morgantown, 191

Crystal Sportswear by Kobe
NJ: Secaucus, 131

Crystal Works
NJ: Flemington, 127
NY: Bellport, 140
NY: Central Valley, 143
PA: Somerset, 206
VA: Williamsburg, 239

Custom Sportswear
PA: Reading, 201

**Daffy's Clothing Bargains
for Millionaires,**
VA: Woodbridge, 242

Dali B
NJ: Secaucus, 133

Damon Creations
NJ: Secaucus, 133

Damon/Enroe
NY: Lake George, 152

Damon Shirts
NY: Monticello, 157

Dan River Outlet
VA: Danville, 223
WV: Martinsburg, 249

Dansk Factory Outlet
MD: Queenstown, 115
NJ: Flemington, 125

NY: Central Valley, 143
NY: Cohoes, 144
NY: Lake George, 153
NY: Mount Kisco, 158
PA: Lancaster, 188
PA: Tannersville, 208
VA: Waynesboro, 237
VA: Williamsburg, 240

Danskin Factory Outlet
NY: Niagara Falls, 161
PA: Wyomissing, 214
PA: York, 217

Danson Jewelers
NJ: Secaucus, 131

Danville Factory Outlet
PA: Danville, 174

Dazzles
PA: Philadelphia, 196

Deb Fashion Outlet
NY: Niagara Falls, 162

Delta Hosiery
DE: Wilmington, 98
NY: Central Valley, 143
PA: Lancaster, 185, 186
PA: Morgantown, 191
PA: Philadelphia, 196
PA: Reading, 201
PA: Waynesboro, 210
PA: York, 217
VA: Fairfax, 224
VA: Fredericksburg, 227
VA: Woodbridge, 243

Designer Jewelry
VA: Williamsburg, 239

Designer Luggage Depot
NJ: Fairfield, 124
NJ: Secaucus, 133
PA: Philadelphia, 196

Designer Wholesale Outlet
PA: Stroudsburg, 208

Designer Yarns
PA: Philadelphia, 196
VA: Woodbridge, 242

Dexter Shoe Outlet Store
NY: Barneveld, 139

Diamonds Unlimited
PA: Philadelphia, 196
VA: Lightfoot, 228

Diane Freis
NY: Malta, 156

Diane Gilman
NJ: Secaucus, 134

Diesse Shoes
NJ: Edison, 124

Dina's Discount Boutique
VA: Woodbridge, 243

Doe-Spun Factory Store
PA: York, 217

Dollar Bills
VA: Woodbridge, 243

Dollar Save Outlet
PA: East Stroudsburg, 175

Donna Karan
NJ: Flemington, 127
NY: Central Valley, 143

Donnkenny
VA: Waynesboro, 237

Dooney & Bourke
PA: Reading, 203

Door Store
NJ: Secaucus, 134

Down East Factory Outlet
PA: Reading, 201

Draperies, Etc.
PA: Erie, 180

Dress Barn
MD: Greenbelt, 108
NJ: Fairfield, 124
NJ: Matawan, 130
NY: Rochester, 163
PA: Lancaster, 187
PA: Philadelphia, 196
VA: Fairfax, 224
VA: Lightfoot, 228
VA: Virginia Beach, 235
VA: Woodbridge, 242

Dress Barn Woman
NJ: Flemington, 126
PA: Lancaster, 187
PA: Philadelphia, 196
VA: Lightfoot, 228
VA: Virginia Beach, 235

Dunham Footwear
NY: Latham, 155

Eagle's Eye
DE: Rehoboth Beach, 96

PA: Lancaster, 187
PA: Wyomissing, 215
WV: Martinsburg, 250

Eastern Shore Uniform Company
MD: Ocean City, 111

East Hampton Clothing
NJ: Secaucus, 133

East Prospect Factory Outlet
PA: East Prospect, 175

Eddie Bauer Outlet
DE: Rehoboth Beach, 97
VA: Williamsburg, 239
VA: Woodbridge, 243

E.K. Bags
NY: Mt. Kisco, 158

Electronics Outlet
PA: Wyomissing, 215

Elegant Boutique
PA: Stroudsburg, 208

Elkay Factory Outlet
PA: Philadelphia, 194

Ellen Tracy
NJ: Flemington, 127
NY: Central Valley, 143
NY: Malta, 156

Emerson Radio Outlet
NJ: Secaucus, 133

Endicott Johnson Factory Outlet
NY: Rochester, 163

Enterprise Golf Outlet
NJ: Secaucus, 134

Eric Allen Factory Store
NY: Central Valley, 143

Escada
NY: Cohoes, 144

Espirit
NY: Central Valley, 143
NY: Niagara Falls, 162

Etienne Aigner
DE: Rehoboth Beach, 97
MD: Perryville, 112
NY: Central Valley, 143
NY: Lake George, 153
PA: Tannersville, 208
VA: Williamsburg, 239
WV: Martinsburg, 249

Euro Collections
WV: Martinsburg, 249

European Designer Outlet
NJ: Secaucus, 134

Evan-Picone
MD: Queenstown, 115
NJ: North Bergen, 130
PA: Lancaster, 188
PA: Reading, 203
PA: Wyomissing, 215
VA: Williamsburg, 239

Evan Picone/Gant
WV: Martinsburg, 249

Everything's A $1.00
PA: Philadelphia, 196
VA: Woodbridge, 242

Executive Neckwear
NJ: Flemington, 127
NJ: Secaucus, 133
PA: Lancaster, 187
PA: Philadelphia, 196
VA: Lightfoot, 228
VA: Woodbridge, 242

Fabric Factory Outlet
PA: Philadelphia, 194

Factory Linens
PA: Lancaster, 187
WV: Martinsburg, 249

Famous Brands
NJ: Secaucus, 133
NY: Watkins Glen,. 166
PA: Philadelphia, 196

Famous Brands Housewares
DE: Rehoboth Beach, 97
NJ: Flemington, 126
NY: Lake George, 154
NY: Mt. Kisco, 158
PA: Lancaster, 187
PA: Morgantown, 191
PA: Reading, 203
VA: Woodbridge, 243

Famous Brand Yarns
NJ: Flemington, 127
NY: Central Valley, 143

Famous Footwear
NJ: Fairfield, 124
NJ: Flemington, 126
NJ: Secaucus, 131
NY: Mt. Kisco, 158

NY: Niagara Falls, 161
NY: Rochester, 163
NY: West Seneca, 166
PA: Philadelphia, 196
VA: Lightfoot, 229
VA: Virginia Beach, 235

Famous Galleries of Williamsburg
VA: Lightfoot, 229

Fan Fever
PA: Philadelphia, 196

Fanny Farmer
MD: Queenstown, 115
NY: Niagara Falls, 161
NY: Rochester, 163
PA: Lancaster, 186
PA: Reading, 203

Farah
PA: Lancaster, 188
PA: Reading, 203

Fashion Bug
NY: Rochester, 163

Fashion Bug Plus
NY: West Seneca, 166

Fashion Express
VA: Woodbridge, 243

Fashion Factory
NY: Niagara Falls, 161
PA: Philadelphia, 196

Fashion Finds
NJ: Matawan, 130

277

Fashion Flair
NJ: Matawan, 130
NJ: Secaucus, 133
NY: Binghamton, 141
NY: Central Valley, 143
NY: Colonie, 145
NY: Malta, 156
NY: Monticello, 157
NY: Williamsville, 167
PA: Lancaster, 185, 187
PA: Olyphant, 193
PA: State College, 207
PA: Williamsport, 212
VA: Lightfoot, 230
VA: Virginia Beach, 235
WV: Martinsburg, 249

Fashion Jewelry Exchange
PA: Somerset, 206

Fashion Shoe Outlet
NY: Niagara Falls, 161

Fenton Art Glass Company
WV: Williamstown, 253

Fieldcrest Cannon
NY: Corning, 143
NY: Lake George, 152
NY: Monticello, 157
PA: Lancaster, 186
PA: Somerset, 206
PA: Wyomissing, 215
VA: Lightfoot, 230
VA: Virginia Beach, 235

Filene's Basement
PA: Philadelphia, 196

Finders Keepers
DE: Rehoboth Beach, 96

Fine Jewelry by Solange
VA: Virginia Beach, 235

First Choice/Escada
NJ: Flemington, 127
NY: Central Valley, 143
VA: Woodbridge, 243

Flemington Fashion Outlet
NJ: Fairfield, 124
NJ: Secaucus, 131
PA: Edwardsville, 178
PA: Lancaster, 185
PA: Morgantown, 191
PA: Philadelphia, 196
PA: Reading, 202, 203

Flemington Fashion Outlet Plus
NJ: Matawan, 130
NJ: Secaucus, 131
PA: Lancaster, 185
PA: Morgantown, 191
PA: Reading, 202

Flemington Petites
NJ: Secaucus, 131

Flemington's Coat World
NJ: Flemington, 127
NY: Central Valley, 143

Flower and Plant Cove
NJ: Secaucus, 133

Garage
PA: Philadelphia, 196

Gem Vault
NJ: Flemington, 127

General Shoe Factory to You Shoes
VA: Lightfoot, 229

Generra
DE: Rehoboth Beach, 97
MD: Queenstown, 115
WV: Martinsburg, 249

Genesco
PA: Morgantown, 192
VA: Fort Chiswell, 226

Gentile Glass Company
WV: Star City, 252

Gentlemen's Wearhouse
NY: Mt. Kisco, 158

Geoffrey Beene
DE: Rehoboth Beach, 97
MD: Perryville, 112
NJ: Flemington, 127
NJ: Secaucus, 133
NY: Bellport, 140
NY: Fishkill, 147
NY: Lake George, 153
NY: Mt. Kisco, 158
PA: Lancaster, 187
VA: Williamsburg, 239
WV: Martinsburg, 250

Georgetown Leather Design
VA: Woodbridge, 243
WV: Martinsburg, 249

George W. Bollman
See Bollman Direct

Georgiou
PA: Philadelphia, 196

Gilligan & O'Malley
MD: Queenstown, 115
NY: Lake George, 153
PA: Reading, 203
VA: Williamsburg, 239

Gitano
DE: Rehoboth Beach, 97
MD: Queenstown, 115
NJ: Edison, 124
NJ: Flemington, 126
NJ: Lafayette, 128
NJ: Secaucus, 133
NJ: Wall Township, 135
NY: Central Valley, 143
NY: Fishkill, 147
NY: Lake George, 154
NY: Monticello, 157
PA: Lancaster, 188
PA: Somerset, 206
PA: Tannersville, 208
VA: Fort Chiswell, 226
VA: Fredericksburg, 227
VA: Virginia Beach, 235
VA: Williamsburg, 239

Gitano Kids Factory Store
NJ: Wall Township, 135
VA: Waynesboro, 238
VA: Williamsburg, 239

Gitano Warehouse Clearance Center
NY: Malta, 156
NY: Niagara Falls, 162
PA: Reading, 201
VA: Waynesboro, 238

Glass Resort Outlet
DE: Rehoboth Beach, 96

Glen-Gery Brick Factory Outlet
PA: Wyomissing, 214

Gloray Knitting Mills Inc.
PA: Robesonia, 204

Gold 'N Things Jewelry
VA: Lightfoot, 229

Gold-N-Silver
WV: Martinsburg, 249

Golden Chain Gang
PA: Morgantown, 192

Golden Talents
NJ: Flemington, 127

Gold Exchange
PA: Lancaster, 186

Gold Outlet
NJ: Secaucus, 133

Gorham
MD: Queenstown, 115
NJ: Flemington, 125
VA: Williamsburg, 240
WV: Martinsburg, 249

Gourmet Kitchen Bazaar
NJ: Secaucus, 133

Great Outdoor Clothing Co.
PA: Somerset, 206

Green Onion Kitchen Shoppe
NY: Niagara Falls, 162

Gucci
NY: Central Valley, 143

Guess? Factory Store
PA: Philadelphia, 196
VA: Woodbridge, 243

Hagerstown Shoe Factory Outlet
MD: Hagerstown, 108

Hahn's Shoes Outlet
VA: Woodbridge, 243

Hamilton Luggage
PA: Philadelphia, 196

Hamilton Luggage & Handbags
VA: Fairfax, 224
VA: Williamsburg, 239
VA: Woodbridge, 243

Hamilton Watch & Clock Shoppe
PA: Lancaster, 188
PA: York, 217

Hamrick's
VA: Woodbridge, 243

Handbag Company Outlet
PA: Philadelphia, 196

Handmade Quilts
PA: Wyomissing, 215

Hanes Activewear
PA: Morgantown, 192
WV: Martinsburg, 249

Hanover Shoe Store
MD: Reisterstown, 116
WV: Franklin, 248

Happy Hatter
NJ: Flemington, 127

Hartstrings
PA: Reading, 203

Hartz & Company Factory Outlet
MD: Frederick, 105

harvé benard
MD: Annapolis, 101
MD: Perryville, 112
MD: Queenstown, 115
NJ: Flemington, 127
NJ: Secaucus, 134
NJ: Wall Township, 135
NY: Central Valley, 143
NY: Lake George, 153
NY: Latham, 155
NY: Monticello, 157
NY: Niagara Falls, 161
PA: Lancaster, 188
PA: Reading, 203
PA: Somerset, 206
PA: Tannersville, 209
PA: York, 217
VA: Fredericksburg, 227
VA: Williamsburg, 239

Harvey Electronics
NJ: Secaucus, 134

Hathaway
NY: Fishkill, 147

Hathaway Olga/Warner
NY: Monticello, 157

Heacock's Deerskin Factory Store
NY: Gloversville, 147

Head over Heels
WV: Martinsburg, 249

Heirloom Lace
NJ: Flemington, 127

Heirlooms
PA: Reading, 203

Helen's Handbags
PA: Philadelphia, 196

Heritage Shop
PA: Stroudsburg, 208

He-Ro Group
MD: Perryville, 113
NJ: Secaucus, 134
NY: Central Valley, 143
VA: Williamsburg, 239

Hilda of Iceland
VA: Woodbridge, 243

Hi-Tec Outlet
PA: Stroudsburg, 208

Hit or Miss
NJ: Matawan, 130
NY: Niagara Falls, 131
NY: Rochester, 163
NY: West Seneca, 167
VA: Fairfax, 224
VA: Lightfoot, 229

H.L. Miller Tops & Tees
PA: Lancaster, 185

Home Again
PA: Tannersville, 209

Jaeger Outlet
NY: Niagara Falls, 161
PA: Reading, 203

Jantzen & Lee Casuals
MD: Chester, 102

J.C. Clintons
VA: Woodbridge, 242

JC Penney Outlet
PA: Philadelphia, 196

J. Crew
PA: Reading, 203
VA: Williamsburg, 239
WV: Martinsburg, 249

Jeans N' Things
PA: Waynesboro, 210

Jessica McClintock
NY: Central Valley, 143

Jewel Master
PA: Philadelphia, 196

Jewelry Connection
VA: Lightfoot, 229
VA: Virginia Beach, 236

Jewelry Outlet
PA: Philadelphia, 196
PA: Wyomissing, 215
VA: Woodbridge, 242

Jewelry Vault
PA: Philadelphia, 196
VA: Woodbridge, 242

J.G. Hook
PA: Philadelphia, 196
VA: Williamsburg, 239

J.H. Collectibles
MD: Perryville, 113
MD: Queenstown, 115
NJ: Secaucus, 132
NY: Niagara Falls, 162
VA: Williamsburg, 239
WV: Martinsburg, 250

Jindo Furs
MD: Queenstown, 115
NJ: Secaucus, 134
NY: Central Valley, 143
NY: Niagara Falls, 162

Jindo Outerwear
NJ: Secaucus, 132

Joan & David
NJ: Flemington, 127
NJ: Secaucus, 133
NY: Central Valley, 143
NY: Malta, 156
PA: Reading, 203

John Henry
MD: Queenstown, 115

John Henry & Friends
NJ: Lafayette, 128
PA: Reading, 203

Johnston & Murphy Factory Outlet
PA: Morgantown, 192

John Wright Warehouse
PA: Williamsport, 213

Jonathan Logan
MD: Chester, 102
NJ: Flemington, 126
NJ: Secaucus, 134
NY: Fishkill, 147
NY: Lake George, 152
NY: Monticello, 157
PA: Lancaster, 187
PA: Somerset, 206
PA: Wyomissing, 215
PA: York, 217
VA: Waynesboro, 238

Jones New York
MD: Perryville, 113
MD: Queenstown, 115
NJ: Flemington, 127
NJ: Secaucus, 133
NY: Bellport, 140
NY: Central Valley, 143
NY: Malta, 156
PA: Tannersville, 209
VA: Williamsburg, 239

Jones New York Women
MD: Perryville, 113
NY: Central Valley, 143
PA: Somerset, 206

Jordache
MD: Perryville, 113
MD: Queenstown, 115
NY: Bellport, 140
PA: Philadelphia, 196
PA: Somerset, 206
VA: Fredericksburg, 227
VA: Williamsburg, 239
VA: Woodbridge, 242

Jordache and Shoe Town
PA: Reading, 201

Judy Bond Blouses
PA: Morgantown, 192

Just'a Sweet Shoppe
PA: Reading, 201

Just Coats 'n Swimwear
NJ: Secaucus, 134
NJ: Wall Township, 135
PA: Lancaster, 188

Just Kids
MD: Perryville, 113
PA: Philadelphia, 196
VA: Woodbridge, 242

Just My Size
MD: Queenstown, 115
PA: Lancaster, 188
VA: Lightfoot, 229
WV: Martinsburg, 249

Kandy Korner
PA: Stroudsburg, 208

Kay Bee Toys
NY: Niagara Falls, 162

Kenar-Nicole Matthews
NY: Central Valley, 143

Kid City
VA: Lightfoot, 230
VA: Woodbridge, 242

Kidrageous
NJ: Secaucus, 131

Kids Barn
PA: Lancaster, 188
PA: Philadelphia, 196
VA: Woodbridge, 243

NJ: Secaucus, 132
NJ: Wall Township, 135
NY: Bellport, 140
NY: Central Valley, 143
NY: Cohoes, 144
NY: Lake George, 154
NY: Malta, 156
NY: Niagara Falls, 161
PA: Lancaster, 187
PA: Morgantown, 192
PA: Reading, 203
PA: Tannersville, 209
VA: Fort Chiswell, 226
VA: Lightfoot, 229
VA: Waynesboro, 238
VA: Woodbridge, 242
WV: Martinsburg, 249

Lenox Crystal & China
NY: Latham, 155

Lenox Crystal Clearance Center
PA: Mount Pleasant, 193

Lenox Shop
PA: Lancaster, 188

Leslie Fay
NY: Central Valley, 143
NY: Monticello, 157
PA: Lancaster, 188
PA: Reading, 203
PA: Somerset, 206

Lightfoot Manor
VA: Williamsburg, 241

Lighthouse Factory Outlet
PA: Greensburg, 181

Lillian Vernon
NY: New Rochelle, 159
VA: Virginia Beach, 236
VA: Woodbridge, 243

Limited Editions for Her
NJ: Flemington, 127

Linens 'n Things
MD: Greenbelt, 108
NJ: Fairfield, 124
NJ: Matawan, 130
NY: Niagara Falls, 161
NY: Rochester, 163
NY: West Seneca, 167
PA: Lancaster, 188
VA: Fairfax, 224
VA: Lightfoot, 229
VA: Woodbridge, 242

Linen Warehouse
MD: Annapolis, 101

Lingerie Shop
NJ: Flemington, 127

Lise J. Fashion Outlet
DE: Rehoboth Beach, 97

Little Red Shoe House
NY: Monticello, 157
PA: Lancaster, 187
PA: Morgantown, 192
VA: Fort Chiswell, 226

Liz Claiborne
MD: Perryville, 113
MD: Queenstown, 115
NY: Central Valley, 143

Middishade Factory Stockroom
PA: Philadelphia, 196
PA: Upper Darby, 209

Mikasa Factory Store
MD: Annapolis, 101
MD: Perryville, 113
NJ: Secaucus, 134
NJ: Wall Township, 135
NY: Niagara Falls, 161
PA: Lancaster, 186
PA: Reading, 202
VA: Williamsburg, 239

Mill Outlets
MD: Ocean City, 112

Moda Fashion Apparel
NY: Central Valley, 143

Mondi
NJ: Secaucus, 134
NY: Central Valley, 143
VA: Woodbridge, 243

Morey's Jewelers
NY: Niagara Falls, 162

Mothercare
NY: Monticello, 157

Munsingwear
Morgantown, 192

Murray's Menswear
NJ: Flemington, 126
PA: Lancaster, 185

Mushroom Factory Store
PA: Lancaster, 188
PA: Wyomissing, 215

Music Den
PA: Lancaster, 188

Names for Dames featuring Adolfo
NY: Monticello, 157
PA: Lancaster, 188

Nanny's Shoppe
PA: Wyomissing, 215

Napier
PA: Tannersville, 209
VA: Fredericksburg, 227

National Locker Room
PA: Philadelphia, 196

Nautica
NY: Central Valley, 143
NY: Lake George, 153
NY: Niagara Falls, 161
PA: Reading, 203
PA: Tannersville, 209
WV: Martinsburg, 249

NBO Warehouse Store
NJ: Secaucus, 134

NCS Shoe Outlet
MD: Perryville, 113

Neiss Collectibles
PA: Lancaster, 187

Nettle Creek
NY: Latham, 155
PA: Lancaster, 188
VA: Williamsburg, 240

Newberry Knitting Co., Inc.
NY: Schenectady, 164

Newport Sportswear
VA: Woodbridge, 242

New York Electronics
VA: Woodbridge, 242

Nickels
MD: Queenstown, 115
PA: Somerset, 206

Nike
MD: Perryville, 113
MD: Queenstown, 115
NY: Bellport, 140
VA: Williamsburg, 239
VA: Woodbridge, 242
WV: Martinsburg, 249

Nilani
PA: Lancaster, 188

$9.99 Stockroom
NY: Rochester, 163
PA: Erie, 180
PA: Lancaster, 188
PA: Philadelphia, 196
VA: Lightfoot, 229
VA: Virginia Beach, 236
VA: Woodbridge, 242

9 West
DE: Rehoboth Beach, 97
MD: Queenstown, 115
NJ: Flemington, 127
NJ: Secaucus, 134
NY: Bellport, 140
NY: Lake George, 153
PA: Philadelphia, 196
VA: Williamsburg, 239
VA: Woodbridge, 242

Noel's Hosiery
NJ: Flemington, 126

No Nonsense
PA: Philadelphia, 196
VA: Woodbridge, 243

Nordstrom Rack
VA: Woodbridge, 243

North Face
NY: Bellport, 140
PA: Wyomissing, 215

Norty's
PA: Lancaster, 188
PA: Morgantown, 192

Norty's Clearance
PA: Reading, 203

Not Just Barrettes
PA: Philadelphia, 196

Not Just Jeans
NJ: Secaucus, 133

N.T. Tahari
NJ: Secaucus, 133

N.W.S. Electronics Outlet
NY: West Seneca, 167

Ocean Avenue
DE: Rehoboth Beach, 96

Ocello Sportswear
PA: Robesonia, 204

Office Furniture Outlet
PA: York, 217

O'Furniture
PA: Greensburg, 181

Old Candle Barn Outlet
PA: Intercourse, 182

Old Mill
MD: Annapolis, 101
NJ: Fairfield, 124
NJ: Matawan, 130
NY: Mt. Kisco, 158
NY: Niagara Falls, 161
NY: West Seneca, 167
VA: Fredericksburg, 227
VA: Lightfoot, 229
VA: Virginia Beach, 236

Old Mill Ladies Sportswear Outlet
PA: Morgantown, 192
PA: Reading, 203

Oleg Cassini
MD: Queenstown, 115

Olga/Warner's
NY: Fishkill, 147
VA: Fredericksburg, 227

Oneida
DE: Rehoboth Beach, 96
NY: Bellport, 140
NY: Central Valley, 143
NY: Lake George, 153
NY: Latham, 155
NY: Sherrill, 165
PA: Lancaster, 187
PA: Somerset, 206
PA: Tannersville, 209
PA: Wyomissing, 215
VA: Fredericksburg, 227

VA: Lightfoot, 230
WV: Martinsburg, 250

Oriental Rug Outlet
NJ: Secaucus, 132

Oriental Weavers
VA: Woodbridge, 243

Original I. Goldberg
PA: Philadelphia, 196

OshKosh B'Gosh
NY: Niagara Falls, 161
WV: Martinsburg, 250

Outer Banks
MD: Queenstown, 115

Outlet Store
NJ: Secaucus, 134

Oxford Brands Ltd.
PA: Wyomissing, 215

Pacific Party Co.
PA: Philadelphia, 196

Palace Music Outlet
PA: Philadelphia, 196

Paldies Young Men's clothing
PA: Reading, 201

Palm Beach Mill Outlet
PA: Waynesboro, 210

Pandora Factory Outlet
MD: Annapolis, 101

Paper Factory
MD: Annapolis, 101
MD: Perryville, 113
PA: Erie, 180
PA: Lancaster, 188
PA: Somerset, 206
PA: Wyomissing, 215
VA: Fredericksburg, 227
VA: Lightfoot, 229
VA: Virginia Beach, 236
VA: Waynesboro, 238
VA: Woodbridge, 243
WV: Martinsburg, 249

Paper Outlet
NY: Central Valley, 143
NY: Niagara Falls, 161
PA: Morgantown, 192
PA: Robesonia, 204

Parade of Shoes
PA: Philadelphia, 196

Paris in Secaucus Perfumes
NJ: Secaucus, 132

Party II
PA: Stroudsburg, 208

Passport Foods Outlet
NJ: Secaucus, 134

Paul Revere Shoppe
VA: Lightfoot, 230

**Payless ShoeSource/
Payless Shoes**
NY: Niagara Falls, 162
PA: Philadelphia, 196

Peddler's Wagon
PA: Lewisburg, 189

**Pennsylvania House
Furniture Factory Outlet**
PA: Shamokin Dam, 205

Perfumania
MD: Annapolis, 101
MD: Perryville, 113
NJ: Flemington, 127
NY: Lake George, 154
PA: Philadelphia, 196
PA: Tannersville, 209
VA: Fredericksburg, 227
WV: Martinsburg, 249

Perrella Factory Outlet
NY: Gloversville, 148

Perry Ellis
NJ: Flemington, 127

Peruvian Connection
MD: Perryville, 113

Petal Pushers
VA: Waynesboro, 238

Petals Factory Outlet
NJ: Flemington, 127
NY: Central Valley, 143
PA: Lancaster, 187
PA: York, 217
WV: Martinsburg, 249

Petite Shop Outlet
PA: Philadelphia, 196

Petticoat Corner
PA: Reading, 201

Pewtarex Factory Outlet Stores
PA: Lancaster, 187
PA: York, 217, 218

Pfaltzgraff
DE: Rehoboth Beach, 96
MD: Chester, 102
NJ: Flemington, 127
NY: Lake George, 153
NY: Niagara Falls, 161
PA: Lancaster, 188
PA: Tannersville, 209
PA: York, 217
VA: Fairfax, 225
VA: Lightfoot, 230
WV: Martinsburg, 249

Phar-Mor
PA: Philadelphia, 196

Phil's Shoes
VA: Woodbridge, 243

Philly Fever
PA: Philadelphia, 196

Piece Goods Shop
VA: Woodbridge, 242

Pier 1 Imports
NY: Lake George, 153

Pierre Cardin
MD: Perryville, 113
NY: Bellport, 140
PA: Somerset, 206
PA: Tannersville, 209
VA: Williamsburg, 239

Pilgrim Glass Corporation
WV: Ceredo, 247

Pinehurst Lingerie
VA: Williamsburg, 241

Plumm's Outlet
PA: Philadelphia, 196

Pocono Candle Shop
PA: East Stroudsburg, 176
PA: Stroudsburg, 208

Pocono Kitchen & Curtain
PA: Stroudsburg, 208

Pocono Linen Outlet
PA: Stroudsburg, 208

Pocono Odd-Lot Outlet
PA: Stroudsburg, 208

Pocono Toy Outlet
PA: Stroudsburg, 208

Pol-O-Craft
PA: Wyomissing, 215

Polly Flinders
NY: Fishkill, 147
NY: Lake George, 152

Polo/Ralph Lauren
NY: Cohoes, 144
NY: Niagara Falls (2), 161, 162
PA: Reading, 203
WV: Martinsburg, 249

Popular Greetings
DE: Rehoboth Beach, 97

Rawlings Sport Goods
PA: Reading, 203

Reading Bag Company
PA: Wyomissing, 215

Reading China & Glass
PA: Lancaster, 188
PA: Philadelphia, 197
PA: West Reading, 211
PA: Wyomissing, 215

Reading Christmas Outlet
PA: Reading, 203

Record World
PA: Philadelphia, 197

Reebok
DE: Rehoboth Beach, 97
NY: Lake George, 153
PA: Tannersville, 209
WV: Martinsburg, 250

Reed & Barton
PA: Lancaster, 188

Regal Outlet Store
PA: Lancaster, 188

Regal Ware Factory Outlet
VA: Lightfoot, 229

Rehoboth Golf Outlet
DE: Rehoboth Beach, 96

Remembrance Shoppe
NY: Niagara Falls, 162

Remington Factory Outlet
PA: Philadelphia, 197
VA: Woodbridge, 243

Ribbon Outlet
DE: Rehoboth Beach, 96
MD: Annapolis, 101
MD: Perryville, 113
NJ: Flemington, 127
NY: Central Valley, 143
NY: Lake George, 154
PA: Lancaster, 187
PA: Somerset, 206
PA: York, 217
VA: Fort Chiswell, 226
VA: Waynesboro, 238
VA: Williamsburg, 239
WV: Martinsburg, 249

Richard Roberts Jewelers
NY: Lake George, 154

Rings N' Things
NY: Niagara Falls, 162

Rite-Aid
NY: Niagara Falls, 162

Ritz Camera
PA: Philadelphia, 197
VA: Woodbridge, 243

Robert Scott & David Brooks
WV: Martinsburg, 249

RockBottom Jeans
PA: Lancaster, 186

Rodier Paris
NY: Central Valley, 143

Rolane Factory Outlet
PA: Edwardville, 177
PA: Robesonia, 204
VA: Lightfoot, 230
WV: Martinsburg, 250

Ronlee
NJ: Secaucus, 134

Rosenbaum Jewelry
NY: Central Valley, 143

Ross Dress for Less
MD: Greenbelt, 108
VA: Woodbridge, 243

Rowe Showplace Gallery
VA: Woodbridge, 243

Royal Book Outlet
NY: Mt. Kisco, 158

Royal Doulton
MD: Annapolis, 101
NJ: Flemington, 127
NY: Central Valley, 143
NY: Malta, 156
NY: Niagara Falls, 161
PA: Lancaster, 187
VA: Waynesboro, 238
VA: Williamsburg, 239

Royal Grouse
NJ: Flemington, 127

Royal Grouse II
NY: Central Valley, 143

Royal Jewelers
PA: Philadelphia, 197

Royal Robbins
MD: Perryville, 113
PA: Wyomissing, 215

Royce Hosiery
WV: Martinsburg, 249

Rubin Gloves Factory Store
NY: Gloversville, 148

Ruff Hewn
DE: Rehoboth Beach, 97
NY: Niagara Falls, 161
PA: Reading, 203
WV: Martinsburg, 249

Rug Outlet
PA: Lewisburg, 190

Rugs, Etc.
MD: Annapolis, 101

Run of the Mill
PA: Stroudsburg, 208

Russell Jerzees Outlet
VA: Lightfoot, 229

Russ Togs
NY: Central Valley, 144

RW's Sweater Outlet
VA: Woodbridge, 242

St. Thomas Inc.
NY: Gloversville, 148

Saks Fifth Avenue Clearinghouse
PA: Philadelphia, 197

Salisbury Pewter
MD: Salisbury, 118

Salt Glaze Pottery
VA: Lightfoot, 230

Sam Goody
PA: Philadelphia, 197

Sam's Tailoring
VA: Fairfax, 224

S & K Brand Menswear
PA: Philadelphia, 197
VA: Fredericksburg, 227
VA: Lightfoot, 229
VA: Woodbridge, 242

Sassafras
MD: Perryville, 113
VA: Woodbridge, 242

Sassco Fashions Outlet
NJ: Secaucus, 134

Satchels Handbags
DE: Rehoboth Beach, 97
NJ: Secaucus, 133

Scotfoam Corporation
PA: Eddyston, 176

Sears Outlet
PA: Philadelphia, 197
VA: Woodbridge, 243

Secaucus Handbags
NJ: Secaucus, 133

NY: Niagara Falls, 162
PA: Philadelphia, 197
VA: Lightfoot, 229
VA: Woodbridge, 242

Sergio Valente
DE: Rehoboth Beach, 97
NY: Central Valley, 144
NY: Malta, 156

Shades of America
PA: Philadelphia, 197

Shady Lamp
NJ: Flemington, 127
NY: Central Valley, 144

Shap's
PA: Lancaster, 186

Sheet & Towel Outlet
PA: Waynesboro, 211

She House
NY: Rochester, 163

Sheri's Moccasin Outlet
NY: Niagara Falls, 162

Ship 'N Shore
PA: Morgantown, 192

Shoe Town
MD: Greenbelt, 108
NJ: Flemington, 126
NJ: Matawan, 130
NJ: Secaucus, 132
NY: West Seneca, 167
VA: Fairfax, 224
VA: Woodbridge, 242

Warehouse
NY: Niagara Falls, 161
VA: Woodbridge, 242

Warnaco Outlet
PA: Altoona, 171
PA: Lancaster, 187
WV: Martinsburg, 249

Watch Outlet
NY: Niagara Falls, 162

Waterford/Wedgwood
NJ: Flemington, 127
PA: Lancaster, 187

Wathne
NJ: Flemington, 127

Waxie Maxie's Warehouse Store
VA: Woodbridge, 242

Webster Warehouse
VA: Woodbridge, 242

Welcome Home
DE: Rehoboth Beach (2), 96, 97
MD: Annapolis, 101
MD: Perryville, 113
MD: Queenstown, 115
NY: Bellport, 140
NY: Fishkill, 147
NY: Lake George, 153
NY: Mt. Kisco, 158
NY: Niagara Falls, 161
PA: Lancaster, 188
PA: Somerset, 206
VA: Fort Chiswell, 226
VA: Fredericksburg, 227

VA: Lightfoot, 229
VA: Williamsburg, 239

Weldon Factory Salesroom
PA: Williamsport, 213

Wemco
MD: Perryville, 113

Westchester Apparel
NY: Mt. Kisco, 158

WestPoint Pepperell
VA: Williamsburg, 240

Westport Ltd.
DE: Rehoboth Beach, 96
MD: Chester, 102
NY: Central Valley, 144
NY: Lake George, 154
NY: Monticello, 157
PA: East Stroudsburg, 176
PA: Philadelphia, 197
VA: Fredericksburg, 227
VA: Lightfoot, 230
VA: Waynesboro, 238
VA: Woodbridge, 242

Westport/Dress Barn
PA: Tannersville, 209

Westport Woman
DE: Rehoboth Beach, 96

West Virginia Fine Glass
WV: Martinsburg, 249

Whims
PA: Philadelphia, 197
PA: Reading, 203

OUTLET MALL INDEX

**Apollo Plaza Manufacturers
Outlet Center**
Monticello, 157

Bellport Outlet Center
Bellport, 140

Burlington Mall
West Seneca, 166

Cohoes Commons
Cohoes, 144

Fishkill Outlet Village
Fishkill, 146

Lake George Plaza Outlet Center
Lake George, 153

Latham Outlet Mall
Latham, 155

Log Jam Factory Stores
Lake George, 154

Mt. Kisco Outlet Mall
Mt. Kisco, 158

Niagara Factory Outlet Mall
Niagara Falls, 160

Panorama Outlet Mall
Rochester, 163

Rainbow Centre
Niagara Falls, 161

Saratoga Village
Malta, 156

Transitown Plaza
Williamsville, 167

**Woodbury Commons
Factory Outlets**
Central Valley, 142

Pennsylvania

The Big Mill
Reading, 200

Crossings Outlet Square
Tannersville, 208

Erie Center Factory Outlet Mall
Erie, 180

Foxmoor Factory Outlets
Marshalls Creek, 175

Franklin Mills
Philadelphia, 195

Georgian Place
Somerset, 206

Lancaster Outlet City
Lancaster, 185

Manufacturers Outlet Mall
Morgantown, 191

Meadowbrook Outlet Village
York, 216

The Outlets on Hiesters Lane
Reading, 201

Pocono Outlet Complex
Stroudsburg, 207

Quality Centers
Lancaster, 186

The Reading Outlet Center
Reading, 202

Robesonia Outlet Center
Robesonia, 204

Rockvale Square
Factory Outlet Village
Lancaster, 187

Vanity Fair Factory Outlet
Wyomissing, 215

Waynesboro Factory Outlet Barn
Waynesboro, 210

Westmoreland Outlet World
Greensburg, 181

Virginia

Berkeley Commons Outlet Center
Williamsburg, 238

Factory Merchants
Fort Chiswell Mall
Fort Chiswell, 226

Great American Outlet Mall
Virginia Beach, 235

Massaponax Outlet Center
Fredericksburg, 227

Outlet Mall at Fairfax
Fairfax, 225

Patriot Plaza
Williamsburg, 240

Potomac Mills
Woodbridge, 241

Waynesboro Village Factory Outlets
Waynesboro, 237

The Williamsburg Outlet Mall
Lightfoot, 228

Williamsburg Outlet
Williamsburg, 240

Williamsburg Pottery
Lightfoot, 229

Wythe Shopping Plaza
Wytheville, 244

West Virginia

Blue Ridge Outlet Center
Martinsburg, 248

Tanger Factory Stores
Martinsburg, 249